Oxford June 1983.

Brief Counseling with Suicidal Persons

Brief Counseling with Suicidal Persons

William L. Getz
University of Washington
David B. Allen
R. Keith Myers
City University
Karen C. Lindner
University of Washington

LexingtonBooks
D.C. Heath and Company
Lexington, Massachusetts
Toronto

Library of Congress Cataloging in Publication Data
Main entry under title:

Brief counseling with suicidal persons.

    Includes index.
    1. Suicide—Prevention.   2. Psychotherapy, Brief.
I. Getz, William L.
RC569.B74   1983   616.85'8445'06   80–8375
ISBN 0–669–04090–8

Published simultaneously in Canada

Printed in the United States of America

International Standard Book Number: 0–669–04090–8

Library of Congress Catalog Card Number: 80–8375

This book is dedicated to our families

Contents

Acknowledgments

We want to say a special thank you to our families for their patience and tolerance during the long months of preparation and writing. They know only too well what it was like. We also want to say thank you to Michael McCarroll, who believed there was a market for what we wanted to say; to Gerry Collins, our typist, who came through on very short notice; to Connie Freeland, who as proofreader cleaned up our act; and to Austin Case, Fritz Hoedmaker, Bob Campbell, Hugh Castell, and others of the psychoanalytic community—we appreciate their insight. Thanks go to our colleagues Ed Goodrich, John Meadows, Evelyn Smith, and Isola Hull, whose support we appreciate. Thanks also go to Emily Titkin and Linda Hartzell for sensitive input on several of the case studies. Thanks to Bob Watt and John Meisel for their special expertise and to Jim Morgan for indexing. And last, but surely not least, we say thank you to our clients past and present. We cannot name you, but you have contributed so much that this book would not have been possible without you.

Introduction

The Problem

Statistics on suicide point to several interesting facts. While the suicide rate for the total U.S. population has remained relatively stable, the suicide rate for teenagers has increased dramatically in the last twenty-five years. Of equal concern is the high rate of suicide among people over age fifty, especially among white males.

In this century the suicide rate for the total U.S. population peaked twice, in about 1910 and again in the early 1930s, each time reaching an overall rate of about 17 suicides per 100,000 people. Since the end of World War II, the suicide rate has remained fairly steady, from 10 to 13 per 100,000. The rate of suicide for males between the ages of fifteen and twenty-four, however, has more than tripled since 1955, increasing from about 6 per 100,000 in that year to over 20 per 100,000 in the late 1970s and early 1980s. The suicide rate for girls of the same ages in the same period rose an equally astounding 250 percent. Suicides in the fifteen to twenty-four age range currently account for almost 20 percent of the 27,000 suicides in the United States, compared with a figure of 5 percent just a few years ago.

Statistics show that individuals over age fifty who commit suicide tend to be white males. People over fifty make up a little more than one-fourth of the total U.S. population, yet account for almost 40 percent of the deaths by suicide. White men over fifty make up about 10 percent of the population and constitute 28 percent of all deaths by suicide. As Henden (1982) points out, the problem of elderly suicide is likely to become even more significant when the post-world War II baby-boom generation reaches the over-fifty age group.

Purpose of this Book

The statistics attest to the significance of suicide as a mental-health problem. Despite the fact that numerous books and articles have been written on the subject, few address the specific clinical issues relating to suicidal individuals who are counseled on a brief or short-term basis. Fewer still acknowledge that a significant percentage of such clients are counseled by paraprofessionals and volunteers at crisis centers across the country and around the world. It is to this segment of the counseling community that we address this book.

As supervisors, trainers, consultants, and clinicians, we have long marveled at the dedication of those who deal with very upset suicidal people: the case worker in Alaska who is the expert in such matters because she is the only mental-health person within 200 miles, the public-health nurse who is the only one to talk with late at night, the housewife who is a crisis counselor because the counseling agency has run out of money and needs coverage on Saturday, and many others. These are the counselors we are writing for.

We have provided theory when necessary, but have tried to focus on the practical side of our work. Our own trial-and-error experiences formed the foundations for this book.

Not everything we have written is applicable to each case of depression or suicide proneness. Nor have we been able to address every setting in which one is likely to see such clients. We hope to convey a set of principles that can transcend the boundaries of time or place, giving clinicians essential sound counseling tactics that will buy time for and return control to the client. To this end we have included many examples from our clinical practice.

Our Philosophy

It is only in the most extreme cases that we would consider the possibility that an individual might have the right to take his own life; and even in such cases we question such a right. For the purposes of this book, no decision to commit suicide is to be supported by you the counselor. The ethical considerations are very straightforward: you are to do everything in your power to prevent suicide. Further, in your role as counselor you are to assist suicidal individuals to understand the real meaning of their self-destructive impulses and ideas. You can show them that their actions are self-defeating and will prevent them from accomplishing the growth and self-actualization they truly seek. We believe this philosophy is best served by the use of sound clinical practices and techniques that transcend varying theoretical orientations.

This book is based on intrapsychic, interpersonal, and environmental/situational theories. We have long admired the contributions of Freud and have relied on his basic works in the formulation of certain sections of this book. We have also drawn from the more recent ideas of Langs and Segal. We have considered the contributions of ego psychology as extensions of Freud's original ideas and in this regard have relied somewhat on Hartman, Mahler, and Jacobson. The interpersonal theories of Sullivan and Rogers have now been incorporated into so many facets of clinical work that it is hard to distinguish them as separate entities. Caplan,

Lindemann, and other proponents of the situational approach are duly recognized and their landmark works referred to often.

These various theories form the basis of our clinical stance. The types of interventions we suggest range from interpretation to restructuring the client's environment. Overall, we feel that to be truly effective with suicidal clients you must be theoretically sound, clinically flexible, and personally active in approach and practice.

Organization of the Book

We have divided this book into four parts: theoretical, clinical, special topics, and case examples. In the first part we cover the issues of why people try and kill themselves, how to understand and make use of the techniques available to prevent this, and specific examples of such phenomena as defense mechanisms, transference, and countertransference. The second part provides structured guidelines for how to organize your interview and how to make and carry out a treatment plan. Part III includes chapters on the special topics of what to do when your client commits suicide and on adolescent suicide. Part IV presents edited verbatim transcripts of actual counseling sessions with suicide-prone individuals. The counselors' private thoughts and authors' comments about the counselors' performance are added to these transcripts.

Finally, appendixes are provided to assist you in evaluating your clients' mental status, suicidal status, depression, and life-changing events. Several examples of suicide contracts that may be useful as clinical tools are also included.

A Final Word

Throughout this book we have attempted to write as though we were talking directly with you. We have used such personal pronouns as *you, your, we,* and *us* whenever possible to help in this regard. For the sake of simplicity, we have used the pronouns *he* and *him* as generic terms to mean either *she/he* or *him/her*.

Part I
Theoretical Issues

1 The Psychology of Suicide

For most suicidal persons, suicide represents the final step of a psychological journey begun weeks, months, or even years before. Along the way, the suicide plan has been elaborated and rehearsed both in fantasy and in trial action. Suicidal acts are virtually never sudden, impulsive, or random. Rather, suicide has an enduring meaning for each client. It is important for the counselor to understand the psychology of the suicidal client and to use this understanding in his assessment and intervention.

It is essential for the counselor to have a sound theoretical base, as well as good clinical skills to bring order to the wealth of information each suicidal client presents and to begin to make sense of the client's inner turmoil. The counselor's theoretical and conceptual framework also helps him avoid becoming overwhelmed and confused himself. Then, as he begins to communicate his understanding to his client, the counseling process is initiated and the client-counselor alliance begins to form. Their mutual efforts at understanding the terrible thoughts and feelings that have so overwhelmed the client form the basis for resolution of the suicidal crisis.

A basic premise of our approach to the psychology of suicide is that it is most often an expression of anger. In most cases, careful analysis of the client's suicidal thoughts and feelings will reveal a dual motivation. Anger has been directed inward against the self and, at the same time, is very likely also directed at some other significant person in the client's life. The client's wishes to destroy himself and to punish the survivor of the self-murder exist side by side and both can be fulfilled by a single act (Henry and Short 1957).

Anger may or may not be part of the suicidal client's conscious awareness, nor for that matter will it always be apparent to the counselor. Nevertheless, the counselor must not forget for a moment that somewhere, perhaps deep inside the person sitting in the other chair, is a seething, murderous rage that has as its aim the destruction of that person. The intensity of the destructive impulse so overwhelms the client that his characteristic ways of organizing and integrating thoughts, feelings, and actions are overshadowed by more immature processes. It will be helpful to describe the nature of these changes in psychological functioning before we examine the content of suicidal fantasies as a means of understanding the motivation to commit suicide.

3

Our ability to love, to work, and to play; our capacity to be happy, effective, and fulfilled, depend on certain life experiences that help us gain psychological maturity. Normal, healthy mental and emotional well-being is characterized by a sense of reality, accurate perception of the world, the ability to recall aspects of experience, and the use of memory together with reason and logic as the bases for judgment. A psychologically mature person is aware of how he is feeling, has some understanding of his feelings, and has the ability to use them as a guide without becoming overwhelmed, excessively frustrated, or frightened by intense emotion. Emotional maturity allows relationships based on love, respect, and empathy without a loss of one's own identity. The normal person functions in an adaptive and flexible fashion without undue anxiety or depression.

The suicidal client has difficulty in many if not most of these areas. As part of his assessment of the client's psychological strengths and weaknesses, the counselor seeks to understand the origins of the problems at hand. Current difficulties in psychological functioning often reflect some combination of disruptive factors during childhood together with the impact of the present crisis. Several technical terms will prove useful in clarifying this point. Periods of either deprivation or overgratification during the formative years are said to produce *arrests* in the child's development or points of *fixation*. This is simply a way of stating that some aspect of the individual's psychological functioning has been adversely affected by his life experience. The following case vignettes illustrate two forms of fixation and their effects on the client-counselor relationship.

As a child, Mr. A.'s every wish and whim were anticipated and gratified by an overprotective and overly solicitous mother, and as an adult he tended to become dependent on others. As a result, he was prone to depression and feelings of helplessness when he lost an important relationship and tended to cling to others in a passive and infantile manner. The counselor working with him felt pressured to make decisions, to tell him what to do, and to actually do things for him that he could, in fact, do for himself. Another client, Mrs. B., had indifferent, unresponsive parents and grew up avoiding close relationships and mistrusting people in general. The counselor found it difficult to establish a counseling alliance with her because she feared and avoided any relationship with a potential for dependency. Each of these examples represents a fixation at an early stage of development. The issues of dependence and independence were unresolved for both Mr. A. and Mrs. B. In each case the fixations produced personality traits that had lifelong consequences for the individuals' self-concepts and relationships.

Clients who have had the benefit of a childhood relatively free of such difficulties can also become less effective in the emotional turmoil that surrounds a suicidal crisis. An individual who has typically functioned in a normal, healthy manner may temporarily manifest a number of maladaptive, ineffective, and self-defeating behaviors during a period of crisis. At such times, his internal state will become characterized more by primitive or less mature emotions and mental processes. This loss of adaptive function and reversion to less effective means of coping is termed *regression*.

The counselor may be surprised at the contrast between how poorly his client functions at the time of the first interview and how much better he looks the following week. For example, Mrs. C., a competent and highly successful executive, had become suicidal and depressed following the sudden death of her husband. For weeks she was incapable of making a decision about the simplest matters. Her need to have others help was a relatively short-lived and temporary regression from her previously high level of functioning, rather than a long-standing pattern of behavior.

The regressed suicidal client's emotional state also includes intense and overwhelming *dependency* needs and conflict over those needs. The helplessness, hopelessness, passivity, and clinging of the suicidal client reflects the severity of the crisis. The client has regressed emotionally and is reexperiencing very immature and even infantile feelings about himself and those around him. Most adult clients have some awareness of these changes in their sense of self, competence, and identity, and are therefore threatened by the experience because it is dissonant and unfamiliar. The wish to give in to feelings of helplessness and to allow others to care for their every need may represent what they imagine as going crazy or losing control of themselves. Regressive tendencies and strong dependency needs are very frightening in that they evoke the most basic of human terrors—helplessness. Most clients also experience tremendous guilt and shame about what they consider to be such childish feelings.

The other central aspect of the suicidal client's psychology is *ambivalence*, the alternation of opposite thoughts and feelings; loving and hating, wanting to live and wanting to die at the same time. It is critical that you recognize the presence of ambivalence in the suicidal client as it is manifested in every phase of the counseling process. The client's ambivalent or mixed feelings contribute to a great deal of confusion for him and for the counselor. They create the sense that the client is not sure how he really feels, cannot say for sure what he wants, and does not know if he will follow through with the treatment plan. This is understandably disorganizing and threatens the client's sense of stability to the point that he may feel as if he is losing his mind. In fact, ambivalent thoughts do interfere with problem solving and render the client less effective in coping with his problems (Shneidman and Mandelkorn 1976).

We have thus far attempted to provide some insight into the suicidal client's inner state in order to better understand the meaning of his suicidal thoughts and fantasies and his motivation to kill himself. Most suicidal fantasies are characterized by *denial* of the fact that death signifies the end of the experiencing self, as though even in death some aspect of the self will survive. For example, a client may relish the thought of how distraught certain individuals will be following his death in a manner that makes apparent his wish for revenge or to punish. It is as if he would somehow be around afterward to say "I told you so!" Again, the motivation disclosed by such a fantasy is to witness and derive satisfaction from the guilt induced in others by the client's death. For example:

An eighteen-year-old man, Mr. D., had suicidal thoughts since the time of his hospitalization for serious injuries sustained in an automobile accident at the age of twelve. During his convalescence he derived a great deal of satisfaction from the attention and sympathy he received. He enjoyed the guilt and remorse his father felt for driving while intoxicated and that which his mother felt for allowing her husband to drive in that condition. The boy learned to play on these emotions and developed a pattern of exploiting subsequent maladies, minor and major, for his own hostile purposes. He often elaborated his illnesses in his mind and imagined the feelings his parents might have if he should actually die. His suicidal preoccupation emerged as an extension of this theme of punishment and retribution exacted by means of his own suffering. He fantasized methods of killing himself designed to have the maximal impact on his family. He took great delight in thinking about how sorry they would all be, how they would suffer, how he could hardly wait to see them at his funeral! It became clear to the counselor that Mr. D. had the fantasy that even though his body would be in the coffin his experiencing self would be present, floating above the scene, unknown to family and friends. In other words, he thought that he could die and stay around afterward to enjoy the results of his ultimate act of revenge.

Whereas the motivation in the previous example had to do with punishing others, another common motivation is the wish to punish oneself out of a sense of guilt. Some real or imagined sin or transgression may form the basis for the underlying guilt. Although the intensity of the guilt may seem to the counselor to be exaggerated and based on a distorted version of a series of events, subjective reality rather than objective reality determines the form the fantasy will take. Through denial of the actuality of death, another possible aspect of this fantasy may allow the person to emerge from the suicidal act redeemed and rid of the terrible guilt and shame.

Mr. E., a forty-two-year-old man, made a suicide attempt when his wife of twenty years died after a six-year bout with cancer. He had fallen in love with another woman years before but could not bring himself to leave his seriously ill wife. During the last year of her life he found himself hoping that death would come to her soon as this would solve his dilemma. He was greatly troubled by these thoughts and tried to keep them out of his head. He went to great lengths to avoid any behavior that could be interpreted as lack of concern for his wife. He stayed with her night and day near the end, saw to her every need, and sought unconsciously to keep her alive by countering his death wish with elaborate caretaking rituals. He was by chance not at her side when she died and he immediately felt an enormous sense of responsibility and guilt. He became convinced that his thoughts had caused her heart to stop. He decided that only through an agonizing death could he expiate his guilt and that if he suffered well enough, God would pluck him from the jaws of death at the last instant as a miraculous demonstration that he was forgiven.

Some of our clients have endured repeated instances of physical and emotional abuse. If this form of trauma is present early in development, one possible outcome is that the child will identify with the aggressive and abusive parent and as a result come to harbor the same antipathy and hatred for himself. Self-destructive behavior, then, may simply repeat an earlier experience at the hands of a parent and suicide may be the eventual outcome. The counselor may sense when listening to statements such clients make about themselves that the words are not quite their own, that they are mouthing a litany of criticism that has its origins in such a parental identification rather than in their own thoughts and feelings.

Ms. F., a thirty-year-old woman, suffered from severe episodes of depression most of her life and had made a dozen suicide attempts in as many years. In the depths of her anguish she would sob repeatedly that there was a demon within her and that Satan had to be driven from her body. The counselor noted that each time that she said this she had a ''far-away look'' in her eyes and he finally asked who was saying these things about her. She responded immediately that it was her mother's voice. She went on to describe how her paranoid-schizophrenic mother considered her to be the incarnation of the Devil and how she was beaten severely for any minor infraction to purge the evil presence. In her suicidal thoughts it was as though she appeared in her mother's guise and killed the demon. Her inner experience all of her life was a struggle between the mother in her head and the devil in her body. When severely depressed, she sought to achieve some sense of control by identification with the powerful mother. It was as though one part of her could be destroyed while the other part survived.

For other clients, suicide is equated in unconscious fantasy with killing some other person in their lives. In a psychological sense, the signficant persons in the cient's life exist internally as mental images and as such become part of the individual. If the client is frustrated or has some other basis for an intense anger but cannot allow himself to express or perhaps even acknowledge that anger, the individual target of the anger who cannot be killed in reality can be killed in fantasy because that person exists as an image in the client's mind. The suicidal fantasy may include the idea that this part of the self can be destroyed while the rest of the self continues to exist free of the other individual involved in the conflict (Wahl 1957).

Such bizarre and mystical internal processes may leave some readers feeling incredulous and in this they have almost complete agreement in the clients' conscious attitudes. These examples of fantasies are generally well below the level of awareness, and in the course of short-term work with suicidal clients ought to remain largley at an unconscious level. They are included here as illustrations of the complex workings of the mind and to establish the fact that the motivation to kill oneself may exist in various forms and at several levels simultaneously.

Among the more familiar and common-sense fantasies encountered in counseling the suicidal client is the fantasy that the client will be rescued. This is, of course, an expression of the other side of the ambivalence about dying that always exists to some extent, namely, the wish to live. Often the fantasy is elaborated in some detail including the events leading up to the suicidal act as well as the details of the rescue. It is not unusual for the suicidal client to have a specific person in mind as the intended rescuer. The fantasy often extends beyond the suicidal events to the wish to have that individual intervene in other life problems.

Miss G., sixteen years old, waited until her mother was out of town on business, wrote a note blaming her mother for her misery, swallowed fifty aspirin, and waited in the living room for her physician father to return from his office. In her fantasy, her father would sweep her up in his arms, lovingly comfort her, and make her well again. Afterward he would realize that she was the most important thing in his life and devote himself to her. Furthermore he would defend her and side with her against her mother, the tormentor. The family had been unhappy from her earliest years and her mother blamed her husband's career-related absences from home for their problems. The girl had long since accepted the notion that if only Daddy were with her all would be well. Casting him in the role of rescuer would force him to be with her, repair their damaged relationship, vanquish her mother, and bring long overdue love and happiness.

Clients who have suffered the loss of someone very near, most often a parent, may harbor the fantasy that in death they will be reunited with the deceased. Another quite commonly stated motivation for suicide is the simple wish to be relieved of suffering and pain. In the mind of a client overwhelmed with unbearable pain and anguish, death becomes the only means of escape. These clients tend to describe death as a peaceful repose, a refreshing sleep that will relieve them of their misery. It is as though death, like sleep, will restore a sense of well-being so that they can somehow go on. Those who choose overdoses of sleeping medications and prepare for death as though they were going to sleep may have this view. Some clients verbalize the wish to go to sleep and never wake up, which clearly equates endless sleep with death. This conception denies the finality of death, because the termination of the ability to experience in sleep is not the cessation of activity but only a turning away from the external world to the rich internal experience we sometimes glimpse in dreams.

The more conscious forms of motivation to attempt suicide may also involve an attempt to evoke sympathy, receive attention, or manipulate significant others. However, these themes can be mistakenly invoked in the service of denying serious intent by the client himself and, unfortunately, in certain cases, by counselors. We must always look beyond the superficial and obvious, entertain the possibility that deeper and darker motives exist below the level of conscious awareness, and recognize that these represent real danger.

An aspect of psychological functioning that deserves comment in this regard is the principle that mental and emotional states are multiply determined. Put more simply, there are several levels of meaning in every thought and feeling that clients present. None of the suicidal motivations discussed are considered to be mutually exclusive. Elements of several motives and fantasies may be observed in the thinking of any one client. Although we consider the theme of anger to be of paramount importance, other themes are intertwined with it.

Equal in importance to the content and meaning of suicidal fantasy is the matter of the client's ability to control his behavior rather than enact the fantasy. Most people at some time in their lives have the thought that they wish to die, but most do not attempt suicide. They control the impulse well enough so that there is little likelihood that the death wish will be translated into action. Dorpat and Ripley (1981) have examined in detail the factors that affect the degree of control the suicidal person has over his impulse to kill himself. They emphasize that the psychological mechanism of denial, which was seen earlier to be central to the content of suicidal fantasy and motivation, is also basic to an understanding of control of suicidal impulses. The client may, in the first place, deny that he has had any such thoughts or wishes even though it is clear to others that he had contemplated suicide. A counseling session with a suicidal client may contain indirect statements of the wish to die followed not long afterward, perhaps in response to a question by the counselor, by an adamant denial of suicidal ideation. At the moment the question is asked, the client becomes unable to acknowledge suicidal thoughts even to himself because too much guilt, shame, or anxiety is associated with such thoughts. Similarly, the client may deny that a recent suicide attempt actually occurred in spite of evidence to the contrary. The client may have no conscious awareness of the cuts on his wrists that a day or so ago threatened his life. He may deny the very existence of the cuts and the fact that he committed a self-destructive act. Finally, the client may deny the seriousness of his intent to destroy himself. Denial allows the client to commit an act that would be unacceptable to his conscious mind by disavowing intentionality and considering the self-destructive act to have been an accident: "I didn't know that I had taken so many pills"; "I don't think that I really wanted to die, I just wanted to go to sleep." After the fact, the conscious mind reconstucts the events surrounding the suicide attempt to minimize the awareness of the wish to die, a wish that has become too terrible to consider. These examples do not involve an attempt by the client to consciously conceal something from the counselor. The thoughts and feelings are concealed from the client himself. In short, the client may deny the fact that he had suicidal thoughts, may deny the fact that he made a suicide attempt, or may acknowledge the thought or action while denying a serious intent to die.

Denial reduces the client's control of suicidal impulses. Dorpat and Ripley describe how a suicidal impulse normally produces anxiety about the possibility of death or guilt over the wish to die. This anxiety acts as an danger signal and mobilizes the individual's coping mechanisms and his attempts to control the impulse in the interest of self-preservation. The normal person in most circumstances is not overwhelmed by self-destructive feelings and can reflect on the thoughts in a manner that affords a sense of control. Denial counteracts the anxiety that normally accompanies suicidal thought, but does not diminish the strength of the impulse. Denial eliminates the danger signal that otherwise would alert the individual to employ his intellect, reality testing, logic, judgment, and other adaptive aspects of healthy psychological functioning. It is normal to feel afraid and ashamed of suicidal thoughts and for these emotions to mobilize problem-solving behaviors that mitigate against the expression of the suicidal impulse. This involves thinking about the consequences of self-destructive behavior, namely, death, injury, humiliation, or punishment. Awareness of these negative emotions has a self-preservative value. Denial short-circuits such controls and increases the likelihood that the thought will become an act.

In summary, suicidal behavior is comprehensible only when placed in its psychological context, that is, in the complex set of suicidal thoughts and fantasies that accompanies it. The suicidal client's internal state is characterized by regressed or less mature expressions of anger, dependency, and ambivalence. Suicidal fantasies generally contain elements of denial of the reality of death such that the suicidal act can be viewed as an attempted resolution of a life problem. Denial serves to increase suicidal risk because it circumvents the anxiety, guilt, and shame that ordinarily would cause the client to reject such impulses as unacceptable. Denial acts further to increase suicide potential when serious intent is disavowed and self-destructive behavior is regarded as only an accident or a gesture rather than a serious intent. Working with the suicidal client demands that the counselor have an appreciation of the complexity and the levels of meaning represented by suicidal phenomena.

References

Dorpat, T., and Ripley, H. "Dyscontrol and Suicidal Behaviors." *Attempted and Completed Suicide*. Unpublished manuscript. Seattle, Washington: University of Washington, 1980.

Henry, H. F., and Short, J. F. "The Sociology of Suicide." *Clues to Suicide*. Edited by E. S. Shneidman and N. L. Farberow. New York: McGraw-Hill, 1957.

Shneidman, E., and Mandelkorn, P. *Suicide: It Doesn't Have to Happen*. West Point, Pennsylvania: Health Information Services, Merck, Sharpe and Dahme, 1976.

Wahl, C. W. "Suicide as a Magical Act." *Clues to Suicide*. Edited by E. S. Shneidman and N. L. Farberow. New York: McGraw-Hill, 1957.

Suggested Readings

Berent, I. *The Algebra of Suicide*. New York: Human Sciences Press, 1981.

Hendin, H. *Suicide in America*. New York: W. W. Norton, 1982.

Resnick, H, ed. *Suicidal Behaviors: Diagnosis and Management*. Boston: Little, Brown, 1968.

Shneidman, E., and Farberow, N. L., eds. *Clues to Suicide*. New York: McGraw-Hill, 1957.

2 The Counseling Relationship

Most suicidal clients have begun to withdraw, renounce relationships, and disavow the meaning and significance of other persons. Because of this, one of your tasks is to make emotional contact and thereby become a significant factor in your client's life by reestablishing and maintaining a relationship. Your client must find a reason to invest in you and the counseling process and form a partnership that has been termed the therapeutic alliance (Zetzel 1956) or working alliance (Greenson 1965). This alliance is based predominantely on the client's rational, reality-based knowledge that he needs help, his friendly feelings toward the counselor, his confidence in the counselor's willingness and ability to help, and the hope which this engenders. On a less mature level, the client also wishes to be taken care of and to be nurtured by the counselor. This, too, contributes to the sense of alliance.

It is a common misconception that such a relationship can develop only over an extended period of time and for this reason is of less consequence in short-term counseling. You must be aware that, even prior to this first contact, your client may already have formed expectations of you and be predisposed to have certain kinds of thoughts and feelings toward you. As you meet and begin to work together, these become modified by your actual behavior and by your client's perception of you, which is partly accurate and partly distorted. You must be prepared to constantly monitor the quality and nature of this relationship and work with an informed appreciation of its impact on the counseling process.

Example: Mrs. H.

Mrs. H., a forty-four-year-old woman, reported to her male counselor that she had called at least thirty counselors and found his voice to have been the only one she could trust. Further, in the interval between her telephone call and the first session she had decided that for the first time in her life she would tell someone her deepest and most personal secrets. This attitude persisted throughout the six counseling sessions and sustained the client during times when she felt that no one else in the world but the counselor had any concern for her.

The strength of the relationship, idealized though it was, allowed the

13

counselor to work with Mrs. H. as an outpatient despite her moderately severe depression and suicidal potential. Had she not established and maintained such a strong attachment, her lack of other sources of support would have necessitated psychiatric hospitalization to ensure her safety. Initially, the counselor was somewhat uncomfortable with the unrealistic nature of the client's positive regard for him and was tempted to comment on the matter in order to help her see him more realistically. Fortunately, he realized that this was an indication of his discomfort at being placed in such a role and that it was in the client's best interest that he not disturb the relationship, nor interpret her positive and idealized transference. Subsequent sessions confirmed just how dearly Mr. H. needed to believe in someone, and her belief in the counselor sustained her in her worst moments.

The nature of the client's predisposition toward the counselor can often be determined to some extent by listening to the client's description of significant others in his life; for example, an employer, spouse, parent, or teacher. Each such comment about another person can be examined as an indirect reference to you. In some instances the implication can be quite clear. A client who says that all psychiatrists are crazy probably has a similar expectation of the counselor. A client's compliant that "no one ever listens to me" should caution you to consider the possibility that you have not let your client know that you are listening and understanding. On the other hand, a very positive statement about a relationship the client feels is helpful and important and can be considered an indication that the counseling relationship is for the moment in good shape.

Your client's perception of you is in part based in reality. It is determined by your actual behavior in the session but to some degree is influenced by distortions from the past. Reactions of your client that are not based on the reality of the counseling situation are termed *transference*. This is the phenomenon of displacement onto the counselor of feelings the client has about other significant persons in his life. Transference is not unique to the counseling relationship. It is, in fact, an important part of all human relationships. The counseling situation does not artificially produce transference. Rather, because the client has little factual basis for his thoughts and feelings about the counselor, the contribution of distortions that have their origins in past relationships are more readily observed than in the client's other close relationships.

Transference feelings may be very positive when the client unrealistically loves or overidealizes the counselor, or negative when the client hates or is very angry at the counselor for no apparent reason. This is not to say that counselors do not behave hurtfully, make errors, or fail. Nor does it imply that these negative feelings on the part of the client are not sometimes justified. A client who is angered by the counselor's tardiness

to a session or his lack of attentiveness is not expressing transference
feelings that belong to some other relationship, but feelings about the real
relationship. It is essential to try to differentiate between those reactions
which are based in reality and those which are transference-based distortions. When you become aware of a client's negative reaction, you
should first silently explore the possible reality of your client's perceptions. If this does not appear to be the source of the client's feelings,
then you should speculate that this is a transference reaction.

Example: Ms. I.

Ms. I., age twenty-four, had been seen three times during the week of
a serious suicide attempt by a drug overdose following her husband's
sudden announcement that he was leaving her for another woman. She
felt very ashamed of her attempt and because of her harsh self-condem-
nation expected that others would be disgusted by her, reject her, and
leave her. Her background included the fact that she was adopted, her
parents divorced when she was four, and a younger brother died a year
later. These events predisposed her to feel there was something bad about
her that not only drove people away but harmed them as well. The
counselor had been alert to this theme and had clarified for the client an
instance where it appeared that she expected the counselor to reject her
because of the suicide attempt. Counseling had proceeded favorably and
in the third session the counselor suggested that they plan to meet twice
the following week. The client agreed that she was feeling better and that
two sessions would suffice. As she went on to summarize the improvement of the past week's work, she began to cry but said she had no idea
why. The counselor was able to suggest to her that she had probably
expected to see him three times again the following week and had experienced this reduction in sessions as the rejection she had feared would
eventually come. The counselor reminded her that it was not surprising
that she would react this way given her background and the recent rejection
by her husband. The counselor acknowledged how frightened and abandoned she must be feeling but went on to say that he still felt it best that
they only meet twice the following week.

Ms. I.'s response to the proposed scheduled was clearly based on a
misinterpretation of the counselor's motives and had more to do with her
own feelings as shaped by past experiences than with the present reality.
Had this transference reaction not been clarified at the time, the client
might well have retaliated by failing to return for any further work. This
would have given her a sense of having left first and thus protected her,
albeit in maladaptive fashion, from the experience of abandonment when

the six-session contract was fulfilled. To have repeated this old pattern would have only served to confirm Ms. I.'s beliefs about herself and what she could expect of others.

The significance of the counseling relationship in short-term situations varies considerably from case to case. It may be that the client is not particularly transference-prone or that the transference that seems to exist is primarily positive in a way that is unobtrusive and seems to further the counseling process. In these situations you would be wise to do little more than monitor the process and make mental notes, thus using the relationship as still another source of information about your client rather than using it in an interpretive manner. For example, an increasing sense of liking and being liked by a formerly withdrawn client is an encouraging sign that he has the potential and the willingness to form a relationship with you.

If you become aware of some negative feelings on the part of your client you must first attempt to understand them and then decide whether to discuss them with him. You will want to ask yourself if those feelings will cause the client to reject counseling and either leave the session prematurely or fail to return for additional sessions. Your interest in such feelings and your ability to accept and tolerate their existence in the counseling relationship can be a unique and powerful experience for your client. In the first place, it conveys that you are not fearful or overwhelmed by his anger and this provides your client with a sense of safety and security. Second, your client may be unaware of such feelings and the danger exists that his decision to leave counseling is experienced only as a vague dissatisfaction rather than as a well-reasoned decision. In such instances, your observation brings the negative feelings into focus and in that way they are more likely to be controlled than if left unacknowledged. Third, his reaction to you may be based on a kernel of truth—an actual lapse of some sort on your part, or some unavoidable interruption or disruption.

Example: Mr. J.

Mr. J., a sixty-eight-year-old widower, had been depressed since his wife's death seven years earlier. At first he was quite uncomfortable talking to someone "young enough to be his grandson," but returned for a second appointment nevertheless. During the second session, they were interrupted by a knock on the door. The counselor opened the door, saw that it was a colleague, excused himself, and stepped into the hall to confer. Following a two-minute conversation, the counselor returned and picked up where he had left off with his client. After a few moments, he noticed that Mr. J. seemed more guarded and less cooperative than he had been a few minutes earlier. He listened for a few more minutes but was unable to find an explanation in the content of the discussion for the shift in attitude. He decided that it might have something to do with the brief interruption. He said to Mr. J., "You know, you seem a little less talkative just now than you were earlier today." Mr. J. grunted that maybe he was and seemed annoyed at the counselor's comment. The counselor asked Mr. J. if he had any thoughts about the change in attitude but got an "I dunno." He then offered an interpretation saying that he thought that Mr. J.'s attitude seemed to change just after the interruption and that he must have been annoyed and felt that the counselor had slighted him and treated him as less important by leaving abruptly without much explanation. Mr. J. responded that wasn't it exactly and he wasn't going to mention it but felt a little like they were talking about him in the hall. He went on to say that he'd heard someone laugh and was sure they were making fun of him. The counselor assured him that it had nothing to do with him and observed that Mr. J. was still concerned, as he was when he first came in, that the counselor considered him to be a "foolish old man" and did not take him seriously. The counselor said that he was sorry that the interruption had been necessary but added that Mr. J. had overreacted to it because of his fear that the counselor would minimize his concerns as others had done in the past. More importantly, he pointed out that Mr. J. tended to do the same thing to himself as a means of coping with his feelings. This seemed to be helpful and was confirmed in the discussion that followed.

This example illustrates that your client, in the midst of a suicidal crisis, can be extremely sensitive and easily hurt by the counselor in whom they have come to place so much faith and trust. A statement on your part that recognizes the disquieting event and your client's reaction to it communicates that you are sensitive to and accepting of his experiences. This manner of handling your client's negative feelings when they are based, in part, on your behavior, strikes a balance between denial or an attempt to treat the reaction as entirely without basis in fact and, at the other extreme, an overly apologetic display of self-recrimination. The former can lead your client to feel that he is wrong to have such feelings and then to feel guilty, crazy, or both.

Excessive apology deprives him of the opportunity to express anger in his own way. Apologies can also serve to disclose more about you than the client wants or needs to know for the purposes of a counseling relationship. Finally, your client's negative reaction to you may have little or no basis in the present reality of the counseling relationship and may properly be termed transference. In such an instance, you should seek to identify the source of such feelings and then work to differentiate between yourself and the original object of the displaced feelings. "You remind me of my ex-husband" should alert you to assess the nature of your client's feelings about that former spouse. If they tend to be negative, look for evidence that your client assumes that you share that individual's undesirable qualities. A comment to this effect can allow him to affirm the anger that exists toward the other person and thereby free you of the preconceptions that accompanied that unfounded assumption. Only when the negative feelings are brought within the context of the counseling setting will the alliance begin to mend and the productive work continue.

Counseling suicidal clients is an intensely emotional experience for the counselor as well, at any level of training and experience. Counselors feel much of what the client feels, share the anguish and the fright, and sense his despair and hopelessness. The counselor's willingness to be helpful and his sense of hope are severely tested by the depths of these feelings. The terrible intensity of feeling can threaten you much as it does your client and evoke a sense of despondency and helplessness. Although it takes an emotional toll, your ability to empathize and identify in a limited fashion with your client's distress is among the most powerful tools of the counseling process. It is the means by which we establish contact with the suicidal person, communicate concern, and achieve a genuine emotional understanding of his predicament.

Another feature of this experience in counseling is your personal feeling about the client and his behavior. It is easy to come away from much of the literature on counseling with the impression that the counselor either has no feelings about the client whatsoever or that he is to be possessed of unconditional positive regard and unqualified acceptance of all that he sees and hears. These lofty sentiments are the stuff of saints and as such serve only to burden mere mortals with undue guilt and anxieity about their human frailty. Worse yet, such notions can encourage you to leave your feelings unexamined and outside of awareness, as though they were simply irrelevant and not part of the process.

We discussed earlier the themes of immaturity and dependence encountered in counseling suicidal clients, the intense anger and murderous rage your client feels, and the irrational quality of his thought processes. Each counselor has his own characteristic reaction to such issues and for this reason self-scrutiny and an ongoing quest for this kind of self-knowledge are integral parts of your work. You must be frank and candid with yourself. You must know if you are uncomfortable with intense displays of anger and how you react in such situations. Do you change the subject, make a joke, withdraw? Are you annoyed by whining and clinging dependence, offended by perverse sexual practices, intolerant of certain religious beliefs? Are you likely to avoid an issue or perhaps talk too much about it? It is essential for you to acknowledge that: (1) you have personal conflicts and unresolved issues, (2) you will have many positive and negative feelings about your clients, (3) you have characteristic defensive and self-protective reactions, and (4) all of these will directly affect your work.

Your perceptions of your client are an admixture of reality and distortion. Those reactions which go beyond reality, those brought to the situation by you, are termed *countertransference*. This is similar to the process of distortion and displacement attributed to the client and referred to earlier as transference. Countertransference is the counselor's transference onto the client of thoughts and feelings that have their origin in some other area of the counselor's life (Freud 1912).

Of paramount concern in counseling the suicidal client is your anger or hatred toward him, especially if you are unaware of its presence. The counselor who does much suicidal counseling will very likely at some juncture wish his client dead, if only for a brief moment. Or your anger may be expressed in the thought that people have the right to kill themselves or that this client's life is so miserable and hopeless that perhaps he would indeed be better off dead. The realization that you may not like this client or that maybe the suffering involved in recovering from the self-inflicted injury will do him good should rise like a red warning flag. Any sense that you are doing, thinking, or feeling something that is a little out of the ordinary should caution you to pay very careful attention. In such instances, consultation with a colleague or supervisor is imperative. As counselors we all have a variety of blind spots and vulnerabilities when we work with potentially lethal clients. Failure to recognize the presence of a countertransference problem or negative reaction to a suicidal client could indirectly lead to your client's death.

You may have a reaction to your client that includes feelings of love, respect, sexual attraction, or a wish for a personal relationship outside of counseling. Such feelings may produce oversolicitousness, overprotectiveness, a tendency to compliment or flatter, or an impulse to overstep the bounds of the counselor-client relationship. It is, of course, preferable to have positive feelings for one another, and fortunately this usually tends to be the case. These feelings, however, need to be monitored to ensure that they do not modify the counseling process and make you less effective. A common tendency is to side with your client and thereby miss other important elements of a problem situation. Joining with him while he places the blame on everyone else and avoids the issue of his contribution to the problems at hand is ultimately not helpful. Under this circumstance counseling has deteriorated into an alliance of inappropriate gratification and mutual admiration rather than an opportunity for constructive change.

The art of counseling is to be found in your sensitivity to the nuances of the counseling relationship. This special relationship is the human contact that forms the basis for hope, the working alliance, and the subsequent work of counseling. Unless careful consideration is given this relationship, the finest technique and most elegant conceptualization will be useless. It requires great sensitivity to be able to monitor your client's emotional reaction and at the same time be aware of your own feelings, while simultaneously a half-dozen clinical tasks press for immediate attention. Such tasks as information gathering, organizing the data, forming diagnostic impressions, formulating a treatment plan, and implementing that plan are interwoven with the interpersonal aspect of this counseling experience. An honest appraisal of suicidal thoughts, fantasies, and acts demands the courage and compassion to become a participant in the process while maintaining an observer's stance. This may sound rather static and rigid. It might better be understood as a constant ebb and flow, moving back and forth between a position of identification and one of greater objectivity.

Summary

In short-term counseling with a suicidal client, extensive examination of the client-counselor relationship is not a primary goal. Such a focus is much more appropriate in long-term, intensive psychotherapy in which the relationship is one of the central vehicles for insight, understanding, and change. For our purposes, the significance of the counseling relationship is in the manner in which it either facilitates the formulation and implementation of the treatment plan or the extent to which the client's feelings might jeopardize the continuance of the counseling itself. Once a generally positive atmosphere has been established and an alliance has been formed the counselor can go on to deal with the essence of the suicidal crisis.

References

Freud, S. "The Dynamics of Transference." J. Strachey, ed. *The Standard Edition of the Complete Works of Sigmund Freud*. Vol. 12. London: The Hogarth Press, 1912.

Greenson, R. (1965) "The Working Alliance and the Transference Neurosis." *Explorations in Psychoanalysis*. New York: International Universities Press, 1978.

Zetzel, E. "Current Concepts of Transference." *International Journal of Psycho-Analysis* 37 (1956) 369–378.

Suggested Readings

Davanloo, H., ed. *Short-Term Dynamic Psychotherapy*. New York: Jason Aronson, 1980.

Epstein, L., and Feiner, A., eds. *Countertransference*. New York: Jason Aronson, 1979.

Langs, R. *The Bipersonal Field*. New York: Jason Aronson, 1976.

Racker, H. *Transference and Countertransference*. New York: International Universities Press, 1968.

3 The Listening Process

Much of the information you will find important in order to understand your client is communicated in disguised and indirect ways. For this reason, you'll need to listen for both the obvious surface meanings and the deeper hidden meanings in what he says. Thus, a portion of your attention will of necessity be reserved for listening "between the lines." In this chapter we will examine some of the characteristics of the interaction between you and your client with a view toward understanding what he is saying and how he is saying it.

In order to be helpful you will need to hear about some of his darkest and most abhorrent secrets and you will ask him to talk about and reexperience all manner of painful, fearful, and confused feelings. Therefore you should not be surprised to find a natural reluctance on his part to freely engage in such an endeavor. But this is only the beginning. Beyond those facts your client may consciously feel uncomfortable about disclosing there exist thoughts and feelings that simply do not come readily to mind even though they are of central importance in the current crisis. Finally, there is an entire realm of human experience, thoughts, feelings, and fantasies that exists quite beyond conscious awareness or, more specifically, in the unconscious. You will encounter three forms of censorship: conscious withholding on the part of your client; the problem that at the moment he is not likely to think of all the facts that relate to the crisis; and mechanisms that actively intervene to keep certain thoughts and feelings from entering awareness. Each of these mechanisms has a definite psychological rationale as a self-protective device and as such represent one kind of coping mechanism.

As a counselor, you necessarily stand in opposition to these natural and, under normal circumstances, adaptive mechanisms. Counseling demands that the client relinquish certain of his characteristic ways of communicating, most notably the censorship employed in normal conversation. To the extent that you have fostered a sound therapeutic alliance, your client will attempt to eliminate conscious withholding and will direct his attention to areas you indicate are important. His wish to be helped allows him to overcome the embarrassment and discomfort that accompanies painful memories and realizations.

Defense Mechanisms

What remain as obstacles to full communication are those mechanisms that operate outside of a client's awareness. These are termed *defense mechanisms* when discussed generally in psychology, and when they occur in psychotherapy they are referred to as *resistances* (A. Freud 1966). They are a normal part of the psychic apparatus and an inevitable factor in counseling. Defense mechanisms exclude from conscious awareness those thoughts, feelings, impulses, and fantasies that would cause the individual anxiety or guilt. They also interfere with the formation of ideas, emotions, and actions that would disrupt psychological functioning. These internal stimuli are either warded off or emerge in disguised form as other ideas, emotions, or actions. In this way, the defenses regulate and maintain a psychological balance and emotional equilibrium which permits us to function, to solve problems, and to get along with people.

Defense mechanisms operate automatically, not as the result of conscious choice. It is important therefore to appreciate that your client does not realize that he is attempting to protect himself from some painful memory or realization when he uses them. This happens at an unconscious level. Understanding this will help you avoid the error of resenting the client's resistances and allow you to use the knowledge to modify your technique to fit his unique needs.

Defense mechanisms are not pathological processes but are an essential part of the normal interplay of internal forces which, in most persons, contribute to effective psychological functioning. For the most part individuals tend to rely on certain defense mechanisms to the extent that they become stable, consistent features of their normal character or personality.

In an emotional crisis these characteristic ways of coping become less effective and the defenses are no longer equal to the task of protecting your client. At such times, the defenses tend to be employed in a maladaptive fashion and character traits become more rigid and extreme. This is, of course, the point at which we first see the client. He is typically experiencing the anxiety and guilt associated with psychological conflict but often without an understanding of the underlying issues. Realizing how defenses operate will help you unlock many of the doors that have stymied your client and have prevented him from solving his problems. Such knowledge and understanding enhance psychological functioning and afford him a greater sense of control. You need, therefore, to recognize and appreciate the significance of the manner in which psychological processes shape what is communicated by your client and how he expresses himself in the counseling session. The following defense mechanisms, with case examples, will help you accomplish this.

Denial

One of the most basic and frequently observed of the defense mechanisms is denial—the refusal of the client to admit the reality of an unpleasant event. The clearest example of denial is the almost universal reaction to the news of a loved one's death: first there is shock; then we hear, "No, it can't be true." The shock is too great, and acceptance of the reality is, at least temporarily, too upsetting to tolerate. Here the wish to have the beloved is in conflict with the harsh reality of losing him, and for the moment reality is superseded. Denial is often the first buffer erected to ward off such an overwhelming and painful experience. It is self-protective and operates psychologically in a manner similar to the physiological process of shock. In most people it is a temporary measure that buys some time until other more adaptive coping strategies can be mobilized. Denial is not very effective when the problem is less transitory because it will eventually fail as evidence to the contrary presses for attention. With greater psychological maturity, the sense of reality is too highly developed to be easily overridden, and for this reason adults must abandon denial as a major defense. The following case study illustrates denial.

Mr. K., a thirty-four-year-old, separated man, had grown up in a family in which his mother had many extramarital affairs throughout his childhood. Though she would be out all night at least once a week, she would return home before breakfast and cook for her husband and children. No mention was ever made of her absences, much less of her whereabouts. When he was younger, Mr. K. was able to adopt the family's wholesale denial of the fact that mother seemed to disappear frequently. Later it became more difficult for him to avoid the facts and he began to surmise the meaning of her behavior. He became very critical and judgmental of his mother and vowed to himself that he would never tolerate infidelity in himself or his future wife. Over the course of Mr. K's twelve-year marriage, his wife had several brief affairs. Mr. K. missed some of the obvious clues, and although suspicion crossed his mind momentarily, he managed to deny the obvious and construct alternate explanations. Finally his wife told him of the affairs, what they meant to her, and that they needed to make some decisions about their present relationship. Mr. K. became depressed, had suicidal thoughts, and was panicked and fearful that he might lose his wife.

After several counseling sessions, it also emerged that he felt humiliated and stupid that he had fooled himself for so long about what now seemed so obvious. Some of the reasons for this reaction had to do with the manner in which he had dealt with the similar situation in his childhood. He recalled his own anger at his mother and a fear that if the whole story were brought out into the open his father would kill her. He remembered that during the early years of his marriage he frequently had the thought that if he "ever found out that she was having an affair, he'd kill her." He had long since forgotten this pledge until the counselor helped him review his feelings. It appeared that only by not finding out about his wife's affairs could he avoid what were tremendously painful feelings and a fear that he might lose control of his anger. He had repeated the lesson of his early life that denial of unpleasant reality is the only safe solution to such problems.

Repression

The second primary defense mechanism is repression, which is experienced by the client as forgetting. But it is motivated forgetting and has a definite psychological purpose. For instance, individuals differ greatly in the extent to which they can recall events of their early childhood, in terms of how far back they can remember and the kinds of memories that are available to them. This is, in large measure, evidence of the operation of repression as a defense against conflicting and painful memories. It is not unusual therefore for a client to report that he has no memory of the year his mother died or when his parents were divorced. This is an indication to you of the significance of such events in the psychology of your clients, and when appropriate you will want to explore it further. Denial and repression will color and distort every recall your client presents bout his life circumstances, past and present. The functioning of repression is illustrated in the following:

Mrs. L., a forty-five-year-old social worker, found herself wishing that she were dead and became very depressed at the time of the first anniversary of her mother's death. She could not stop thinking that she had not been good enough to her mother in her later years. There was nothing in what she described to the counselor that seemed to warrant her tremendous sense of guilt. It appeared, rather, that she and her mother had a warm and loving relationship. Mrs. L. agreed that this was the case and could not explain the basis for her guilty feelings. In the third session, the counselor asked about the circumstances of her father's death and learned that he had killed himself when Mrs. L. was eight. The counselor wondered aloud if Mrs. L. might not have had some of these same feelings then that she was having now. She replied that she couldn't remember much about her father's death and funeral. The counselor asked about her relationship with him. She responded immediately that they had a good relationship, then paused and said that she had completely forgotten until that moment that he had engaged in sexual touching with her for years and had once, when she was seven, asked her to engage in an act of oral sex which she refused. Mrs. L. had told no one about this because she feared that if her mother found out she would leave.

Considerable time was spent discussing these issues over a period of eight months of counseling. One outcome of this work was some clarification of her reaction to her mother's death. With the counselor's help, she was able to reconstruct the repressed memories of what had happened with her father. Though she had tended to have the conscious attitude that her childhood was happy and uneventful, she recovered her actual memories. Of central importance was the idea that her father had killed himself because of what he had done to her. Although this thought had long since been repressed, the enormous guilt that was associated with it had continued to be part of her life and had contributed significantly to the difficulty she had resolving her grief over her mother's death.

Regression

This mechanism is defined as a return to earlier modes of psychological functioning in response to a traumatic emotional experience. In adults, for example, this may take the form of clinging dependency on others. Individuals who have been perfectly independent and entirely self-sufficient may, in an emotional crisis, become indecisive and unsure to the point of immobilization. Such clients will often ask you for advice on decisions and seem to be constantly in need of reassurance. These are regressed ways of relating to others and tend to be temporary.

M., a high-school senior, had broken up with her boyfriend after going steady for three years. She took an overdose of aspirin two weeks later because she "couldn't live without him." In those two weeks she had not gone to school because of a stomachache she seemed to have every morning. She stayed in bed most of the day and read, selecting some of her younger sister's storybooks. She refused to join the family at meals and demanded that she be brought her meals in her room. Her mother noticed her several times sitting on the edge of bed rocking while she stared off into space. She began to carry an old Raggedy Ann doll with her when she had to leave the house and would only go if her mother was close by. She was calm and relaxed only near her mother, and particularly liked her to brush and braid her hair.

Her parents were at first worried and later somewhat annoyed at their daughter's childish whining and clinging. They felt that she was just doing it to get attention and that they didn't want to reinforce the behavior or let her get away with it. The counselor was able to explain to the three of them that this was a severe, but not unusual, reaction to the emotional trauma of losing her boyfriend and that it would be temporary. He reminded them of the many kinds of regressions that are typical and familiar in any child's life. Placed in this context, they could better accept her need to return to earlier forms of safety and security. The parents' tolerance and support and the counselor's guidance allowed M. to take the time she needed to return to her previous level of functioning and was much better within a month.

Isolation

Clients will sometimes recount experiences that evoke considerable emotion in you without seeming to have any such reaction themselves. In this circumstance, the client is consciously aware and able to discuss the events clearly but has managed to construct a narrative devoid of emotion in order to isolate feelings from the content of a memory. You may have the sense that something is missing in the story; by placing yourself in the client's shoes for a moment you realize that you would react with considerable emotion to such events.

One counselor, for example, found herself uncertain about her client's suicide and homicide potential. Mr. N. had talked at great length about killing himself and wife and children and had elaborated his plan to do so in great deail but without any hint of emotion. She was puzzled because in her experience suicidal clients were usually depressed and unhappy and those who threatened murder were generally angry. Mr. N., on the other hand, was rational and coherent and had no thought disorder. In fact, aside from the topic of conversation he appeared to be entirely normal. As she listened further, she noted that he never talked of feelings of any kind, only facts. His analysis of his situation was objective and detached, as though he were an outside observer. His intellectualization showed a dramatic isolation of thoughts from the feelings that should have been associated with them. He acknowledged that this was his style but saw no particular reason to change it. He declined the counselor's offer to work with him on his family problems, saying it was simply a matter of making up his mind.

Reaction Formation

This mechanism is defined as turning an unacceptable thought or feeling into its opposite. The client may consciously express an excessive concern for someone else's safety in order to counter an equally intense underlying anger and wish for harm to come to that person. The following case illustrates reaction formation.

Mr. O. found himself preoccupied with the welfare of senior citizens and had become increasingly more active in championing their rights. The counselor sensed a driven quality in these activities. Examination of his relationship with his parents revealed that there had been a major falling-out and that the client had been disinherited and disowned. When his father died, the client was inconsolable for a week or so, until his interest in the cause of the elderly developed. His concerned attitude was finally recognized as a reaction formation that protected him from experiencing his intense hatred for his father, which had caused him more than once to wish him dead. These thoughts were entirely repugnant to him and were turned into their opposite. The intensity of his concern for the elderly bespoke an equally strong anger and rage toward his father that could not be acknowledged.

Undoing

If the client has the sense that he harmed someone or behaved in some unacceptable way, certain of his actions may be attempts to undo the misdeed. Such behavior often has an exaggerated quality because it derives its impetus and intensity from its psychological opposite.

Lady MacBeth's compulsive hand-washing, for example, was an attempt to rid herself of the psychological blood that stained her hands, the guilt that could not be cleansed from her soul. Shakespeare has provided a classic example of an attempt to undo a deed, to symbolically and magically eliminate its consequences and make it as though it had never happened. Undoing is related to reaction formation in that each represents a contradiction of the original idea. In undoing, the expression is in terms of action which, actually or magically, is the opposite of what was done before, either in fantasy or reality. This is the basis for many compulsive rituals that are repetitive behaviors to ward off an unacceptable wish.

In the previous case example Mr. O's attitude of concern for the elderly was seen to be a reaction formation against his hatred for his father. The translation of this attitude into action, namely his work on behalf of the elderly, represents an undoing insofar as the defense involved actual behavior.

The case of Mrs. P. further illustrates undoing. Mrs. P. found that she had to end every telephone call to her parents, husband, and children with "I love you." She also said this whenever any member of the family left the house, if only for a short while. There were countless times during the day when she would verbalize her love in this way. Taken together, these instances totaled over one hundred such statements each day. The counselor was of the opinion that this was somehow excessive but found it difficult to criticize someone for the mere expression of loving feelings. When he attempted to bring the subject into the discussion, Mrs. P. was, indeed, offended. Only when her fears of anger and rejection were better understood could she see her repetitive statement as a plea for others to continue to love her and to not leave her. As a result of these fears she had bottled up a tremendous amount of resentment and anger that she was afraid to acknowledge. She employed reaction formation and undoing in the service of opposing what seemed to her to be terrible forces within her. Her ''I love you'' ritual took on almost magical meaning as a way to keep the family together.

Projection

This mechanism is considered a more severe psychological disturbance than some of the other mechanisms we have described. Here a thought or feeling that the client has at some level but cannot accept or tolerate in himself is attributed to some other person. A client in the midst of a homosexual panic may perceive others as wanting to attack him homosexually and becomes very fearful even to the point of having persecutory delusions.

Mr. Q., a man whose religious beliefs and strict conscience could not admit any sort of attraction to a woman other than his wife, found himself anxious around his female supervisor. He had no idea what was bothering him other than the thought that he was anxious to perform well on the job. At about the same time, he became preoccupied with the notion that his wife was having an affair. It was true that the marriage had been unsatisfactory for some time but there was no basis in fact for his jealousy. The counselor felt that the man was sexually attracted to his new superior, and though he was not consciously aware of these feelings, this was the basis for his uneasiness at work and probably explained his suspicions at home. Mr. Q. had projected the wish he could not accept as his own onto his wife. The counselor recognized how contradictory these feelings were, felt that an attempt to clarify and interpret them would arouse more anxiety that Mr. Q. could tolerate during the crisis, and decided to work on the marital relationship in the short term, leaving the other intrapsychic issues for later.

Acting Out

Sometimes an impulse finds expression in actual behavior in some indirect fashion though its meaning never enters conscious awareness. For example, a client who is disappointed and angry with a counselor but has difficulty experiencing and expressing such feelings may be chronically late for appointments. Such expressions of feeling through action provide partial gratification of the wish to strike out in anger, relieve the feeling, and ensure that the issue remains out of conscious awareness. Acting out can also be a displacement of a response from its original context to another. It is, therefore, possible that acting out involves more than an isolated feeling or a single action but is the reenactment of a memory. In counseling, transference is a form of acting out. It is the displacement onto the counselor of feelings and ideas that originally arose in another situation.

R. came for counseling because he knew he needed help with relationships with women. Although he acknowledged this readily, at the same time he struggled with the wish to end the counseling after nearly every session. This was puzzling to the counselor. Exploration of his feelings in relation to the counselor revealed that he felt that the counselor would reject him and tell him not to return or, worse yet, simply not be there for the next appointment. R. was protecting himself from this possibility by leaving the counselor before the counselor could leave him.

Further clarification of these feelings provided the opportunity for R. to recall countless times in his life when he had felt abandoned by people he depended upon dearly. He began to recognize just how central an issue this was, and its far-reaching implications for his relationships in general. Acting out the traumatic childhood situation allowed the memory and feelings of abandonment to remain out of his conscious thoughts. The acting out afforded some partial relief in that he was doing the leaving but had the same familiar outcome, being alone again.

Listening to the Client

Defense mechanisms obscure certain events and their meanings in a self-protective way. As a result, your client's communications to you have both obvious and hidden meanings that need to be recognized from the process as well as the content of the interview. Clients disguise their feelings without knowing they are doing so. For example, a depressed client who has made no reference to his own depressed mood may go on at length about all of the terrible things in the news that day, how the whole world seems to be going crazy, and that some catastrophic event is certain to occur in the near future. With this brief information you can be reasonably sure that the client is telling you something about himself. *The principle here is to listen to every statement the client makes as though it applies in some way to himself.* A detailed account of how badly "his junk heap of an automobile runs and how no one seems to be able to fix it" is a fairly direct metaphor for the client's mental state and his sense that there is no help for him either. Descriptions of the client's home often contain similar clues. What a client may have to say about some problems his child may be having and the child's feelings should likewise be considered true of the client.

Another powerful clue to the meanings hidden in the obvious content of the interview is the sequence of the client's thoughts. For example, your client may mention in passing his involvement in a fatal auto accident some years ago and then proceed to change the subject and talk about how one of his sister's children died eight years ago of sudden infant death and how many times over the years he has wept at the thought that if he had been close by and had only mentioned an article he had read about precautions just the week before, the child might have lived. He goes on at length about the terrible guilt he feels each year on the anniversary of the baby's death. You should be alert to the likely possibility that what appears to be a change of subject is in fact not the case at all. Therefore you'll remain open to the possibility that there is some less obvious connection between the two topics. Here the obvious link is the element of death in each incident. The hypothesis that follows is that the client's emotional reaction is the same to each, that he has a great sense of guilt and responsibility for the auto accident as well. Your client may not be aware that he had displaced his feelings about the accident onto the death of his sister's child. And you may choose to clarify this, especially if it has some value in helping the client whose related feelings have precipitated his suicidal impulses.

You must attempt to maintain the kind of attention and receptivity that allows the greatest number of possible connections. When the client talks of the past, you wonder if the statements also apply to the present. If the client speaks of the present, you consider the possibility that he refers also to the past. When the client discusses other people, you entertain the possible hidden reference to either the client himself or to you.

In most counseling sessions, several themes will emerge as more important than others and will tend to be more fully elaborated. The client's initial statement will, more often than not, provide the elements basic to the dominant issues to be discussed in the remainder of the session, and while in the throes of a crisis he will have little awareness that there is a connection between these topics. You may miss the thread that runs through the session and these multiple issues if you pay exclusive attention to the surface meanings or only to the feelings being expressed. This will result in a less than adequate treatment plan. And instead of helping your client you will only prolong his suffering.

Speaking to Your Client

One of the most important factors in the client's counseling experience is *what you say to him* and *how you say it*. We wish in no way to attempt to dictate style. Each counselor must rely on and develop his own characteristic way of relating to clients. The counseling relationship demands genuineness and honesty above all else, and there is little room for role playing. Your sense of respect for the client is conveyed in your attitude and in the manner of speech you use. At a time when the client is extremely sensitive and vulnerable, it is imperative to avoid any hint of condescension. To the extent that you are comfortable with it and it is appropriate, use some of the client's own idiom and manner of expression, especially key phrases that evoke the client's exact meaning. Your attempts to communicate succinctly and directly relieve both parties of many of the social conventions and niceties that characterize such discussions in social conversation. Simple declarative sentences also convey your meaning with the greatest impact and ensure that one clear message is transmitted at a time.

The interval following your comments is of crucial significance in monitoring the counseling process. This is the time that you must ask yourself whether the client's verbal and nonverbal response confirms in some way that the comment was helpful. The client may overtly agree or disagree, remain silent for a moment, begin talking about the topic under discussion, or change the subject. As always, you listen both to the surface response and to the hidden reaction. For example, you may make an interpretive statement or attempt to clarify what seems to be an issue for the client and its signficance for his current crisis. Confirmation of such a remark should ideally take the form of the client's elaboration of the theme you alluded to.

Often your insight, if accurate, well-phrased, and well-timed, will stimulate the client to recall some similar event from the past but with a new understanding. This shows that he has, in fact, taken your comment and made some use of the information to increase his understanding in a manner that integrates intellect and emotion. It may appear on the surface that he has disregarded your statment and has simply gone on to change the subject. But the client's response always contains some commentary on your remarks, though it may be indirect and disguised.

Summary

Communication in the counseling session is subtle in its nuances and intricate in the complexity of its levels of meaning. You must listen to both what the client is saying and how he is saying it with an appreciation of the psychological factors that shape the communication process. Defense mechanisms disguise and distort underlying motives such that they are not expressed directly in thought, feeling, or action. Much important information is, therefore, hidden. This is true not only of the content of the counseling session but of the client's reactions to you and your interventions.

References

Fenichel, O. *The Psychoanalytic Theory of Neurosis*. New York: W.W. Norton, 1945.

Freud, A. *The Ego and the Mechanisms of Defense*. Revised ed. New York: International Universities Press, 1966.

Munroe, R.L. *Schools of Psychoanalytic Thought*. New York: Holt, Rinehart and Winston, 1955.

4 Counseling and Interviewing Techniques

Our discussion of counseling techniques begins with some characteristics of the optimal counseling environment. The office should provide comfort, freedom from interruption, and privacy. Your client should be assured of whatever measure of confidentiality you can realistically offer. You should be aware of the possibility that tape recording and note taking during a session may detract from the client's sense of privacy. Furthermore, excessive note taking may interfere with your ability to listen. Telephone calls should not be taken during the client's time, if possible. Starting and stopping times and fees for sessions should be discussed explicitly. When these ground rules are adhered to, they contribute to the client's feeling of predictability in the counseling relationship and promote a sense of safety and security.

The possibility that tape recording and note taking may create some disruption needs to be balanced against the clinical demands placed upon you as a counselor and your agency's recordkeeping procedures. Notes that outline the essential facts of the case ensure that you have the information you need while working with the client, for your records, and for the purposes of supervision. Tape recording is also tremendously useful as a training technique and benefits your clients as it helps you to improve your skills. But be prepared to discuss your policy on both matters with your client and listen for his feelings about it. Tape recording should be introduced at the beginning of the interview and only after obtaining your client's written consent.

Some comments regarding your general attitude and behavior are also in order. As a counselor, you are an expert and this places you in a position of authority in the counseling relationship. It is in your client's best interest that this role be maintained. It is common for counselors to feel somewhat uneasy in the expert's role and as a result to seek to create a more equal relationship with the client. One expression of this discomfort is to define the counseling relationship as a friendship and then indulge in excessive self-disclosure. This attitude may address your needs but deprives your client of the kind of professional relationship that is most helpful. Such an understanding of your role creates an environment that expresses warmth and concern through a professional degree of formality.

The counseling process begins with the initial greeting. In keeping with the professional attitude, an adult client is always called by appropriate title and surname. Similarly, you introduce yourself either by first and last name or by title and last name, never by first name alone. A smile, firm handshake, and invitation to accompany you into the office are all that need transpire in the waiting area. Once in the office it is often helpful to direct your client to the chair you wish him to take rather than allow him to make the choice and possibly create some unnecessary tension and uncertainty.

Basic Interviewing Techniques

After you have introduced yourself and asked the client to come into your office there are several choices about how to start the session. Do you sit down and then without another word wait for your client to say something? Or do you start things off with some kind of explanation of who you are and what you do? In crisis work you are less likely to have the luxury of remaining silent. The limited number of sessions, the brief amount of time, and the potential seriousness of the crisis all demand that you take a more active role in the counseling process. This extends to the way you structure the opening of the interview, regardless of whether it is the first or the last session (Ivey 1971).

Open Invitation to Talk

Open-ended techniques are designed to give the client as much latitude as possible when he begins talking. They presuppose that he knows what he wants to say and that all you need to do is give him permission to begin. This method offers the client the least amount of structure, enables him to begin wherever he wishes, and does not interfere too much in the process. An additional advantage of open-ended techniques is that they give you the opportunity to sit back and listen to what is being said. Further, they make the indirect statement that you want to find out something about how well your client can function on his own. You give him the least amount of structure necessary in order for him to get started. You might say, "Tell me why you wanted to talk today." or "What can I help you with?" If the client shows signs of not being able to handle the open-endedness of your introduction, then become more focused and directive. Your focus will then give his anxiety the containment it needs in order for him to function.

Closed Invitation to Talk

By contrast, the closed-ended approach is direct and very pointed. It is best used when you want some very specific information or when the client is saying that he cannot handle the vagueness of the open-ended approach. You might open by saying, "Your doctor said you have been having trouble with suicidal impulses?" or "Tell me about your suicide attempt." Closed-ended questions are best used sparingly particularly when you are beginning the interview. Too much specificity will signal your client that you intend to do all the work and that he should remain passive and relatively uninvolved. Use the closed-ended approch only as it seems appropriate to your client's needs. Whenever possible, move away from it and substitute a more nondirective approach. Later on use it as the process of the interview determines that you need it. For example, you might need to say, "Tell me who is staying at your house now."

With depressed and suicidal persons, the closed-ended technique can prove very valuable. Whenever you suspect that the client may be withholding crucial information about a suicide plan, use closed-ended questions, for example, "You said you have pills at home?" With the client who is chronically depressed do the same thing. Given the time constraints in crisis work, your skill at interspersing the closed and open invitations to talk will help the session get going and at the same time help you get all the important information along the way.

Examples

Open

Counselor: Tell me about yourself.
Client: Well, I'm twenty-nine years old. I have three children and a husband. I live on Denice Hill. I am a native here. . . .

Closed

Counselor: Where do you live?
Client: On the East Side.
Counselor: How long have you lived there?
Client: About five years.
Counselor: Where did you move from?
Client: Los Angeles.

Open

Counselor: Why don't you begin wherever you would like to.
Client: OK. I lost my job two months ago and everything has

been going downhill since then. My husband has a pretty
good job but we need the money from my work too.

From these examples you can imagine that there are an infinite variety
of ways to begin a session with either the open- or closed-ended approach.
Sensitivity and skill will help you decide what the needs of your client
are and thus which approach you should use at any given time during the
session. Getting specific facts and feelings does not mean that you have
to put your client on guard. You can be closed-ended without being
aggressive.

Combining Interviewing Techniques

There are ways to use these two techniques in tandem to facilitate the
smooth and easy flow of the interview once it begins. If for example you
start open-ended and then your client comes to some kind of abrupt halt,
you may want to assist him a bit by shifting to the closed-ended approach:

First Interview

Open

Counselor: What can I do for you?
Client: Well I'm not really sure. My wife left me the other day
            and has moved in with her boyfriend. She says she doesn't
            love me anymore and I don't know what to do. (Pause)
Counselor: Tell me more about your marriage.
Client: Well I'm not sure where to begin. We've been married
            for fifteen years and I always thought we had a good
            marriage . . . until this. Now I don't know. We have
            three kids and they are pretty upset about this and I just
            don't know what to tell them.

This back and forth shift in interviewing techniques can be used by
you throughout the session. Sometimes you will have a client who does
not need your help to get started and keep going. Others will require that
you constantly intervene in order to keep them talking. There will also
be times when it will be absolutely necessary for you to be quiet and stay
that way for prolonged periods. This happens most often when you are
dealing with someone who is grieving. You are more likely to use these
silences therapeutically during the middle sessions of crisis therapy than
you are in the first session.

Bridging Techniques

Once you have your client talking, you need some additional ways to keep him going. Bridging statements are designed to do just that, and at the same time minimize interference from you. Bridging is a facilitating technique that requires very careful listening in order to pick just the right time and way to say something that will clarify, elaborate upon, or continue the themes you have already identified, in a smooth and useful way. As your skill improves, you will develop a better sense of when to say something and when to keep quiet. Most clinicians can tell when a client is rambling, rather than saying something important. That is the time to carefully intervene and redirect the interview in a more productive direction. By the same token you should also be able to sense when your client is struggling with emotionally laden material and could use your assistance to continue. In either case common sense will tell you that in a crisis setting you only have so much time and so many interviews in which to get your job done. Bridging techniques can be short and to the point or they may be longer and more complex. Clients will give you many opportunities to use bridging techniques, and there are any number of variations that will be useful. While we can only give a few here, be assured that others will develop with your own style, experience, and clinical exposure. The more choices you have, the more effective you will be with this aspect of the interview. Here are some examples:

Client: . . . I'm not completely sure how I got in this terrible state of mind but I feel awful most of the time. (Pause) The other day I even had thoughts of suicide. (Pause)

Counselor: Suicide? (Voice rising)

Client: . . . he's got my two little ones upset so this is the reason we took him to the hospital Thursday. His mother is scared. She is scared to be in the house with him.

Counselor: Scared! (Voice dropping)

Client: She is not necessarily scared of being in the room with him. . . .

At other times the situation may require that you make a brief statement in order to direct the interview without interfering.

Client: . . . it just seems that everything has been going wrong lately.

Counselor: When you say *lately,* what's the time period you're referring to?

Or

Counselor: Earlier you said that *everything seemed hopeless*. Let's go
              back to that.

One Question at a Time

We have noticed that counselors often try to crowd several questions into
one statement. This almost without exception adds confusion to the session. The client is already overloaded. Multiple questions will seem more
like a police grilling than sensitive counseling technique. In addition to
this disturbing element your client is most likely to respond only to the
last question you ask. In our previous book (Getz et. al. 1974) we gave
the following examples:

Examples: One Question

Counselor: What caused the divorce?
Client: I didn't like him at all. We got along OK. I don't know
              if it was because I was so young and didn't know the
              difference or what. I knew it wasn't really what I thought
              love was. But, I just stayed with him. . . .
Counselor: What did the drugs do to you?
Client: Nothing. I just didn't like them. I found some weed in my
              house one time and I literally blew it. I told my sister-in-
              law . . . I've just always been so scared of drugs. . . .

Examples: Multiple Questions

Counselor: Why did you come to this area? Do you have friends here?
              Any relatives?
Client: My aunt and uncle, but it's really my boyfriend's aunt and
              uncle.
Counselor: Have you been served with papers? Are you certain that
              this is a fact? You can't visit them?
Client: Oh, no! It's not that. I'm sure that he'll even let me visit
              them. I don't worry about him having them, because I
              know he'll be good to them. But it's the fact I love them
              too. . . .
Counselor: Let's return now to the discussion of slugging. Is that
              something new? It's obviously something you have dif-
              ficulty in dealing with. Has it gone beyond that?

Client: No. In many areas there's so much that is wonderful between us . . . in this communication bit. It just seems
like we fight each other. We're both strong people per-
sonality-wise. . . .

Silence

Of all the techniques we have outlined so far this one may cause the
greatest amount of confusion and anxiety. Remaining silent for any length
of time at all gives rise to considerable anxiety in the counselor. We
usually feel that we should be doing something and if we remain quiet
it often feels as if we are not. In certain circumstances that is the only
thing you should be doing. Your mind is working, organizing, collating,
keeping track of things externally and internally while you remain silent.
The pause allows the client to reflect and gather himself. He can decide
what it is that he wants to say. Your silence may be the first time anyone
has allowed him this chance to reflect without barging in with some
advice. Silence gives you an opportunity to understand where your client
wants to go with the time. You can learn how much or how little structure
to offer him. During the first session it can prove invaluable as a diagnostic
tool. Silence is to be used to get to know your client better. If you see
that silence causes too much anxiety for him to deal with effectively, then
say something appropriate and in keeping with the spirit of the interview.
Wolburg (1969) suggests that a pause in silence of longer than thirty
seconds requires an intervention. This depends on the circumstances of
the interview and on the clinical material. If you think that the client is
stuck and needs some help, step in and say something. During silence
you will want to stay in tune with yourself and the client. Do not let your
mind wander to other things. Concentrate on what you are doing and try
to fathom the reasons for the break in the flow of things. Plan your next
comments.

Summarization

Summarization is a technique that has a dual function very much as
silence does. In the context of all the sessions it can serve as a review
of what you think the client has said. If you ask your client to use it, it
can serve as a pause in the otherwise pell-mell pouring out of facts and
feelings. In a therapeutic sense it my prove to be useful in allowing the
client a psychological pause. For you it will provide a sense of whether
you are on the right track with this person. It can also go a long way in

helping you establish that all-important contact we have mentioned. Perhaps there is nothing quite so reassuring to a client as hearing from you that you have been listening and are able to repeat back to him precisely what he is feeling and what he has been trying to say. Summarization must be used with discretion. Too frequent usage hinders the smooth flow of the session. If not used enough, you may miss important facts that have been said only once.

When a client is showing a great deal of mental disorganization, it will be crucial that you use summarization both as an ego-organizing tool and as a diagnostic tool. The inability to remember what was said a few moments ago will have tremendous significance for your treatment plans. If your client cannot remember what you said as a way of helping him then your time and his effort have been wasted. The client can end up feeling misunderstood and even more helpless than when he came to your office. You can end up feeling useless as well. The correct appreciation of summarization will serve to thwart these negative outcomes. Here are some examples of summarization:

Counselor: Mr. Jones, let me cut in here for just a moment. So far you have told me that you feel like dying because your wife has left you, you are broke, and they are trying to repossess your car. Is that correct?
Client: Yes. And there is more . . .

Counselor: Mrs. James, let me see if I understand what you have said so far. You're frightened. You feel alone. You think that no one cares.
Client: That's it in a nutshell.

Counselor: Are you saying that because of the car wreck, your mom will throw you out of the house and that you'll get your friends in trouble for being with you?
Client: Well not really. My mom knew that I had the car and I have wrecked it once before and nothing really bad happened. I'm really worried about what my friend's parents will do to my friend.

In this last example you can see how useful (and sometimes embarrassing) the technique can be. In a high-stress situation such as crisis counseling there will be many times when you may think that you have heard what the client was trying to say only to be jolted by a response to summarization such as, "No, that's not what I meant." It is always better that your client be able to verbalize this. You then have a chance to correct the situation and thus cut down on the possibility of having your client act out his feelings of not being understood by not returning for the next appointment, or, at worst, making a suicide gesture.

Statements that summarize what your client has said demonstrate that you are listening and understanding. This can be a unique experience for your client and often has profound effects. Summarization also encourages elaboration of the feelings you refer to and contributes greatly in establishing a sense of emotional contact and rapport with your client.

Mrs. S., for example, paused following a detailed account of her depressed and suicidal feelings following her mother's recent death. The counselor took this opportunity to restate what he had heard, saying, "it sounds like feeling depressed reminds you of your father's mental problems and makes you afraid you'll end up like he did spending the rest of your life in an institution." Mrs. S. agreed and went on to add that she had feared throughout her childhood that she was like her father in this way and described how her mother had used it against her. This vignette illustrates how the counselor's summarization conveyed his understanding and acceptance of her feelings and encouraged her to tell more of her story.

Counseling Techniques

Statements that explicitly express empathy and understanding are always interwoven with the interviewing techniques just mentioned depending on the unique needs of the individual client. For some clients, the interspersed nod and "um-hmm" are sufficient while others need you to express your understanding more frequently in words. Such remarks as, "That must be very frightening for you" or "I think I understand why you were angry about that" demonstrate your understanding and acceptance of the feelings under discussion and serve to clarify issues for your client. You will find that it is not unusual for a client in the midst of a suicidal crisis to pour out his feelings in your office without being able to make much sense of what is going on. Though you may consider his feelings to be perfectly apparent, your client may respond to an observation that he is quite angry with a look of surprised recognition. In such instances, your identification of a feeling or an issue serves as a *clarification* and represents another important aspect of counseling technique.

As seen earlier, Mrs. S. responded to the counselor's summarization with relief and then went on to elaborate some feelings she had about her mother. The counselor listened and then commented that she seemed quite angry and resentful of her mother. Mrs. S. reacted to this clarification by saying that she had never realized just how deeply she was affected by her mother's sadistic comments. She then became somewhat agitated and said that it made her a little ashamed to say such things about her mother, especially now that she was dead.

The use of clarification often sets the stage for *interpretation*, which is designed to facilitate your client's further understanding of his feelings and behavior. An interpretation goes beyond a descriptive approach to what is on the surface and seeks to address the underlying meaning and significance of what the client is saying. This usually involves an attempt to direct his attention to a possible explanation for feelings and behavior based on motives of which he is less aware. An example from the same case will illustrate.

Later in the same interview with Mrs. S. the counselor offered her the interpretation that he thought her mother's death had brought back the hatred she felt as a child and her childhood wish that her mother were dead or in the institution in place of her father. He went on to say that she was probably feeling terrible about herself for having such thoughts and that her guilt was part of the reason she was depressed and suicidal. After a moment of silence and reflection Mrs. S. went on to describe how she had always felt as a child that she was somehow the cause of her father's problems and that she was the reason he had been taken away. The counselor made the interpretation that, in much the same way, she probably felt as though her murderous thoughts had finally caused her mother's death, and perhaps she was feeling as though she had actually killed her. He suggested that this had led her to feel that she did not deserve to live. Mrs. S. nodded in acknowledgment and sobbed quietly for several long minutes.

It is fundamental to verbal therapies that psychological and emotional phenomena have causes that are often outside of the client's awareness, and that these can be ascertained and utilized in the counseling process. Your client's confirmation of an interpretive statement and his subsequent ability to integrate and make use of the new knowledge emotionally as well as intellectually is termed *insight*. Clarification and interpretation of his emotional experience can provide a framework by which he can recognize, organize, understand, and thereby achieve some measure of control over his life based on his psychological and emotional resources. Always seek to determine the extent to which this emphasis is useful to a given client. Your ability to formulate and apply insight-oriented techniques is naturally dependent on the nature and severity of the suicidal crisis. We consider this to vary considerably from case to case but feel that clarification and interpretation have a most important place in short-term counseling with suicidal clients.

At times you may have to resist the impulse to offer interpretations in short-term work with suicidal clients. In the first place, the short-term model requires that the essential problems be addressed first, often to the exclusion of less central secondary issues. Time restrictions simply force you to let a number of things go. A second constraint has to do with your client's ability to make use of an interpretive statement. Many clients are not psychologically minded and have little interest in understanding underlying motives for their behavior; others are too anxious to participate in an insight-oriented approach. Finally and most importantly, to the extent that an interpretation makes something conscious that was heretofore unconscious, it will arouse some anxiety. This may range from slight embarrassment or mild discomfort to nearly overwhelming and intolerable guilt and fear. In short-term counseling it is seldom wise to uncover additional areas of conflict for the client. However, interpretations that help him cope with the issues and feelings of which he is already aware are supportive and enhance his sense of competence and control.

Our discussion thus far has focused on several basic interviewing principles and counseling techniques designed to facilitate the establishment of the counseling relationship. They are also designed to communicate your understanding and to utilize your client's insight as a means of bringing some order to his emotional upheaval. We turn next to several additional techniques that require much greater activity and directiveness on your part. Selection of the most appropriate techniques is based on an assessment of your client's strengths and weaknesses such that you do for your client only what he cannot do for himself. This again is the principle of employing the minimum intervention necessary to produce the best effect. Implicit in this principle is an expression of respect for your client and the expectation that he will assume a share of the responsibility for the process and outcome of counseling. This attitude maximizes the potential for growth through resolution of the crisis. You must therefore continually seek to intervene in a manner that avoids any sense of infantilizing your client or minimizing his personal resources.

Reduction of Anxiety and Depression

From the first moment of the initial meeting, pay attention to your client's level of anxiety and depression and monitor the intensity of his distress throughout the session. Anxiety disrupts and interferes with thinking about the problem at hand, with communication of thoughts and feelings, and with problem solving. Attention, concentration, and memory are especially vulnerable to the effects of depression. Without these tools your client will be unable to exercise judgment and his ability to understand what is going on will be severely diminished. In working with the suicidal client, anxiety and depression are your primary concerns.

Providing your client with the opportunity to *ventilate,* to say what he has to say about his circumstances, can be tremendously helpful early in the counseling process. In the course of your client's account of his story, you should seek to respond in a manner that communicates that what your client is going through is not unusual or unique. In this way you *normalize* your client's experience in order to reduce his sense of being different from the rest of humanity. You let him know that anyone in his situation would feel the same way and that many people have similar reactions to stress in their lives. You will find that it is common for a client who has considered or attempted suicide to feel shame and embarrassment about it. This can very easily be generalized to an expectation that others, including you, will disdain and reject him. The resulting sense of isolation and alienation compounds his problems and for this reason this issue becomes one of your initial concerns. The message that he is not the only one to have ever been in such emotional straits can significantly reduce the level of anxiety and facilitate the counseling process.

Following quite naturally and an extension of normalization is the technique of offering *reassurance* to your client. Here you convey not only that the crisis is a familiar one to you and has been shared by countless others but that because of this you can make some predictions about the likely course and outcome of the situation. Obviously, this applies in cases where your client has largely unrealistic fears and as a result is suffering from an unjustified and needless anxiety. Offering reassurance relies on your confidence that such is the case, the strength of your expert role, and your client's willingness to accept a different view of his situation. In no way are we advocating a psychological pat on the head or any attempt to deny the reality of the crisis by offering empty words of encouragement where none is warranted. Reassurance must be based on the realities involved and attempt only to correct your client's faulty perception of the situation as it contributes to his level of anxiety and depression.

Reassurance, then, contains an element of another technique, that of *educating* your client about psychological matters related to the crisis. As an expert, you have a fund of information, knowledge, and experience about the kind of problem your client is experiencing. Educational techniques assist him in using his intellect as a means of coping and problem solving. This has the effect of immediately strengthening and supporting his psychological resources and thereby reducing his anxiety. You should consider whether it would help to provide information in the form of recommended books for those clients who can make good use of written materials. In general, printed materials are best used to reinforce that which you have already communicated directly, rather than as a substitute for presenting new ideas in the counseling sessions. In short-term counseling, education can be an effective demonstration to your client that you have something to offer that can make a difference. Additionally, a significant portion of your client's anxiety is usually bound up in distorted and inaccurate ideas about himself and the world, and when this is the case an educative approach can be the most direct and effective technique.

Skills Training

A third group of techniques is applicable in short-term counseling and facilitates your client's acquisition of skills that will be useful in dealing more effectively with the events that have precipitated the suicidal crisis. *Relaxation training* deals directly with the intensity of your client's anxiety (Jacobson 1934; Benson 1975). Many of your clients will not have the ability to tolerate and effectively manage strong emotions. Deep muscle relaxation, meditation, self-hypnosis, and related techniques can be taught in the office and used by your client on a daily basis to ameliorate his anxiety and to function more effectively. In cases in which your client's thinking includes intrusive ideas that threaten his psychic equilibrium or incite him to act in a maladaptive fashion, *thought-stopping* can be a useful tool (Wolpe 1973). For example, a client who has a repetitive sequence of thoughts that begins with a litany of his faults and weaknesses, proceeds to an inner sense of terrible wrongdoing, and results in suicidal ideation as the appropriate punishment, needs help in stemming the flow of reproofs. In the counseling session you can ask him to engage in the self-recrimination and begin the self-destructive mental process. On your signal, he then is to stop and divert himself to more constructive thoughts. This procedure is repeated until he can employ it to interfere with such thoughts and in this way reduce the likelihood that he will act on the impulse to harm himself.

Most suicidal crises are precipitated by some form of interpersonal difficulty and for this reason techniques that improve skills useful in resolving such problems are helpful. Communication and negotiation skills can be acquired in the office by the *modeling* of behavior and *role playing* with your client (Bandura 1969). Representative problem situations can be constructed and various solutions rehearsed and practiced in the relative safety of the counseling session. This allows you to observe your client in a sample of actual behavior and give him constructive feedback. A good example of this approach is *assertiveness training* (Alberti and Emmons 1978).

Environmental Manipulation

The final class of interventions we will address falls under the heading of environmental manipulation. Here you devise a treatment plan that alters the client's environment with the goal of reducing the immediate risk of suicide. An intolerable living situation may be a major factor in the crisis and you may help your client decide whether to find an alternate place to stay for a while and how to implement the plan. It may be necessary to help him find a place to stay where he can be observed and, if need be, protected from his impulse to kill himself. Another method of directly modifying your client's behavior is to negotiate a *contract* in which he agrees to do certain things and not to do others. The language of the document includes an explicit agreement that your client will not kill himself, either accidentally or purposefully, for a specific period, usually until the time of the next appointment, and that he will avoid situations and behaviors that have been determined to increase risk. These may include drinking, driving, and seeing certain persons; and may also provide that he rid himself of the means by which he might destroy himself. The contract is then signed and dated and renegotiated at the next counseling session (see appendix E).

Your assessment will have provided you with a great deal of information regarding your client's *social support system*. You will know which members of the family and which friends, if any, can be called upon in the crisis. The background information you have will include those professionals and agencies that may already have some involvement with your client. Previous counselors and therapists, clergy, family physicians, probation officers, and caseworkers are frequently significant figures in your client's past and current problems. As such they are resources and potential sources of information. Your decision to contact any third party must of course take into account the effect such action will have on your counseling alliance, professional ethics, and confidentiality.

The client's family is generally the most significant of the available social supports, but the family may interfere with counseling. Systems theory is the most adequate conceptualization of the dynamics of the family. According to this theory, you must shift from an individual focus to an understanding of patterns of interaction. The basic tenet of systems theory is that man is not an isolated being but is part of a system, the most basic system being the family. Furthermore, since man is part of a system, anything he does affects everyone else in his system. Because of this, a suicide attempt must be considered in the context of the individual and his system. Crucial to this understanding is information regarding who is in the family (the configuration) and what each family member's interaction is with your client and with everyone else in the system.

The family seeks to maintain the status quo or homeostasis. Each family has its own balance and works to maintain that balance when it is upset as it is when one member attempts suicide. The typical response of a family to an upset in this balance is to protect the individual and sometimes that means protection from counseling as well. In an attempt to help the individual, the family can actually sabotage counseling. You will need to recognize this and take steps early to determine how the family works, what the suicide attempt means within the context of the family, and what the typical family response to crisis is. Your knowledge of this system will assist you in formulating a realistic treatment plan and will help you determine whether or not the family is a source of environmental support for your client. An understanding of family systems theory also provides you with the skills necessary to work with the family when indicated (Bowen 1978; Minuchin 1974; Haley 1980; Madanes 1981).

Control over the possible enactment of suicidal impulses can in some cases be enhanced by the use of *psychotropic medications*. If you work with severely disturbed persons you should educate yourself about the types of medications available and the indications for them in order to make better-informed referrals for medication consultations with a physician (Mason and Granacher 1980).

Finally, we must consider the instance in which all of the above techniques fail to provide you and your client adequate assurance that he will not kill himself. The remaining option is psychiatric *hospitalization* on either a voluntary or involuntary basis. Because you are working with potentially lethal clients you need the security of having hospitalization as backup. This requires that you understand commonly accepted criteria for voluntary hospitalization as well as for involuntary commitment. Each hospital has its own set of admission procedures. Involuntary treatment laws vary from state to state but generally require that a person be imminently dangerous to himself or others or gravely disabled and unable to care for himself. In the state of Washington, for instance, this determination is made by mental-health professionals employed by the county who can be requested to evaluate a client. In most agencies this decision will be with a supervisor and a consulting psychiatrist if possible.

Summary

The characteristics of the optimal counseling environment, appropriate office procedures, and the counselor's professional attitude were discussed as they contribute to a successful counseling outcome. Four general classes of counseling techniques were presented: (1) verbal interviewing techniques, (2) techniques that reduce the client's anxiety and depression, (3) techniques that provide the client with coping skills, and (4) environmental manipulations that are supportive of the client. The interviewing techniques are employed to accomplish several goals. They elicit the information you need to assess your client's problems and formulate a treatment plan. They communicate your empathy and understanding, which are the basis for a counseling alliance. These techniques help your client by clarifying and interpreting the meaning of his experiences with the goal of providing some insight. Depending on the nature and severity of the crisis, techniques that reduce feelings of depression and anxiety can be utilized. Some clients can benefit from skills training in specific areas. Finally, in some cases you will employ methods that increase your client's social support or, in extreme instances of potential danger, will arrange to have your client in the protected environment of the hospital.

References

Alberti, R.E. and Emmons, M.L. *Your Perfect Right: A Guide To Assertive Behavior*. San Luis Obispo, California: Impact Books, 1978.

Bandura, A. *Principles of Behavior Modification*. New York: Holt, Rinehart and Winston, 1969.

Benson, H. *The Relaxation Response*. New York: Avon Books, 1975.

Bowen, M. *Family Therapy in Clinical Practice*. New York: Jacob Aronson, 1978.

Getz, W., Wiesen, A., Sue, S., and Ayers, A. *Fundamentals of Crisis Counseling*. Lexington, Massachusetts: Lexington Books, 1974.

Haley, J. *Leaving Home: The Therapy of Disturbed Young People*. New York: McGraw-Hill, 1980.

Ivey, A. *Microcounseling, Innovations in Interviewing Training*. Springfield, Illinois: Charles C. Thomas, 1971.

Jacobson, E. *Progressive Relaxation*. Chicago: University of Chicago Press, 1938.

Mandanes, C. *Strategic Family Therapy*. San Francisco: Jossey-Bass Publishers, 1981.

Mason, A., and Grenacher, R. *Clinical Handbook of Anti-Psychotic Drug Therapy*. New York: Brunner/Mazel, 1980.

Minuchin, S. *Families and Family Therapy*. Cambridge, Massachusetts: Harvard University Press, 1974.

Wolberg, L. *Short-Term Psychotherapy*. New York: Grune and Stratton, 1965.

Wolpe, J. *The Practice of Behavior Therapy*. New York: Pergamon Press, 1973.

5 The Role of Diagnosis

Your selection of interviewing techniques and intervention strategies will be determined largely by your assessment of the nature and severity of your client's difficulties. In this chapter we introduce the concept of *diagnosis* and its role in working with the suicidal client.

The term *diagnosis* has two related meanings, both of which are important for our discussion. Diagnosis is first of all a process of investigaton; it is the clinical procedures employed to make known the facts as they relate to your client's problems. The second meaning of diagnosis has to do with the product of that investigation process. In this latter sense, a diagnosis is a condensation of what is known about the client in a succinct and organized form.

In medicine, a diagnosis contains several kinds of information: the *syndrome* or set of symptoms, the underlying cause or *disorder*, the *etiology* or factors that have produced the disorder, the appropriate *treatment*, and the *prognosis* or probable course of the disorder. The diagnosis thus relates what is known about a client to the existing body of scientific knowledge. Though psychiatric and psychologic diagnosis is at present less precise and complete than the medical diagnosis, the diagnostic process and its goals are analogous. The most thorough and widely accepted systematization of psychological problems is the *Diagnostic and Statistical Manual of Mental Disorders* (third edition) (DSM-III) published by the American Psychiatric Association in 1980. We will follow the DSM-III in our discussion of schizophrenic disorders, depressive disorders, and personality disorders. We will also illustrate how counseling techniques differ according to the nature and severity of the client's problems. These three categories of disorders are selected from among the dozen or so major diagnoses because they present special difficulties commonly encountered in working with suicidal clients.

Schizophrenic Disorders

The DSM-III lists eight essential features in schizophrenia. In chapter 6 we will discuss many of the same issues as part of the mental status evaluation. For a complete description of these and other terms in the psychiatric nomenclature, see Spitzer's "Mental Status Exam Record" (MSER) in appendix A.

Content of Thought

The schizophrenic client has unusual and bizarre ideas known as *delusions*. Persecutory delusions, which involve a belief that someone seeks to do him harm, are among the most common. There are also delusions of grandeur, in which the individual believes that he actually is the extraordinary person such as Jesus or the Virgin Mary that he identifies with. Delusions of reference are beliefs that events that are in reality unrelated to the client have great personal significance. The presence of a clearly delineated and well-elaborated delusional system is one of the chief diagnostic criteria for schizophrenia.

Form of Thought

A second characteristic of schizophrenia involves disordered thought processes, of which a *loosening of associations* is a primary feature. This is when ideas and subjects follow one another without any logical connections. The result is speech that is confused and incomprehensible in the extreme.

Perception

A third hallmark of schizophrenia is the presence of *hallucinations*. These are sense perceptions in the absence of an actual stimulus and they can occur in any or all of the five senses.

Affect

Mood or *affect* is an evaluation of the emotional tone you observe in your client. In schizophrenia affect is frequently blunted, which means a severe reduction in the intensity of emotional expression. If there is no emotional expression, the term *flat* is used to describe it.

Sense of Self

A fifth feature is the schizophrenic's preoccupation with his *sense of self*. He has serious concerns about his identity and the meaning of his existence. Underlying much of his fear about himself is a sense of panic that he will cease to exist, disintegrate, or be destroyed.

Volition

Most schizophrenics have some degree of difficulty with goal-directed behavior and with demands placed on them to fulfill roles. They will appear ineffective at best and at worst may be incapable of making the simplest decisions. In the extreme the result is virtual immobilization.

Relationship to the External World

Schizophrenic clients tend to turn inward and to withdraw from the external world. This may appear to be a depressive reaction but here it represents a preoccupation with internal life. Thoughts, perceptions, and feelings are based on irrational ideas and fantasies rather than on reality. This sort of thinking is also called *autistic*.

Psychomotor Behavior

The schizophrenic person may show a reduction of spontaneous movement, maintain a rigid posture, or make stereotyped, repetitive movements. Unusual mannerisms and facial expressions may also be observed. These are often your first clues as to the severity of the client's difficulties. Recognizing these signs from the first moment you see your client allows you to modify your approach and greeting according to his needs and helps to avoid frightening or threatening him.

   These eight features constitute the group of symptoms (the syndrome) of schizoprenia. The schizophrenic disorder is, then, considered the underlying cause of these observable signs. The etiology of schizophrenia is generally considered to involve some genetic predisposition that interacts with certain dysfunctional communication and family patterns. The prognosis or course of the disorder includes a period of deterioration followed by an acute phase characterized by the symptoms described above. A residual phase follows during which some of the symptoms persist but usually in a less severe form. According to the DSM-III, a complete return to the client's level of functioning prior to the onset of the disorder is unusual. This implies that the client never fully recovers and is always vulnerable to a recurrence of the symptoms. Treatment for schizophrenia often includes hospitalization and psychotropic medication during the acute phase as adjuncts to or precursors of psychotherapy.

If you detect symptoms of schizophrenia in a client referred for suicidal thoughts or behavior, you must adapt your interviewing technique to take into account the nature of his difficulties. If the possibility exists that he has paranoid or persecutory delusions, you need to be most sensitive to his fears and concerns. You certainly do not want to do anything to arouse his fear or suspicion of you. First of all, you should avoid touching, crowding, or confining the paranoid client. You should avoid sudden moves and should explain any movement or sound inside or outside of the office that appears to have distracted or troubled him. If he is startled by a sound made by the air conditioner or reacts to a door shut in another part of the building, you should matter-of-factly comment on the sound and its meaning in order to reduce the possibility that he will form his own less benign explanation.

The schizophrenic is sometimes disoriented, unsure of the day and time, where he is, or who you are. You should explain each of these if there is any question about them. For example, "Mr. T., my name is Joan Gray. I'm a counselor and we are at the Westside Mental Health Center. Your wife brought you here about 10:00 this morning so that I could talk to you. It's Wednesday morning and it's about 10:30 now."

You should then proceed to conduct a much more structured interview than you would with most other clients. Because of the nature of the thought disorder, the schizophrenic client will likely be unable to answer questions that rely on memory, complex or abstract thinking, or on awareness of his subjective state. Simple, closed-ended and direct questions about the particulars of his situation are preferred. It will be less frustrating for both you and your client if you stick to matters of fact and avoid questions that require opinions, conclusions, or logical analysis. It may be helpful to conduct the interview in much the way you would with a child, depending on your assessment of the client's level of functioning.

Depressive Disorders

Following your determination as to whether or not your client is schizophrenic, your attention turns to the severity of your client's depression. Most suicidal clients present symptoms of depression and for this reason a detailed assessment of the client's mood is essential in every case. The following diagnostic criteria again follow the DSM-III:

1. The client's mood is characterized by hopelessness and sadness, often with anxiety and agitation.

2. Some clients lose their appetite and as a result have a significant weight loss. Others experience an increase in appetite when depressed and gain weight.
3. Sleep disturbance takes two forms: insomnia, which is the inability to sleep; or hypersomnia, which is excessive sleep or unusual patterns of sleep frequently associated with depression. Some clients may have difficulty falling asleep, others wake up early in the morning, some are restless, and some sleep during the day and stay awake at night.
4. The depressed client almost always complains of low energy and constant fatigue. This is not necessarily related to sleep and even when he has had an adequate amount of sleep, he is likely to feel tired upon awakening.
5. Problems with attention, concentration, memory, and the ability to think clearly are almost always present to some degree.
6. A pattern of decreased effectiveness at school, work, or home is typical in an assessment of daily activities.
7. The depressed client expresses a loss of interest and enjoyment of activities he once found pleasurable.
8. Feelings of inadequacy, self-depreciation, and low self-esteem are common in depression.
9. Social withdrawal results from a lack of interest in other people as well as the belief that no one else would want to associate with him.
10. Increased irritability is generally reported by family and friends, if not by the client himself.
11. The depressed client may appear to be slowed down in terms of thought processes and phsyical movement. This is referred to as psychomotor retardation.
12. The depressed client is often preoccupied with thoughts of death or suicide.

Assessing the severity of your client's depression will be based on having gathered information about each of these twelve symptoms. This information is supplemented by your subjective experience in sitting with and listening to your client.

You will find that his mood can have a profound effect on you. It is not unusual to begin to feel hopeless about your client and his distress, to feel that nothing will help this person, and that it simply seems inevitable that he will kill himself. You need to recognize that the source of such thoughts and feelings is your client and *not you*. This experience is the basis for empathy and an accurate assessment of your client's mood. As long as you are able to keep these emotional reactions in their proper perspective, they will not threaten to disrupt your work. If you do not monitor such feelings they can immobilize you and cause your intervention to be completely ineffective. Your client will sense the point at which you have lost hope, and the possibility of change so essential to the counseling alliance will vanish and with it your chances for success.

Your detailed inquiry into the manifestations of your client's depression will in itself be reassuring. It demonstrates that you have familiarity with and understanding of such problems by the kinds of questions you ask. Your ability to recognize the pattern will help your client appreciate the full import of his distress. Much of this information will be supplied quite naturally during the course of the interview. However, if some of these areas are unclear, be sure and ask; you have everything to gain by doing this.

You can help your client with his depression by allowing him to ventilate his feelings, by making him feel understood, and by trying to clarify what he is going through. For the mildly distressed client whose depression is less severe, this supportive relationship may suffice and form the basis of your treatment plan. However, in most situations that have deteriorated to the point that the client is having suicidal thoughts, verbal counseling techniques will need to be supplemented by more active and directive methods.

In cases of moderately severe depression you will need to combine several approaches in your inervention plan. In such cases the depressive symptoms interfere with your client's ability to analyze his situation and his ability to participate in formulating a plan. His problem-solving skills are diminished by his difficulties with attention, concentration, memory, and logical thought. In a very real sense you function as an auxiliary source of such skills whenever you encounter such deficits in your client. Another major area of concern is his motivation to take the steps necessary to resolve his crisis situation. Here again, you must intervene in a most active and directive manner.

The list of symptoms derived from the DSM-III serves as a beginning point for counseling the depressed client. He can often benefit from a normalizing statement that his symptoms are quite common and that the pattern of his problems is very familiar in depression. Many clients will not have realized the nature of their feelings or recognized their experience as depression. For this reason educating your client about depression will often be one of your first counseling interventions. This mutual understanding then becomes the framework for your interviewing techniques and for the treatment plan.

In most cases in which depression is a central issue, part of your plan will incorporate methods of depression management. We recommend that, at a minimum, the following four elements be included:

Sleep

Your assessment of sleep patterns will establish exactly where your client is having difficulty. Your educative approach should have included an emphasis on getting rest during an emotional crisis. Try to use methods that have been helpful to your client in the past. Common sense will lead you to such remedies as hot baths, reading, physical exercise, prayer, deep-muscle relaxation, a glass of wine and so on. Some clients may already have sleep or tranquilizing medications that can be used when necessary. Others may be able to request medication from their physicians. As will be seen, the discussion of sleep patterns and your prescription for better rest is quite detailed and thorough. This communicates to your client just how important you feel this issue is and how involved in creating solutions you are willing to become.

Food

When your client's appetite is diminished and he neglects his diet, physical strength and stamina suffer. Lack of nourishment, of course, creates a condition of low blood sugar and compounds feelings of depression. Many depressed clients simply forget to eat, often for a day or two at a time. Others find that they become nauseous when they try to eat and give up trying. The crucial importance of getting adequate nourishment to keep up physical strength and to lessen depression cannot be overstated to your client. You may have to sit and help him plan a menu, inquire about what food is available at home, and help with a shopping list. In the midst of a depression, your client may have great difficulty with these relatively simple tasks. You must not take for granted that he has the wherewithal to take the action necessary to provide an adequate diet.

Activity

It is generally accepted that physical activity can provide relief from mental and emotional problems. The need to stretch one's legs, get some fresh air, have a change of scene, or get out of the house are familiar folk remedies. Medical science has recently begun to corroborate that physical activity has uplifting effects. More specifically, it has been shown that jogging can reduce depression. This may be something the client is already aware of and may have practiced in the past but has neglected during his emotional crisis. The benefits can be almost immediate and some form of activity is available to almost everyone.

Contact with People

The depressed client has more than likely withdrawn socially and begun to avoid people. He may not be aware of this if it has been a gradual process and no one has pointed it out to him. The basic human need for contact should be part of your educative discussion of depressive symptoms. Either by encouragement, advice, or by written contract, daily social contact should be included in the depression-management portion of your intervention plan. As an assignment between sessions human contact can contribute significantly to a reduction of the client's depression.

The inclusion of these four lifestyle issues in counseling the depressed client has several advantages. First of all, the issues are based on common sense and are likely to be accepted readily. Second, they give your client the sense that there is something within his control that he can do to better his situation. This begins to counter his feelings of helplessness. Finally, the prescriptions work and can be the early success that will foster hope and further his belief that you can make a difference (Seligman 1975).

In cases of severe depression, more extreme measures are necessary. The client who is immobilized will require constant supervision in the home, or if this is not feasible, in a hospital. Antidepressant medication is often indicated for the client who is seen as an outpatient. Consultation with a psychiatrist about the indications for medication and hospitalization should be standard procedure with such clients. Finally, in cases of severe psychological distress, a referral for long-term psychotherapy will almost certainly be integrated with your other interventions in the short-term model.

Personality Disorders

Next we consider aspects of the client's psychology that have to do with the kind of person he is and how he characteristically reacts. The DSM-III describes *personality traits* as enduring patterns of behavior exhibited in a range of situations, traits that involve consistent, stable ways of perceiving, relating to, and thinking about oneself and the environment. When personality traits become inflexible and maladaptive to the extent that they impair functioning or create distress, they constitute a *personality disorder*. This category of psychological phenomena has particular significance for those who do brief counseling with suicidal persons. It is crucial that you recognize that the problems associated with personality disorders are highly resistant to change. If you understand this description, it will ensure that you will not confuse issues that might distract you in your plan to address the acute situation. These well-established, entrenched patterns are among the chronic issues that are not amenable to modification in short-term counseling.

The DSM-III lists eleven specific personality disorders. We will present only those which are most frequently encountered and require special handling in counseling.

Paranoid

The paranoid personality is suspicious, mistrustful, and hypersensitive. You cannot expect to be accepted readily or to become very close to this client. More than likely, you will represent a threat of some kind and find that many of your interventions will be rejected. The paranoid client tends not to be expressive and therefore will not be able or willing to provide you with the information you need to assess his psychological state and, most importantly, his suicide potential. Your expectations and goals for working with this client have to be set in light of the restrictions he places on the process. You can only hope to avoid anything that might make him more suspicious, could be interpreted as criticism, or might be seen as an invasion of his privacy. This client will not see much benefit in any form of counseling and will be unlikely to return for further sessions. Acknowledging these facts will contribute to a more realistic treatment plan and will minimize any sense of rejection or feelings of failure on your part when the outcome falls short of your goals.

Histrionic

Clients in this group are overly dramatic and express themselves in an exaggerated manner. They are given to excitability and seek stimulation. This client tends to be egocentric, demanding, and manipulative. There may also be a need for reassurance together with a communicated sense of helplessness. Such clients tend to become seductive with the opposite sex. You will need to moderate what you hear and what you see with such clients and remember that most of it is exaggerated to some degree. Some confrontation of the more outlandish claims may help such clients adopt a more realistic perspective. They tend to operate in terms of impressionistic thinking based on global reactions and feelings. It is helpful, therefore, to be somewhat more logical and analytical in your interventions.

It is not useful for the client to get carried away in a flight of excited fancy. The immediate danger, of course, is that this style can produce an impulsive suicide attempt. Suicidal behavior is also more likely to have a manipulative motive, especially to coerce attention, concern, or love. You can expect to feel the pressure of the demands and dependency that characterize most of the histrionic client's relationships. You must be aware of and recognize any manipulation designed to modify the counseling relationship or to influence you to step outside of your professional role.

Antisocial

An antisocial individual has a history of behavior in which the rights of others are violated. There may often be an inability to sustain consistent work performance, problems in parenting, participation in illegal acts, poor personal relationships, a failure to plan ahead, a disregard for truth, or recklessness. One caution, however, about the antisocial personality. There is a stereotype that holds, in part, that such individuals do not experience personal distress in the form of guilt, remorse, depression, and anxiety. This is not true. They do experience anxiety and depression and it follows that suicidal ideation needs to be taken as seriously with them as it would be with any other client. At the same time, a healthy distance if not skepticism should be your stance. Mental-health professionals are frequently conned by clients who wish to avoid responsibility for the consequences of their behavior. In medical settings such individuals sometimes make requests for medications with the intent to abuse them. Alcohol and drug abuse are frequent complications in working with the antisocial personality.

The antisocial personality is not likely to relate to you in an open and straightforward manner unless his level of distress is such that he is desperate. This can place you in an uncomfortable position in which you are aware that you are being deceived to some extent, and this can cause you to feel that you are being made to appear foolish in the interview. It is natural to take this personally and to react with some anger and frustration. The danger here is that your hostility will render you ineffective or, worse yet, be expressed indirectly in ways that encourage the client to kill himself. Such countertransference issues are always prominent when you are working with a client who treats you not as an individual but as an object to be used and abused. Your personal makeup and experience will determine which of two strong reactions you are likely to have. Some counselors react in an overly sympathetic manner. Others are hostile and rejecting out of fear of being manipulated.

Passive-Aggressive

This individual passively expresses his covert aggression. He typically harbors a great deal of resentment but does not express it openly. Chronic lateness, forgetting to fulfill obligations, procrastination, stubbornness, and intentional inefficiency are expressions of his aggressive feelings. These are often not recognized as such by the person himself. Clarification of the connection between anger and certain of these behaviors is an important first step in interfering with this maladaptive pattern of behavior. Often, passive-aggressiveness is a mode of handling aggression that is the consequence of a poor self-concept and a lack of social skills. It can, therefore, be useful to try and teach the client communication and assertiveness skills as alternative behaviors. You must recognize that such traits are not easily modified even in long-term psychotherapy and that you must generally forgo a discussion of the origin of such issues in favor of skills that are more limited in scope and directly relevant to the current crisis.

Passive-aggressive clients may appear to be most cooperative, if not compliant, in relation to you and counseling. Their reservations and objections will be expressed in behavior rather than in words. You must be alert to any such instance of covert reluctance and clarify the issue. Otherwise, the unexamined anger may cause the client to devalue you and decide to discontinue your work together. There are also very serious implications of this personality style for suicide, namely, the use of suicidal behavior as the ultimate passive-aggressive act.

Summary

The role of diagnosis is crucial in the development of your interviewing techniques as well as the formulation of your treatment plan. A *diagnosis* is an organized and condensed presentation of what is known about a client. It contains information about symptoms, causes, appropriate intervention, and the likely future course of the problem. This statement of the nature and severity of the client's difficulties determines the selection of counseling techniques and goals. We illustrated the role of diagnosis with schizophrenic, depressive, and personality disorders.

References

American Psychiatric Association. *Diagnostic and Statistical Manual of Mental Disorders.* Third ed. Washington, D.C.: American Psychiatric Association, 1980.

Seligman, M. *Helplessness: On Depression, Development, and Death.* San Francisco: W.H. Freeman, 1975.

Suggested Readings

Schizophrenia

Arieti, S. *Interpretation of Schizophrenia.* New York: Brunner, 1955.

Burnham, D., Gladstone, A., and Gibson, R. *Schizophrenia and the Need-Fear Dilemma.* New York: International Universities Press, 1969.

Burton, A, ed. *Psychotherapy of the Psychoses.* New York: Basic Books, 1961.

Lidz, T., Fleck, S., and Corneleson, A., *Schizophrenia and the Family.* New York: International Universities Press, 1965.

Salzinger, K. *Schizophrenia: Behavioral Aspects.* New York: John Wiley and Sons, 1973.

Searles, H. *Collected Papers on Schizophrenia and Related Subjects.* New York: International Universities Press, 1965.

Depression

Beck, A. *Depression: Clinical, Experimental and Theoretical Aspects.* New York: Harper and Row, 1967.

————. *Cognitive Therapy and the Emotional Disorders.* New York: New American Library, 1976.

Becker, J. *Depression: Theory and Research.* New York: Holt, Rinehart and Winston, 1974.

————. *Affective Disorders.* Morristown, New Jersey: General Learning Press, 1977.

Gaylin, W., ed. *The Meaning of Despair.* New York: Science House, 1968.

Kline, N. *From Sad to Glad.* New York: Ballantine Books, 1974.

Mendels, J. *Concepts of Depression.* New York: John Wiley and Sons, 1970.

Personality Disorders

Giovacchini, P., ed. *Psychoanalysis of Character Disorders.* New York: Jason Aronson, 1975.

Hare, R. *Psychopathy: Theory and Research.* New York: John Wiley and Sons, 1970.

Wishnie, H. *The Impulsive Personality: Understanding People with Destructive Character Disorders.* New York: Plenum Press, 1977.

**Part II
Clinical Aspects**

6 The Deductive Model

In the first part of the book we presented some important facts and ideas about suicide and reviewed some basic techniques for dealing with material that might come up in an interview with a suicidal person. In this part we will offer you very specific ways of organizing and thinking about what your client says throughout your counseling sessions.

In our previous work (Getz et al. 1974) we offered a system for organizing and recording crisis-interview material. The deductive model (figure 6–1) evolved over a period of years and is applicable in crises involving suicidal thinking and behavior as well as in other crises. This model consists of four basic steps plus assessment of the client's mental status and suicidal status. The basic steps are as follows (see also figure 6–1).

Step 1: Record facts and feelings as the client presents them.

Step 2: Connect related themes.

Step 3: Isolate major themes.

Step 4: Formulate a treatment plan.

The additional mental- and suicidal-status assessments will be discussed in detail later in this chapter.

The deductive model is designed to help you keep track of facts and feelings in an organized way so that when it is time for you to act to help the suicidal person resolve the crisis, you will be able to do so with confidence. As you listen to your client you can use any shorthand method you choose for recording the information; we use the client's own words as much as possible but shorten them to fit our own needs for time and space. Not every crisis will fit neatly into this model but it is nevertheless an excellent training device.

The deductive model places a great deal of emphasis on the first ten minutes of each interview, particularly the initial minute. With practice you can learn to identify the major issues and get ideas about other important elements of the client's situation in that span of time. At the end of ten minutes you should be able to identify the precipitating events, the severity of the crisis, and assess your client's psychological resources,

Step 1 *Facts and Feeling as Client Presents Them*	Step 2 *Connecting Related Themes*	Step 3 *Isolating Major Themes*	Step 4 *Treatment Plan*
1._____	1._____	1._____	1._____
2._____	2._____	2._____	2._____
3._____	3._____	3._____	3._____
4._____	4._____		
5._____	5._____		*Suicidal*
		Mental Status	*Status*
6._____		concise	concise
7._____		statements	statements
8._____			
9._____			

Figure 6–1. The Deductive Model

suicide potential, and mental status. You will not always be able to get all of these things accomplished in this time span, but people in crisis reveal a great deal about themselves by their mood, fluctuations in their affect, and other things such as their posture and facial expression. If you are alert and observant you can become highly skilled at picking up the variety of cues available.

You will not stop formulating your clinical impressions after ten minutes. Clients are not likely to stop talking or feel less pain when this arbitrary period of time has passed. In all instances, give your client your full attention for the entire session. What we are urging you to do is to train your mind to begin organizing the crisis information immediately, with the expectation that you will receive much of the important information in the early part of the interview.

It is not uncommon to find that after the initial few minutes you will begin to hear the same themes repeated. The words may be different or the context may change but the themes are nevertheless there. In our discussion of the sixteen basic questions in chapter 7 you will find that it is not always necessary to mechanically structure the interview to secure answers to questions. The client will tell you what is troubling him in his own way not just once but several times. The skilled counselor will collate the information and identify the key points, placing them in the context of the affect the client is expressing. You will also be listening with what Reik called "the third ear" (Reik 1948); or "reading between the lines." You will wonder about what *is not* being expressed; what the client is not talking about. You will often ask yourself, "Where is the anger? The sadness? The guilt?" These themes and the questions about what is missing are all found in those first few minutes when the client's story begins to unfold. There is so much material and so much to think about that there is real potential to lose your way. The wealth of material is what makes the first few minutes so important in brief counseling. In longer-term therapy you would have the chance to come back to something you may have missed and either clarify or explore it further when it came up again in a later session. This is a luxury that crisis counselors rarely have. In a crisis situation in which an individual may be threatening his very existence you must use every possible moment in the most constructive way.

There are several advantages in using the deductive model (Getz et al. 1974) in your attempts to use crisis-intervention time as constructively as possible. They are

1. It is a systematic and visual method of keeping track of the facts and feelings the client is presenting about his crisis.
2. It will help prevent the counselor from forgetting or getting confused about what is important, particularly in the early stages of the interview.
3. The model is flexible enough as a teaching instrument that once mastered, the counselor can set the guide aside and still be able to garner all the important information without a loss of confidence or the sacrifice of accuracy.

The deductive model is based on the following set of assumptions. First, you must have the facts of the crisis before you can take any action (formulate or enact a treatment plan). Second, you must simultaneously recognize the feelings that accompany the facts. Third, you have to know what mental status is and how to determine it. Fourth, you will have to know something about diagnostic categories. With these tools you should be able to develop a coherent treatment plan that has a high probability of working. By investing extra time you will be able to master the intricacies of this model so that you can use it throughout an interview, leaving you free to recognize the essential components of the session.

Applying the model to a suicidal crisis is in many ways no different than applying it to any other crisis. Your client will present the facts and feelings as they occur to him. It will be your responsibility to separate the relevant from the trivial, formulate a tentative diagnosis, and then come up with an effective treatment plan. In those cases in which you know beforehand that the client is suicidal, you will simply move more deliberately into assessing his danger to self and others. With individuals who disguise their depression and self-destructiveness, you will have to be more skilled and work harder. In either case the deductive model will help you know how to proceed.

It is easy to diagram a case with a suicidal person, analyze it, and fit each part of the puzzle neatly together on paper. In an actual clinical situation things are often different. People are not that predictable nor do they often fall exactly into textbook categories. Sometimes you may feel that the deductive model has little relevance. But remember to take it for what it is, a teaching and training device. If you are flexible, the model should help reduce your frustrations considerably. As we have mentioned, clients in crisis are so often overwhelmed with their situations that once they start telling you about themselves, it is hard to shut them off. The model is not designed to be a tape or video recorder. If you miss some of the material the first time, do not worry too much about it. The client will tell you again in one way or another and then you can record it. Simply concentrate on separating the important from the trivial and on remembering things reasonably accurately. With good supervision you will not miss much no matter which organizational model you use.

Several additional comments must be made in order to elaborate on the mental status and the suicidal status aspects of this model.

Mental Status

Simply put, mental status is "the psychological and behavioral appearance of a person" (Hinsie and Campbell 1970). In historical perspective, it describes the results of a psychiatrist's mental examination of someone in a clinical setting. Currently it is a concept and organizing tool that is being used by other mental-health professionals as well. With the proper appreciation of its strengths and weaknesses, it will have its place in your hands as well.

The following abbreviated outline is based on Spitzer's Mental Status Exam Record (MSER), which can be found in its entirety in appendix A. We have streamlined it here to make it useful for you, given the amount of time you will have with each client and the level of skill you possess. This format covers the important areas. But you should not feel that you have to be an expert in order to use it effectively. Nor should you feel that you will be out of your realm by becoming familiar with it. Simply know the significance of assessing mental status in the crisis interview and its place in determining your intervention plan.

Appearance

Dress and Grooming. Involves an evaluation of the client's clothing, hair, makeup, jewelry, accessories—all those things that catch your eye on first meeting.

```
┌─────────────────────────────────────────┐
│  1. Appearance                           │
│     a. Dress and grooming                │
│     b. Eyes and face                     │
│  2. Motor Behavior                       │
│     a. Slow                              │
│     b. Agitated                          │
│  3. Speech                               │
│     a. Rate                              │
│     b. Quality                           │
│  4. Orientation                          │
│     a. Person                            │
│     b. Place                             │
│     c. Time                              │
│  5. Mood and affect                      │
│     a. Feeling tone                      │
│     b. Quality                           │
│  6. Thought disorder                     │
│     a. Content of thought                │
│     b. Perceptions                       │
│  7. Dangers to self/others               │
└─────────────────────────────────────────┘
```

Figure 6–2. Mental Status

Is there anything unusual about any of these aspects of the client's appearance? If so what might be the explanation? Is it cultural or personal preference? Is it the counselor's bias? Does it reflect a general life-style or is it part of the symptoms reflecting the client's crisis state? Is there something inappropriate about his appearance? Something that seems out of place or odd (such as two different shoes or one sock or extremely long fingernails)?

Face. What do you notice about the client's facial expression? Is it expressionless or is there some grimacing? Are the jaw muscles working constantly as if they were chewing gum? Do you see tension in the face? What about facial color? Is he pale? Tanned?

Eyes. Are the eyes bright and clear or dull and lifeless? Are they downcast or staring straight ahead? Do they make contact with yours or is there avoidance? Does the client appear extra vigilant, staring very intently at you?

Motor Behavior

Motor behavior includes characteristics of bodily movement that are observable.

Slow. Is it a generalized slowdown or is it more marked and rigid as in a catatonic state?

Agitated. Is it a generalized overactivity whereby the client is unable to stay in one place and must move around? If so, is this his normal rate of activity or is it related to his crisis? Is it purposeless? Involuntary? Inappropriate and bizarre?

Speech

Rate of Speech. Is it fast, moderate, or slow? Is this a normal pattern or is it crisis-related? Does it have something to do with this professional visit?

Quality of Speech. Is it monotonous and flat, devoid of feeling? Is it incoherent, irrelevant, evasive? Is there evidence of *blocking* (the sudden cessation of speech in the middle of a sentence for which the client has no explanation)? Is there a *flight of ideas* (abrupt and rapid change of topics during conversation so that the client's ideas are not completed)?

Orientation

Personal Orientation. Does the client know who he is and is he able to identify others correctly? Can he identify the counselor, others in the room, family?

Place Orientation. Does the client know correctly where he is and what kind of place he is in?

Time Orientation. Does he know the year, season, month, day, and time of day?

Mood and Affect

This is an evaluation of the emotion or feeling tone that you observe or your client reports. *Mood* is the client's state of mind, while *affect* is the quality of that mood.

Mood. The predominant impact that the client presents. Is it depression, which is sadness, a sense of hopelessness, and worthlessness, or is it anxiety, which is apprehension, worry, nervousness, fearfulness, or panic? Or is it anger, euphoria, or loneliness?

Affect. Affect includes characteristics of the client's particular mood. Is the client's affect appropriate for the mood that you see or that your client reports? For example, is he laughing while he talks about someone's death? Is there a flatness, an absence of emotional responsiveness? Is your client *labile* (showing unstable emotions that shift rapidly without adequate internal control)? Are there outbursts of laughter and then rage and then crying, all fairly uncontrolled?

Thought Disorder

This concept broadly defines disturbances in thinking. It is thinking that becomes haphazard, confused, seemingly purposeless, or bizarre.

Delusions. A delusion is a conviction in some important personal belief that is almost certainly not true. They can be of the following types.

1. *Persecutory.* Beliefs that people are organized against the client, are cheating, harassing, attacking him, and so on.
2. *Somatic.* Convictions of strange things happening to one's body such as beliefs that the body is rotting, or someone is inside the client's brain.
3. *Grandeur.* The client believes he has knowledge and power beyond credibility; believes he can read minds, and so on.
4. *Influence.* The client claims his thoughts and feelings are controlled or influenced by others or by strange forces.

Hallucinations. These are sensory perceptions that are without identifiable stimulation and which primarily affect the five senses. Hallucinations can be visual (unformed lights and flashes or people, animals, cars, and so on), auditory (sounds), olfactory (smells), gustatory (tastes), tactile (touch), or visceral (hallucinations of sensations arising within the body).

Depersonalization. This includes feelings of strangeness about one's own body. For example, the client feels he is outside his body or that it somehow does not belong to him.

Potential Danger to Self (Suicidal Status)

The assessment of danger to self is a judgmental area where no one set of questions will help you be absolutely sure about who will or will not kill themselves. We urge you to err in the conservative direction. In appendix C we have included a scale for the assessment of suicide potentiality from the Los Angeles Suicide Prevention Center to help determine your client's danger to himself. It is not the only such scale available but it will give you a place to start. In crisis work you will probably not have the luxury of administering such a scale. Given the time you have to do a thorough job, we suggest including the following outline in your mental status exam.

Those Who Are in the High-Risk Category

1. The client who wishes to die and openly says so. ("I have no reason to live and everyone would be better off if I were dead.")
2. The client who appears to be psychotic. ("The voices tell me that I should kill myself.")
3. The client who is depressed and shows the following signs:
   a. Excessive guilt (especially over a dead relative).
   b. Exaggerated feelings of worthlessness and despair.
   c. An expressed wish to be punished (as a way of reducing his guilt).
   d. Withdrawn and hopeless feelings.
   e. Extreme motor agitation and anxiety.
   f. Significant weight loss in the past thirty days (ten to fifteen pounds or more).
   g. Disturbed sleeping patterns (different from his normal routine).
   h. Significant disturbance in eating behavior (loss of appetite, picking at food, nothing tastes good).
   i. Flat affect or talking about important issues without much life in the voice.

In addition to these signs, *previous suicide attempts* should be taken into consideration. Make sure you investigate every aspect of your client's previous attempts. Previous suicide attempts in the past ninety days are especially significant.

The "Five W's"

In our own clinical experience we have found that the *five W's* will help assess the degree of seriousness and danger in a client's present or past suicide intent. The five W's are who, what, when, where, and why now.

At times suicide attempts seem to be a kind of distorted communication to important people in the suicide attempter's life. Even if you discover that a suicide attempt seems to be directed at an important person in the client's life rather than at himself, always take it seriously. Even people who are trying to manipulate important others die if their communication goes awry. The five W's will help you sort out the reasons for the suicide attempt and clarify other important problems in the client's life.

Who? Who was around at the time the act was considered or attempted? Was the client alone or with someone significant to him? Was someone significant expected? If the client was alone, how lethal was the method considered or used?

What?   What was the method? Methods that allow little margin for error include guns, hanging, jumping from dangerous places, and drowning. Methods that have a greater margin for error and provide time for someone to intervene and save the person include pills, slow poisoning, and other methods.

When?   When did the attempt take place? Was it late at night when no one could have possibly intervened, or was it in the middle of the day with everyone watching? What was the time?

Where?   Where did the suicide attempt take place? What was the physical setting? Where were the significant others?

Why Now?   Why did the client select this particular time to take this action? What was the message he was trying to express? Why did he act now instead of a week ago? How much of what he was expressing in the suicide action was conscious? How much was unconscious? What did he hope to accomplish by taking this action now? What in fact has been the outcome?

As you can readily see, there is some overlap in these five questions. Do not worry about that. We want you to be able to remember these questions so that they can serve as a base for making an accurate assessment of which suicide attempts are life-threatening and which are not. As you listen to your client and talk about his situation, his private feelings about the degree and intensity of his suicide ideation will unfold. These private thoughts must be carefully assessed. If you have any suspicion at all that he may be harboring suicidal thoughts that you have not heard about, *do not* hesitate to ask about them. It is a myth that if you ask about suicide you may give the client suicidal ideas that he did not have before. This is not the case. Your responsibility is to bring out into the open any self-destructive material that may exist. It is no different than when you are working with a client you know is very sad and is unwilling or unable to express it. You would point this out to him and then empathically help him to come to grips with whatever was making him sad. Your place in the context of crisis intervention is to help the client verbalize his psychological state so that he does not have to act it out. To do this you obviously have to ask questions based on what the client has or has not told you. If any client who by history or feelings implies that he is vulnerable to the suicidal state, ask him about it. Have this clear in your mind so it will be easier to explain to the client if he challenges your need to ask certain questions or your right to certain information.

Timing, Tone, and Style

Timing, tone of voice, and style are key elements in all phases of the counseling process, but they are particularly important whenever you want to investigate suicide material.

Timing is probably the most difficult concept to master because it is so much more an art than a technique. Who is to say for sure when the right time comes to make an interpretation, a confrontation, or to offer support? Or when to ask a question about suicide? Of course there are those very obvious instances when even the least experienced counselor will recognize that he should say something. That is not what we are talking about here. Rather it is those times when you ask yourself, "Should I interrupt him now and ask about his previous suicide attempt or should I wait a little longer?" or "She sounds depressed but I don't know if she is hiding suicidal material or not. When and how should I bring it up?" or "Do I have enough rapport yet to ask some questions about her suicidal ideas?" In addition to these questions, there is the matter of the amount of time left in the interview, and the amount of material that has already been offered that is not specifically suicidal. Do you always know when to squelch such material in favor of asking questions about someone's thoughts of self-destructiveness? It is better to risk cutting off the client than it is to risk being without the information you need to assess the client's danger to himself.

Tone of voice is also important. How can you be firm and yet warm at the same time? How does one express gentleness and respect about such a subject and at the same time probe with the knowledge that it is likely to be upsetting to your client? How can one be incisive but not mechanical; caring but not tentative? All are part of the art of communication. If you are not comfortable with your interviewing style we suggeest you read the books by Mayeroff and Jourard listed at the end of this chapter.

Style is your particular mode of expressing yourself in a clinical situation. It is your individualized and personal way of phrasing your questions, expressing empathy, and offering advice. It is the way you have modeled yourself after certain people, particularly those you admire and respect. It is the way you imagine they might respond to this particular situation. Above all, it is the way *you* say things. It is the way you figure out the best time to make a clinical interpretation and ask a penetrating question. It is based on a certain feel that you have about the way the interview is going. It is the result of the way you have processed the client's information and have concluded that the time is right to ask about his suicidal thoughts. Though you recognize the place that your role models have played in your life, you do not act just like them. Do not try to conduct a family therapy interview as if you were Virginia Satir, or an interview with a schizophrenic as Frieda Fromm-Reichmann would. Take what they have to offer, but always blend it into what you would do. From this amalgam you develop your own style and pay attention to its effectiveness in the clinical setting.

Summary

There are a number of clinical models available for use with clients in crisis, (Mann 1973; Lieb, Lipstitch, and Slaby 1973; Sifneos 1972; Budman 1981; Aguilera, Messick, and Farrell 1970). The deductive model is primarily a way of helping the counselor organize crisis information in such a way as to make it clinically useful. It focuses on the early moments of the interview and gives the counselor an effective way of looking at and pulling together facts and feelings associated with a crisis state. The place of the mental status assessment in this type of work was outlined as well as the significance of a suicidal assessment. We intended to convey that a firm grasp of such theoretical models would serve to give the counselor a sense of mastery over a difficult situation. We stated that talking about suicide would not give the client suicidal ideas. It is when the counselor does not talk about such ideas that damage occurs; in effect this says to the client that he should be afraid of such ideas, that to have such notions is defective or crazy. Nothing could be further from the truth, of course. It remains for the counselor to keep this in mind whenever he works with someone in a highly depressed state. Finally, we considered the implications of the use of timing, tone of voice, and style, and concluded that this was as much an art as a science.

References

Aguilera, D., Messick, J., and Farrell, M. *Crisis Intervention Theory and Methodology*. St. Louis, Missouri: C.V. Mosby Co., 1970.

Budman, S. ed. *Forms of Brief Psychotherapy*. New York: Guilford Press, 1981.

Getz, W., Wiesen, A., Sue, S., and Ayers, A. *Fundamentals of Crisis Counseling*. Lexington, Massachusetts: Lexington Books, 1974.

Hinsie, L., and Campbell, R. *Psychiatric Dictionary*. Fourth ed. London: Oxford University Press, 1970.

Lieb, J., Lipsitch, I., and Slaby, A. *The Crisis Team: A Handbook for the Mental Health Professional*. New York: Harper and Row, 1973.

Mann, J. *Time-Limited Psychotherapy*. Cambridge, Massachusetts: Harvard University Press, 1973.

Reik, T. *Listening with the Third Ear*. New York: Grove Press, 1948.

Sifneos, P. *Short-Term Psychotherapy and Emotional Crisis*. Cambridge, Massachusetts: Harvard University Press, 1972.

Suggested Readings

Jourard, S.M. *The Transparent Self*. Revised ed. New York: D. Van Nostrand, 1971. See especially parts 5 and 6, pp. 133–207.

Mayeroff, M. *On Caring*. New York: Harper and Row, 1971.

7

The Sixteen Basic Questions

Goals of the First Interview

As we stated elsewhere (Getz et al. 1974), "The goal of every initial crisis interview is to gather, collect and organize" the crisis material.

To assist you in this task, we have outlined sixteen questions that cover many fundamental areas in determining why the crisis occurred and how you can help resolve it. We suggest you memorize the questions if possible. They will prove very useful during the actual interviewing process. The sixteen questions will help you get the information you need and give you a specific goal. Additionally, the structure provided by the questions will give you confidence in the first session and should reduce your anxiety accordingly.

A word of caution: do not try to get answers to the sixteen questions in a methodical, question-and-answer way. The questions are not meant to be given and responded to in sequential order. A crisis interview is not a job interview; it is a very sensitive interchange between someone who is asking for help and someone who is offering help. You will want to listen for the answers as your client is talking. Clients talk, sometimes in a rambling way, sometimes in a coherent way, but seldom in the logical and organized way the questions are outlined here. This is where your skill as an interviewer will serve you well. You will have to remember which questions your client has already answered and find the proper time to ask about those that still remain unanswered. Sometimes you will have to be very structured in accomplishing this. At other times you will not have to say a word. You will just listen, remember, and try to organize what you hear according to the deductive model.

These elements of the first interview are one reason that brief counseling is such hard word. In long-term counseling you can take time to get all the information necessary to formulate a diagnosis and treatment plan. In the crisis model you must make every moment count as you may have only one session with this person. That does not give you much leeway. You cannot afford to overlook key elements of the client's crisis.

The Sixteen Basic Questions

1. What prompted the identified client to seek help now?

    a. Family, community pressures?
    b. Self-referral?
2. In the client's words, what happened that caused this crisis?
    a. What are the unconscious determinants as you understand them?
    b. ˙What are the dynamics involved?
3. How is the client trying to solve this crisis? Is it working?
4. How was the client functioning before this crisis?
5. Is there any noticeable difference between then and now?
6. Has anything like this happened before?
    a. How effectively or ineffectively was it handled?
    b. What was the outcome?
7. How has this client handled other similar situations?
    a. What worked?
    b. What did not work?
8. What are the client's environmental supports? (Family, friends, church, work, recreation?)
9. Is this a *chronic* or an *acute* situation?
10. What does the client say is the most important problem to be worked on right now? Do you agree?
11. What do you the counselor see as the most important issue(s)?
12. If there is a difference between what the client sees as important and what you see as important, what if anything can be done to resolve the difference?
13. Are you and the client working together?
    a. Do you have the potential to form a working alliance?
    b. Do you have the support of the client's family and friends?
14. What is the client's suicidal status?
15. What is the client's mental status?
16. Are there community resources available to help?

The following case example will give you some idea of how these questions are answered during an actual interview. We have only presented the first several minutes of the session, but it will give you some idea of the workings of a session and how the information is presented. Through careful analysis of what is being said and the way it is being said, the counselor is able to get answers to some of the key questions. Although we cannot replicate all the nuances of thought and feeling the client offered, you will be able to see the information the counselor focused on for very obvious reasons.

For practice, see how many of the questions are answered in these first few minutes. It will give you some fine experience in a protected way and at the same time sharpen your clinical skills.

Margaret, age thirty-five, married with several children, walked into the crisis service and asked to talk with someone. She was dressed in blue jeans, tennis shoes, a pullover turtleneck sweater, and brown jacket. She wore little makeup, no fingernail polish, her hair was brushed in a short, shag style, and she looked tired and upset.

Counselor: Why don't you tell me why you came here today?

Client: (Speaking slowly) I was cited for shoplifting several months ago and then again on Sunday, and I know something is wrong and I think I need help. (She pauses, looks at her hands, wrings them tightly.) It also happens that I have been entertaining thoughts of destroying myself so I decided I needed someone to talk to.

Counselor: What type of thoughts of destroying yourself have you been having?

Client: I would just dearly love to take a bottle of aspirin and say forget it. (Pause) I don't really know why I have been having these thoughts. (Pause) (Still looking at her hands) I would really like to leave this area. It has been nothing but a disaster since we got here, and this has been going on for the past four years. The last two have really been rotten.

Counselor: How serious were you when you thought about suicide?

Client: I think I was pretty serious.

Counselor: Did you take any steps?

Client: No. I sat there with the aspirin and I had a five-year-old that was due home from school, so I kept putting it off and putting it off.

Counselor: Why do you think you put it off?

Client: Because I knew I had responsibilities to my children and to my husband. And I've got a little one five months old plus the five-year-old plus four older ones. It was foolish to begin with . . . the move out here. We didn't really know the people we were going to do business with, but we thought it was a chance to start over and my husband thought he could do all right selling real estate. But it sure hasn't turned out that way. (Pause) (Looks up from her hands but not directly at the counselor) I've been depressed before and to cope with that I just keep busy. I've got sixty million projects started and none of them finished because I hop from one thing to the next only because I'm looking for something different to keep my mind occupied, I think. (Laughing) Now I've got two projects started and nothing completed. I'm trying to get the baby's crib and the bedroom for the two little boys put together before the summer and I'm not making much progress.

Counselor: I get concerned when I hear somebody has been thinking about suicide.

Client: That's basically why I'm here. I got scared of my own

> thoughts. (Pause) I think what's happened in the last six
> weeks has got a lot to do with my way of thinking because
> I had thought this way before. (Pause) I don't know why
> I do the things I do. I really think I need help. I have a
> nice family and good husband and why destroy them. (She
> begins to cry and holds her hands to her face.)

Your notes on the questions for the first few minutes of this interview might look something like the following.

1. *Why now?*—Shoplifting and suicidal thoughts.
2. *Cause?*—Move?
3. *Solutions?*—Keeping busy is not working.
4. *Prior functioning?*—Need more information.
5. *Differences?*—Suicidal thoughts; need more information.
6. *Before?*—Yes.
7. *Method of dealing with crisis?*—Projects helped before; need more information.
8. *Supports?*—Family.
9. *Chronic or acute?*—Six weeks this time but has had suicidal thoughts before.
10. *Client says:*—No answer yet.
11. *Counselor says:*—Suicide potential.
12. *Differences?*—No answer yet.
13. *Working together?*—Probably.
14. *What is the client's suicide status?*—Thoughts, plans, means (aspirin in large quantities is lethal).
15. *Mental status?*—Mood depressed.
16. *Community resources?*—New in community.

If this were a complete interview, there would be ample time to answer in detail the questions that are only partially answered so far. Our point is that in most instances your client will tell you in one way or another what is troubling him. What remains is for you to be patient and attentive and to intervene with the proper empathy and interviewing techniques as the case unfolds.

Breaking for Consultation

Consultation is a technique that can be very useful while you are developing confidence and skill in your crisis work. Prior to the completion of the session (approximately ten to fifteen minutes) excuse yourself and discuss the case with a peer or supervisor. This break need take no longer than five minutes, and the potential benefits are enormous.

Consultation will help you get perspective on the crisis and help you finish your planning more professionally. We have advocated consultation in our published works and in our training programs and seminars. We feel that it is inappropriate and dangerous for any clinician who is not professionally trained and properly experienced to assume full responsibility for direct crisis work without supervision and the opportunity to consult with someone who has the training and experience. The risks are too great for the counselor, the agency, and especially for the client. Once you are comfortable with the need for consultation, it will be no hindrance in your clinical work: you will simply incorporate it into your overall approach. There are several ways to handle the interruption for consultation and each must be carefully considered in the context of what is most appropriate to the clinical situation you are in.

Although you can consult at any time during the interview, you are more likely than not to want to accomplish this break toward the end of the session. There are no rules that say you must wait until then. If you feel that you have all the data you need in the first thirty minutes, then say "excuse me" and step outside. Since you are often working against the clock, there will be times when you will by necessity have to be quite assertive and interfere with the client's need to keep talking, asking in effect that your client pull himself together for a brief time while you consult. Timing and diagnostic sensitivity are important variables here. You should always be attuned to such therapeutic issues as abandonment, acting out, and loss of impulse control whenever you excuse yourself from the office, regardless of the reason. If you are unsure of your client's ability to keep himself together long enough for you to discuss the case, then (1) ask your supervisor to come into the counseling office, always being sure that your client understands what you are doing and why, (2) have the client accompany you to the waiting area, or (3) if you have been working with the person alone and he has a supporting person waiting, have that person come in. There are any number of crisis situations that cannot be anticipated in this discussion. But if you know your client and can to some extent predict how he will react to your absence, then you can devise appropriate and helpful ways to take the few minutes necessary to discuss the case.

Take heed about the length of time you are gone. To you it may be only a few minutes. To the client it may seem longer or shorter, depending on the nature of his crisis. In either case be prepared to say something to the effect that you appreciate his patience while you are gone. Aside from its potential therapeutic value, this thank-you is also a small courtesy. In those situations in which you feel it is not safe to leave the client, call your supervisor and have him meet you just outside your office. You can position yourself so that you can see and hear the client. Certain clients (psychopaths, for example) may try to take things from your office without your knowledge. So too might more passive-aggressive clients or those who feel they have something to gain by upsetting you. If your client resists your request to be excused, respond as you would to anything else that has therapeutic meaning. Ask him why, then deal with the material and make a choice about how and when you will consult. Do not make the mistake of promising a client that you will not consult. Such a request is more than likely a manipulation of some sort and therefore is not therapeutically legitimate. If your client turns your request to leave for consultation into a power struggle or a paranoid plot of some kind, then you must adjust your consultation session accordingly. If the client is too frightened and you feel endangered, do not push the issue too hard at that moment. Deal therapeutically with his fears and misunderstandings while you sort out just how and when you will consult. Here are a few examples we recommend to prepare your client for this brief interruption.

> "If you will excuse me for a few moments, I would like to consult with my supervisor. I'll be right back."

> "As I mentioned at the beginning of the interview, I would be discussing your case with my supervisor. I'll be back in just a few minutes."

> "I would like to talk with my supervisor now. How would you feel about that?"

> "If it is all right with you, I would like to talk over this case with one of my colleagues. Would you mind waiting here for a few minutes plese?"

> "Mr. Jones, I would like you to wait in the waiting room for a few minutes while I consult with Dr. Smith. I want to check on your medication questions and then I'll get right back to you."

There are of course endless variations on these themes, each one determined by your style and the client's needs. Once out of the office you should be consistent in what you cover with the consultant. Each supervisor has his own preferences about how he would like you to discuss the case, some emphasizing one aspect of the case over another. But in each situation he will want to know the basic facts, the client's state of mind, and what you plan to do. Figure 7–1 outlines a consultation model designed to give some structure to those few minutes and, once memorized, can prove useful in getting at the essentials of the case. Remember, you want to give your consultant a mental picture of your client. You will want him to have a real feel for your client by the time you are finished giving him the essentials.

This consultation model contains many aspects of the deductive model, expressed in abbreviated form. The elements can be juggled around to fit the demands of each case, and with skill the information can be gathered and recorded within five minutes. Here is a fictional example of a consultation report.

> Mr. J. Jones, age 35, is married with two children, a boy fourteen and a girl twelve. He lives in Broadmore with his wife of fifteen years and her elderly parents. He came to the clinic with a sense of depression that has been getting worse in the past month, following the loss of his $40,000-a-year-job as an engineer. He reports he is having difficulty sleeping through the night, his appetite is down and he has lost eighteen pounds so far. He was accompanied by his wife, who has urged him to get help for the past several weeks. With the exception of the clinical depression, his mental status is unremarkable. He denies suicidal plans and expresses a willingness for further counseling. He has several job leads coming up in this next week and I can see him for another appointment in a few days. My treatment plan is to use Seligman's Learned Helplessness Model as a partial explanation and at the same time work with what must be a great deal of internalized anger."

Do not worry about including everything in your consulting model. It is designed to give a brief overview rather than an in-depth discussion of every detail.

The Counselor's Feelings

As important as the facts about the client are your intuitive feelings about the case. Do not hesitate to verbalize the impact of this case on you with

Name	Age	Marital Status
If Significant: Nationality, Race, Religion		
Living Where		
With Whom		
Came to Agency for What Reason		
Brought by		
Referred by	Family Dr.	

Counselor's statement of the problem(s) and the dynamics involved including a mental status and suicidal status plus a proposed treatment plan:

Figure 7–1. Consultation Model

your supervisor while you are giving him the facts. Countertransference feelings, as we have already pointed out, are powerful forces that affect what we hear, what we remember, how we diagnose, and what we propose as a treatment plan. In stressful situations it is particularly important that you discuss how you are reacting to what you are being told in the office. The relief that can accompany a sharing of these feelings is refreshing, energizing, and provides the motivation to continue with what you were doing.

In addition to this aspect of sharing your feelings, you may also get a fresh view by simply talking to your supervisor about what you have been experiencing in the past hour or so. Insight comes about in a variety of ways, and every counselor can recall the times that he or she was talking about a case and several things became apparent that were neither previously clear nor conscious. This is the so-called "A-ha!" effect. It can be a very powerful learning experience, particularly during consultation.

When You Return to the Client

As we have already mentioned, a word of appreciation to your client about accepting your absence will be a good place to begin. This must be said in earnest or you may be open to several levels of criticism. The end result may be defensiveness on your part or worse, a disruption in the fragile alliance you have with the client. Having commented appropriately, do not allow the comment to serve as an apology or to obscure how your client has handled the pause. While you were gone he had a chance to catch his breath and reflect on what he has and has not told you. Be prepared to deal with more information, some new, some old. In either case incorporate it into the overall picture just as you would if it had been presented in the first ten minutes. Separate the important from the trivial and look for confirmation of facts you have already heard. Deal with the accompanying feelings as appropriate for the situation.

Make any necessary adjustments in your diagnostic formulations if the facts warrant it. Some clients will wait until the very end of the session before they talk about what they consider to be shameful or embarrassing issues. Do not be surprised if this happens when you return from consulting. Just be flexible and keep in mind that while you now have a plan that you wish to implement, this may not be what the client wants. You will have to be sensitive to what new information means and deal with it as if you have not left the office.

In a partially reported case in our previous book (Getz et al. 1974) we diagrammed a first interview, showing how to use step 1 of our deductive model. In this chapter we want to repeat that same interview but carry it through to steps 2, 3, and 4, as well as breaking for consultation. At the end of the interview, try filling out on a separate piece of paper your analysis of the interview according to the deductive model. Then compare it to our analysis (figure 7–2). Of course there will be differences. However, we are more interested that you acquire a feeling for this model and its clinical usefulness than we are in absolute accuracy.

Case Example: Mrs. S.

Mrs. S., forty-five, married, is employed as an office clerk/assistant manager and was referred by her family doctor. Her address indicates that she lives outside the clinic's catchment area and therefore must be referred if there is the indication for further contact. Under the heading of problems, she writes that she has had suicidal thoughts for the past several months. Upon meeting the counselor, her handshake is weak, her smile is forced, and she looks sad. For the most part she avoids the counselor's eyes. Dressed in slacks and a patterned blouse, she appears to weigh 125–130 pounds and stands approximately 5 feet 4 inches tall. She walks slowly and carries herself with a slight stoop.

Counselor: What can I do for you?

Client: Well, first of all I always start crying. (Begins to cry) I don't really know what my problem is. I just get upset all the time. I started to go through the change some time ago. I take medication for that. My kids left home and I quit smoking and now it's all caught up with me, and I just can't handle it any more. That's about the size of it. But to really tell you what is wrong, I can't because I don't really know. I just get upset and cry a lot. Thank God my husband understands. He's very understanding.

Part of my problem could be because he has changed jobs so much that it has really upset me and I probably at this point have just reached the point where I can't take any more of it, but I wouldn't leave him. He means too much to me. Now we've worked this out. When he finds a job this time, he won't change any more because Matt has changed. He knows he has done wrong, and he realizes that in his changing jobs he was just searching for something that wasn't there. Now he realizes that, so when he does get a job this time it should solve the problem. Now whether it solves mine or not, I don't know. This remains to be seen. Maybe it will. That might be the whole basis of my problem. Maybe it that was wiped away I wouldn't feel like I do. But I don't know that yet.

I work and right now I don't like my job. I don't like
people, and yet I know I can't be alone. I can't stand to
be alone. So, I have to have people around me, and yet
I get very irritable and upset with them, but I think it's
because I'm upset with myself, not with them. I find fault
with them because I'm finding fault with myself. Like
today. I was going to take the whole day off for a vacation.
Well, right away this morning I was upset, wondering
what am I going to do with myself? So I was going to go
back to work this afternoon. But then my doctor sent me
over here and I don't think I'm going to make it, but I do
get upset at work too because I'm under quite a bit of
pressure, but I've been able to take it up to now. It bothers
me at the time but I get over it. I do feel taken advantage
of this year, where I didn't before. This one girl is working
part-time, and I have to do her job as well as my own,
which I don't find fair. I don't think it's right, and they've
had to bring another in to train because of this and I have
to train somebody on my desk, and that has been a good
thing because somebody had to learn my job. Up until
now nobody has known my job, so I never felt free to take
a vacation or anything because nobody knew what I did.
This has been good in that sense, because somebody has
been forced to learn my job.

I still resent having to do this other girl's work, and she
knows how I feel. I told her I didn't like her job and I
didn't want to have to do it, but I did. I've stuck with it
anyway. I've hurt her feelings and she thought she was
losing me as a friend. Well, she hasn't lost me as a friend,
but I feel a little taken advantage of by her because some
time ago she was using me as a scapegoat to run with a
fellow, and I don't appreciate that at all. She's a very nice
person and happened to make a mistake and I have no
right to judge her, but I do and I shouldn't do it, because
she's a very nice woman who happened to make a mistake.
I just can't judge her, because she's just not that type.
(Pause)

What else? I don't know, maybe if Matt gets a job and
everything works out, I may not have to come back here.
I hope not. Maybe just talking to you will be enough. But
it has been a problem. I've had a bad past which haunts
me sometimes, but I realize that I can't look back because
I can't undo anything that's already done and even though
I had problems before, I know what they were and I've
been able to cope with them so far. There's no reason why
I can't continue to cope with them. It's just that I've gotten
to the point where I can't seem to take any more. That's
all. And I don't know what to do about it.

Counselor:	How did you handle your problems before?
Client:	I just went from day to day battling with them, I guess. That's about all. Probably not solving anything. I've had help before. A doctor that I went to in Ashton gave me hypnosis, which helped immensely, but that was thirteen years ago, and this was before I married again, and I was afraid to get married again. This was the crux of the problem. I realized that I could go on the rest of my life, being afraid to get married again because of what happened to me and I just had to go ahead and try again. And outside of Matt's changing jobs, I couldn't find a better guy. He's been very good to me. So, that's the only complaint I have about him. Sexually, every way, except changing jobs, we get along fine. There has never been any problem that way. Compatability is great and I don't know what else to tell. (Starts to cry)
Counselor:	What do you think you are crying about?
Client:	I don't know. Probably nothing. When I think about it, I have so much to be thankful for that I don't know why I'm crying, really, to tell the truth, because Matt's got a job. It is only temporary, but he has a good job. We don't make enough to live on, but we can get by with both of us working . . .
Counselor:	On your intake you said that you'd had suicidal thoughts since October.
Client:	Yes.
Counselor:	Could you explain that history?
Client:	Well, I have tried suicide before, years ago, with pills . . . they were pain pills, and sleeping pills, and everything I could get my hands on.
Counselor:	How old were you then?
Client:	About nineteen. Then I tried again a couple of years later when my husband was going to kill me and I was going to do it instead of him. That's why I did it that time. Otherwise, I wouldn't have done it the second time, but it didn't work. I just slept for three or four days most of the time. Nobody knew about it. Nobody knew about the first time I tried it either. I did tell my doctor about it later, and he was a big help to me at the time. I used to be able to go in and talk to him, and he was a big help . . .

I've been married three times. This is my third marriage and that's probably one reason for the shape I'm in. I think your past has a lot to do with it. The day comes when it all catches up with you, but as far as actually planning any suicide lately, no. I've thought about slitting my wrists, but I'd never have the guts to do it. I'm sure I wouldn't. I'd have to get much worse than I am. If it wasn't for my husband, I probably would do it. (Voice breaks) He keeps |

me going. (Starts to cry) If I couldn't cry to him and tell him how I feel, I wouldn't make it. I just feel so desperate most of the time and I don't know what to do about it. If I could just get rid of that feeling, but I can't explain it. I can't even tell you what it's like, except that I feel desperate.

Counselor: You were referred by Dr. Reed today?

Client: Yes. Well, he feels that I'm trying to—and I believe he's right—blame the change and not my mental attitude on what's happening to me.

Counselor: Because of the time I want to step out of the office for a minute and consult with my supervisor. I'll be right back.

How would you diagram the case so far? And then what would you discuss with your supervisor? Fill in the consultation model (figure 7–2) and compare it with the consultation discussion that follows and the use of the deductive model that follow.

In consultation with the counselor we asked her to get some more information on her client's suicidal potential. We also wanted to know if the client showed any signs of clinical depression (disturbed sleep, eating patterns, and significant weight loss all in the past thirty days or so). We reminded the counselor that the client would have to be referred to another agency as she lived outside this agency's geographical service area. And we wanted the counselor to get verbal permission to contact the client's physician. If time permitted, the counselor should get more information on previous therapy, which would also include a psychiatric history. It would also be helpful if the counselor could deal with the client's feeling about referral for counseling.

Counselor: Thanks, Mrs. S., for waiting.

Client: That's all right. It gave me some more time to think about my problems.

Counselor: What were you thinking about?

Client: Oh, just about some of the things I said. I don't want you to think that I'm angry with anyone, because I'm not. I have a lot to be thankful for and if I can just get a hold on myself I think I'll be all right.

Counselor: Well that's one of the things I wanted to talk over with you. We want to help you get a hold of yourself too. So I wanted to find out how you would feel about letting me refer you for some ongoing counseling? You mentioned that you have gone before and it seemed to help you a lot.

Client: Well yes it did. But that was a long time ago, so I don't know about right now. It costs so much.

Name	Age	Marital Status

Name   Age   Marital Status
If Significant: Nationality, Race, Religion
Living Where
With Whom
Came to Agency for What Reason
Brought by
Referred by   Family Dr.

Counselors statement of the problem(s) and the dynamics involved including a
mental status and suicidal status plus a proposed treatment plan.

Figure 7–2. Consultation Model

Counselor: I think I can help along that line. There are a number of
places that will charge you based on your ability to pay.
And given that you sort of feel at the end of your rope,
I could arrange that you could get right in.

Client: Can I come back here?

Counselor: Well that's a bit of a problem. You see you live outside
of the area that we serve so I would have to set up an
appointment for you closer to where you live. Now that
won't be a problem actually. I can make the calls from
here, while you are out in the waiting room and can make
sure that you don't fall into the cracks and get forgotten
about.

Client: (Pausing) Well I guess that would be all right.

Counselor: I'm glad to hear that, but does it feel like we are shuffling
you around a little bit?

Client: Well yes. But then that's all right. You have listened to
my problems and if you think I should see someone else
than I'll go along with what you say. My doctor told me
that you'll be able to give me some good advice.

Counselor: And speaking of your doctor, I need your permission to
discuss your case with him. I'll let him know what happened and how we had to refer you to a place closer to
home.

Client: Yes, that will be all right. Do you want me to sign anything?

Counselor: Yes, we have a release-of-information form at the front
desk if that will be OK?

Client: Yes, I've signed those before.

Counselor: There are one or two other things I want to ask you before
we stop. First of all, have you lost any weight lately? And
do you have any trouble sleeping since you have been
feeling so upset?

Step 1	Step 2	Step 3	Step 4
1. Always starts crying	1. Upset (crying)	1. Suicide danger	1. Don't abandon in referral
2. Don't know problem	2. Suicidal History	Feels deserted	process
3. Change of life	Previous attempts	Internalizes frustration	2. Call referral agency
4. Kids left	Method	Passive method	3. Follow-up calls to client un-
5. Can't handle anymore	Motives	2. Dynamics	til she gets connected
6. Husband understands	Previous events	Related to husband?	
7. Many job changes	3. Previous Counseling	Related to work?	
8. Unhappy at work	When	3. Acute vs. Chronic	
9. Doesn't like people	Where	Everything sounded chronic	
10. Upset to self	Outcome		
11. Dr. referred	Feelings		
12. Previous counseling	4. Present suicidal state		
13. Husband good	Losses		
14. Suicidal history	Not impulsive		
15. Menopause	A bit chronic		
16. Married three times.			

Mental Status: Dressed appropriately, slow motor behavior, speech appropriate, oriented in time, space, person; moderately depressed mood, no evidence of thought disorder, possible danger to self. *Suicidal Status:* Moderate danger. Do not abandon. Appears on surface as fragile.

Figure 7–3. Analysis of Case by the Deductive Model

Client: I sleep real well. In fact I've been sleeping more lately
              than I usually do. My appetite has always been good and
              Matt is always teasing me about a second dessert. I suppose
              I could stand to lose a few pounds but my weight is OK.

Counselor: One last question please. You've told me that recently
              you've felt desperate and kind of at the end of your rope.
              And with your history of suicidal thoughts and actions I'm
              kind of worried about what may happen to you once you
              leave the office.

Client: Well that's very nice of you . . . to worry about me. But
              I feel better now. I guess just talking to someone really
              does make the difference. Matt sometimes gets so worried
              about me that I just can't take my problems to him all the
              time. And I don't like to take my doctor's time. He's a
              busy man and sees a lot of patients. And I can't go running
              to him all the time with my problems either.

Counselor: What about you suicidal thoughts?

Client: As I said before, I guess I'm just too much of a chicken
              to cut my wrists or something like that. We all get de-
              pressed I guess, but the way I'm thinking that's not going
              to help me get straightened around. I'm just going to have
              to learn to let bygones be bygones and put things behind
              me and go on.

Counselor: Well, before you go will you let me get you tied in with
              the Mental Health Center close to your house?

Client: Yes, that will be OK. Do you want me to wait outside
              while you call them?

Counselor: If you wouldn't mind?

Client: No, that will be fine.

Case Comments

Before we turn to the final section of this chapter, we would like to offer
some clinical comments about this case. Looking first at the sixteen basic
questions, we see that the first question (what promoted the client to seek
help?) turns out to be the key to the entire case. In all probability the
physician's referral was the precipitating event of this crisis and the client
once again felt abandoned and rejected. We can only surmise how draining
this client was to the doctor. But if it was anything like the material she
presented to this counselor, it is easy to understand that he was frustrated
and overwhelmed with the multiple problems she presented to him. Of
course his referral was quite appropriate and we do not wish to imply
any criticism for his action. We simply point out here that in the counseling situation the referral source and the referral itself can be the underlying core of the crisis, particularly with someone who feels
chronically displaced and misunderstood.

A second point to consider is the significance of answering this first question fully. As we say, it has so much to do with determining the real reason for the client's appearance at the counselor's office. And in this case it would seem that her motivation for real counseling was rather low. That she came to the session more out of compliance with the doctor's wishes than her own felt need supports this conclusion. However, as she reports a suicidal history, the counselor must not assume that the client is to be taken lightly, simply because of the way she got to the counselor. Question 9 (Is this a chronic or an acute situation?) makes this same point. And it is one we have stressed in earlier chapters. Thus these two questions taken together with the rest of her story indicate how difficult this case would be to work with beyond the first few contacts. As soon as the counselor began focusing in on her defenses, she would begin acting out and the counselor would be left without a patient. However, it would be unprofessional for the counselor to abandon either this client or the treatment plan in spite of this clinical information. Regardless of the chronicity of the situation, completion of the intervention plan must be effected, and in actual practice it was. An appointment with another counselor was made, and the present counselor kept in touch by telephone until the client kept her first appointment. After the first session the referring crisis counselor terminated the case.

Bringing the First Session to a Close

Being able to bring the first interview to a successful close requires a sense of timing that is geared to the realities of the actual length of the session as well as to the needs of the client. It requires skill, experience, and a mastery of the art of being in touch with your client's feelings. You must be able to tell the difference between the client who really does need some extra time in order to tie his loose ends together and the client who is simply manipulating in order to sustain an inappropriate relationship with you.

It takes practice, close supervision, and a willingness to learn from your mistakes. It also means that you must be able to accept criticism from your clients—in subsequent appointments—that you were either correct or incorrect in the way you handled the ending phase. Sometimes clients will verbalize it, and sometimes they will express themselves by missing appointments or displaying some other form of acting-out behavior. All of this represents some aspect of the more complex issue of the counselor's failure to make and sustain therapeutic contact with the client before he left the office. Thus there is considerable art and subjective feel in handling the first contact.

There are a number of very real issues that ought to be dealt with at this stage. Broadly speaking they are under two major headings: clinical and administrative matters. Though there is certainly overlap between them, this arbitrary separation will serve to illuminate their respective importance. Under the clinical heading we would include the next appointment, the number of sessions, follow-up telephone calls, notifying referral sources, and counselor availability. Under administrative matters we would list discussion and setting of fees, release of information, and cancellation policies and missed appointments.

Clinical Issues

As you begin formulating your treatment plan, you should automatically be thinking of how and when to introduce it. And you should be prepared to explain why you have chosen that specific intervention plan. Depending on how complicated the case is, you may have to set aside considerable time in which to accomplish this. Or it may be so well understood from what has already been said that little more than reiteration need be used. Whichever is the case you will want to double-check with the client that he understands what the next step is going to be.

Next Appointments

The next appointment will depend entirely on the facts of the crisis. It can be the next day, the next week, or even the next month. But whenever it is, make sure that it fits the dynamics of the case. This is true of all clinical situations, but it is especially true when the client is depressed and suicidal. It will help if you write down the time and the date of the next appointment and hand it to the client, even though he has assured you that he will remember it. In times of crisis it is easy to interchange Tuesday and Thursday or one o'clock with four o'clock. Handing him something very specific will reduce that potential. When you present the next appointment, make sure that you have his agreement that (1) he sees the need for another visit and (2) it is a time that is reasonably compatible with his schedule. Violation of either of these two principles will lead to missed appointments. Be therapeutic with the client who shows some resistance to a next time. He is probably telling you something very important, and it should be dealt with before you go any further. Is he saying that he really does not want to return? Or is it that the next appointment is too far away? Whichever the case you will want to leave open for discussion the client's reaction to the next appointment this way, by saying something like, "I would like to see you next Thursday at five o'clock. How do you feel about that?'' Then observe him carefully, making sure that his verbal response is compatible with his body and facial language. If you sense a discrepancy, then ask about it. Do not let it go by silently. If you feel that the client is simply manipulating you and just asking for more immediate time, then you may have to stand firm and end the interview as you had planned. But make note of this and be sure to listen for its emergence in the next session, assuming that by your firm action you have not made him so angry that he will not return.

Follow-Up Telephone Calls

In crisis cases the telephone can prove to be one of your most effective clinical tools. A few moments on the telephone to your client can serve as the much needed bridge between the client's chaotic feelings of abandonment and a quiet calm until the next appointment. When desertion and abandonment are central issues in suicidal individuals, a telephone call can mean the difference between life and death. Therefore do not hesitate to use this means of communication as needed. A telephone appointment over the weekend, for example, will often be just the thing for a client. It keeps him in touch with you and lends some much needed structure to that time of the week when there is ordinarily not as much planned as during the rest of the week. This same reasoning can be used for holidays, vacation times, and other times (in snowstorms, rain, and so on) when it is almost impossible for the client to make it back to the clinic. If part of your treatment plan was to refer the client to another counseling source, then telephone calls from you can ensure that the client does not lose touch while he is getting connected to the next service agency. Finally, the follow-up call is an excellent method to monitor how your client is doing so that you can see him sooner or later than his next scheduled appointment. Even though you may feel you are clinically right by the time the client leaves the office, there is nothing like a call to either confirm or correct this impression. And with so much hanging in the balance, a little double-check can go a long way toward the healthy resolution of the crisis.

The Number of Sessions

Depending on the clinical elements of the case, you may or may not want to contract with your client for the number of sessions you expect him to fulfill. If you think that a certain number of interviews are necessary to work successfully with this client's crisis, then present it along with the rationale for the proposal. If on the other hand you sense a more open-ended approach will be fruitful, then leave it open and say so as part of your established treatment plan. There are proponents for either approach (Malan 1963; Sifneos, 1972; Budman 1981; Wolberg 1980). The basis of any approach should be what is best for the client, but do not be so naive as to assume that agency policy and practice will not have something to say about this. However, even recalcitrant administrators will listen and yield if they are given sufficient information to support an adjustment in policy.

The number of sessions should be considered early in the interview. If it sounds like the case can be handled using the acute crisis model we have proposed, then you may wish to say so, letting the client know that X number of visits should prove helpful. This should be followed by the comment that if more visits seem needed, an extension would be considered. If on the other hand you appear to be confronted with a chronic situation, you may choose to keep the number of visits open-ended, expecting the client to terminate prematurely. If you are sure of your diagnosis, and in light of the research supporting the futility of expecting much commitment from such clients, then you will be able to stand your ground regardless of the client's disapproval. The key to this stance is of course the correct diagnosis and supporting data.

Notification of Referral Sources

Professionals who send clients to agencies for service and then never hear what happens to them may get irritated or antagonistic. If the person referred happens to be suicidal, you can expect to make an enemy if you do not contact the referral source. Nothing is quite as infuriating to the referral source as to find out second-hand what happened when he sent a client to another agency. First, the client is likely to distort the picture somewhat simply because of his state of crisis. Second, the referral source has no accurate data on which to base any further work with this person. In most instances this means he will have to make a telephone call and try and track down just what you said and did. Not only is this embarrassing for you, but also it is aggravating to the referral source. And if there happens to be another, more professional service in the community that will let him know what happened, he will probably use that one the next time. From a therapeutic standpoint, it is always best to talk directly with the referral source and tell him what you have done. This way nothing is left to third-party distortion, and the client, if manipulative, cannot play one helper against the other. It may take several calls, but the effort will be well worth it in the end.

Counselor Availability

Since you already know from your client contact that desertion is a basic issue, you will want to make sure that the client understands the rules about contacting you. In private practice the clinician has a twenty-four-hour answering service and is thus theoretically just a phone call away. If the setting in which you practice is not so well equipped, then other arrangements have to be made. We strongly recommend you do not give out your home telephone number to any client except when there is no other choice. As a professional clinician your distance from the client is essential if you are to be helpful. In suicidal cases you cannot allow your personal life to become tangled up with your professional life. Direct telephone calls to your home open you up to such questions as "How's your wife and kids?" or "It sounded like the family is ill. I hope everything is all right with you," and so on. This diverts you and the client from the real task, which is to help him understand why he is in the crisis and what he can do about it.

If you will be on vacation or out of town, make sure that you arrange for a substitute counselor and tell your client this. Be specific and take special caution to make sure that your client has access to a counselor. If your situation is one in which a substitute counselor is not available, then use a community resource such as the suicide-prevention center, the walk-in clinic, or even the emergency room of the local hospital. Be sure to notify the source(s), telling them what to expect and asking how they feel about helping you in this way.

Taking calls in the middle of the night is all part of the therapist's role. At such times make sure that you are alert before you start offering advice. A technique we recommend to counselors who have a hard time waking up is to position the telephone some distance from the bed. This forces you to get up and walk before you begin responding to the caller. Walking should clear the cobwebs of sleep sufficiently for you to offer effective advice.

Administrative Issues

If you work for a social-service agency, your crisis practice is influenced by the policies that govern that agency. That is the way it should be. The rules are meant to protect both you and the clients the agency serves.

Although you may not always agree with such policies, they can be very useful when it comes to working with crisis-phone clients. You will enter every session with a set of expectations that are based in reality and that are reflective of the real world, guidelines for fees for services, release of information, and so on. If you are uncomfortable about any of these issues, you can always sidestep the confrontation by stating that it is agency policy and that everyone must abide by that ruling. This can be particularly helpful when it comes to the issue of charging for your time.

Fees

Whether you charge $0.50 or $50, your client knows that he will get what he pays for depending on his resources. This pay-your-own-way ethic is so deeply ingrained in Americans that to pretend it does not exist is a disservice to your clients and a denial of this reality. Paying for a service that involves life and death counseling can be a hard issue to face. But face it you must. To leave it unattended is to create a false impression that it plays no part in the therapeutic transaction. Even if the client is on welfare, there must be some acknowledgment that a medical coupon will be submitted for the service he is about to receive or has already received. The client who asks for a free ride, so to speak, will be the same person who will seek any shortcut rather than abide by the general rules of society. He will use this request to pay to resist further counseling and will be happy to blame you for his unrewarding clinical experience. Never mind that his requests were unrealistic or out of the question, or that his motivation was suspect from the beginning. These are the exceptions. But even with these persons we advise you to follow agency policy and try to secure some form of monetary payment for your time. If your client is actively psychotic and is unable to comprehend his world, however, do not make the mistake of asking for a fee. Neither should you be so callous as to ask for money from a person whom you are about to hospitalize. Use some discretion. But in the main, consider the charging of fees as important as any other adminstrative function and perhaps even more so. In a clinical sense money carries with it some important implications. It can be power; it can be slavery; it can be the road to personal freedom or it can be a curse. Whatever the case, you will want to appreciate its significance to your client, and as such must be recognized and dealt with in a therapeutic way. Clients who cannot pay for their services are likely to feel guilt. They may deal with this phenomemon by claiming they are healthy so that they do not run up a bill. Or they may terminate counseling prematurely because they feel they cannot afford the cost of the services. Either course is inappropriate because it does not really address the underlying issues of why the client came for counseling in the first place.

Monetary issues can be used as a defense, and the person simply perpetuates the problem he came to you with in the first place. From the administrator's point of view, money must be brought in to pay for overhead. Allowing a client to receive a service that he does not pay for simply means that the services may terminate sooner than expected. If you practice in a setting other than an agency, the same rules apply. There are always overhead expenses. Someone is going to have to pay the bill if you are going to keep practicing. This is a reality that all clients can understand.

Release of Information

When clients query you about who has access to their case material, you must be careful what you say in the way of guarantees of privacy. Unless you are familiar with the statutes where you practice, you had better not commit yourself. It causes a great deal of therapeutic disruption when you promise something and then have to backtrack later in light of the legal or administrative laws. The request for privacy might be considered a therapeutic inquiry, however. Is a client afraid you might reveal something that will prove embarrassing? Is it an issue of shame or vulnerability? Or manipulation? These must be explored before an accurate answer can be given. And even then you must be cautious until you are familiar with all aspects of the request.

Another aspect of to this issue is the necessity for authorization to contact a resource in order to be helpful to the client. We have already mentioned the importance of contacting referral sources. We also want to underscore the importance of having signed consent to participate in the referral process in case you must send the client elsewhere. To simply send a client on his way with just a referral name is close to unconscionable and downright hostile. If you have not secured the client's permission to make this contact, then you have erred administratively as well as clinically. In a previous research study (Getz, Fujita, and Allen 1975), we found that the active referral process was largely responsible for the referred client following through and getting connected at the next service agency. Without the administrative support related to release of information, this practice would be impossible.

Missed Appointments

Most clinical agencies are rather lax on this subject. The prevailing attitude is that there is not much one can do administratively or clinically about missed appointments. You will of course use your good judgment and not bring up this problem when the client is leaving the office in tears. But you will want to consider several of the implications of a policy toward appointments and the several ways it can affect the clinical side of your interviews. If it is clear to you that the client is ambivalent about a next appointment but has agreed to it anyway, then a reminder that cancellation twenty-four hours in advance is required in order to avoid being charged for a missed session is quite therapeutic and proper. It may be that the client misses the appointment anyway. But by your statement you have reflected a position that shows you have a value system that can be depended upon to reflect reality, and that the professional advice you give him as it pertains to his crisis is just as reliable. An additional element here is the use of the cancellation policy as a test of the client's motivation and commitment to the counseling process. You do not want to waste your time with "mental-health shoppers." The missed-appointment edict will serve as something of a screening device for such persons. Further, you will be implying that your time is valuable and that this meeting is set aside specifically for him, and you expect him to show up; if he does not he will be billed for it. It is a policy that is used in the private community and works quite well. There is no reason that you as a crisis counselor cannot use it also.

Summary

In this chapter we incorporated an actual interview using some of the mechanics of the deductive model. We spelled out some key questions that need to be answered during the first interview and emphasized the technique of consultation to check out how a supervisor or colleague sees the case. We offered several ways for counselors excuse themselves from the office, and cautioned them what to be sensitive about once they return. We mentioned some of the clinical and administrative issues in ending the first interview and cautioned the counselor about the complexities of pulling it all together successfully the first time.

References

Budman, S.H., ed. *Forms of Brief Therapy*. New York: The Guilford Press, 1981.

Getz, W., Fujita, B., and Allen, D. "The Use of Paraprofessionals in Crisis Intervention: The Evaluation of an Innovative Program." *American Journal of Community Psychology*, 3 (1975):135–144.

Getz, W., Wiesen, A., Sue, S., and Ayers, A. *Fundamentals of Crisis Counseling*. Lexington, Massachusetts: Lexington Books, 1974.

Malan, D. *A Study of Brief Psychotherapy*. London: Tavistock Publications, 1963.

Sifneos, P. *Short-Term Psychotherapy and Emotional Crisis*. Cambridge, Massachusetts: Harvard University Press, 1972.

Wolberg, L.R. *Handbook of Short-Term Psychotherapy*. New York: Thieme-Stratton, Inc., 1980.

8 The Treatment Plan

The next important step in the counseling sequence is the preparation of a treatment plan. In many ways this aspect of brief counseling is the core of helping your client resolve his crisis. Therefore you will want to be very accurate in diagnosing his problems and proposing solutions. It follows from the deductive model that having amassed the information (step 1), listened for related themes (step 2), and isolated the major themes (step 3), that formulating a treatment plan (step 4) would be the next logical task. But it is not as easy as it looks. Regardless of your skill, crisis clients do not always follow such a sequence. Any plan must be accompanied by a built-in attitude of flexibility, flexibility in when to offer treatment as well as what to offer and why. Anything less will cause you clinical troubles in later sessions. In actuality all treatment plans may come together in your mind in rapid-fire succession or concurrently. Here we have chosen arbitrarily to divide the important issues into separate components in order to clarify them.

Developing a Treatment Plan

As a result of your work in steps 1, 2, and 3 of the deductive model, you now have some idea of the direction to take in your treatment plan (step 4). You have identified what you feel are the most important issues to address if the crisis is to be resolved, and you are prepared to suggest and implement treatment. But first we would like to review some of the key elements of the process of developing a treatment plan.

Acute versus Chronic

You must decide which problems are acute and treatable within the crisis model and which are chronic and relatively unchangeable within this system. Such problems as chronic alcoholism, long-standing marital problems, or extensive criminal history are not amenable to change in a few sessions. Of course these clients can be counseled, but with a different orientation. If the problem is alcoholism, referral to such agencies as Alcoholics Anonymous (A.A.) or alcoholism treatment centers is preferred. For chronic marital problems you will probably want to refer clients to a family counseling service. If the client is in any way involved with the criminal-justice system, it is best to work with that system in an ancillary rather than a primary way and get the client reconnected with that service as soon as possible. It is often the case that these chronic, problem-prone clients carry acute distresses as well. If such a client seems to be suicide-prone, you must be prepared to deal with that issue before sending him elsewhere, and then check that the referral connection is made.

If the client's problems are acute, you must be prepared to make some similar decisions. Do you hospitalize or refer? If you refer, when and to whom? With acute clients you should be prepared to intervene in a direct way, knowing that the problems to be addressed are likely to show change fairly quickly. It is not often that acute problems will be further complicated by unforeseen circumstances. You and your client will be able to focus on the key issues and proceed without careening from one disaster-filled moment to the next.

Goals and Objectives

Your first priority is to keep your client alive. Remember that suicidal ideation is not an isolated factor set apart from your client's many other stresses. It simply is the most dangerous and therefore must be addressed first. Keep in mind that there will be other problems as well. In dealing with a self-destructive client you must be able to accept the totality of his problems but focus on the few that are the most threatening. For example, while your client may present a long history of drinking that must be acknowledged, it may also be true that he is suicidal. The acute situation is his life-threatening behavior—drunk or sober. Therefore inpatient treatment with suicidal precautions is indicated and should be immediately considered. In this treatment formulation, you recognize the chronic problem (alcoholism) overlaid with an acute problem (suicidal ideation) and should devise a plan to deal with both problems. Your first objective is to keep him alive and secondarily to keep him sober.

Caplan (1961) and others (Getz et al. 1974; Parad 1965) state emphatically that the purpose of counseling is to return the client to the same or a higher level of functioning than before his crisis. Recognizing when your client has accomplished this will require that you adequately answer question 4 of the sixteen questions, "How was the client functioning before the crisis?" No matter how many sessions this takes or what other problems *you* would like to work on, your function is complete when your client has returned to his precrisis state. In most cases this will be your client's goal as well.

The Client's Strengths and Weaknesses

If your intervention plan is to be effective, it must take into account your client's capabilities and limitations. From a traditional point of view this refers specifically to your client's *ego strengths*. There are eleven ego strengths including intelligence, accuracy of reality testing, the ability to attend and concentrate, unimpaired memory, sound judgment, the ability to tolerate intense feelings, effective impulse control, quality relationships, an adequate self-concept with self-esteem, and an awareness of and insight into one's own problems.

Several authors support these concepts (Jahoda 1958; Maslow 1968; Allinsmith and Goethals 1956). Basically you look for adaptive skills that have served your client successfully in the past. It is also wise to refer back to questions 6 and 7 of the sixteen basic questions for additional evidence of what is likely to work (Has anything like this happened before? and How has the client handled similar situations?). In an interesting study, Cohen and Walder (1971) experimentally demonstrated that one successful experience will lead to another, much the same way that one failure leads to another. This will prove to be an important consideration as you set your treatment plan into action.

You will also want to consider the client's environmental strengths. We are referring to the client's family, friends, church, and employment affiliations. You should consider anyone the client has some connection with as a resource to be called upon to help him over rough spots. If he is on welfare, think of his caseworker. If he has legal problems, think of his lawyer. What about a school counselor? Does the client have a family doctor, previous or current counselor, or religious affiliation you can call on? In short, look for anyone who will be supportive and helpful for a short period of time. We do not suggest that you forge ahead and contact these people indiscriminately. As with all resources, some are better than others. Make sure that your client identifies these resources as individuals who have the potential to help. Be prepared to integrate them into your overall treatment plan via a telephone call, a letter, or even a face-to-face meeting.

Do not contact these resources if your client is able to do this for himself. If, however, you feel the client's state of distress will confuse the resource person, then ask for permission to make the contact yourself. A simple explanation from you may go a long way toward securing the support your client needs. Be especially sensitive to how the resource person may interpret this request to become involved. Listen for fear, anger, apprehension, and other forms of possible resistance, and deal with them in much the same way you would if this resource were your client. The vast majority of people are anxious about suicide. Such fears as "will he kill himself on my doorstep?" or "What will I talk about that won't upset him?" are common reactions. These fears lead resource persons to say "I don't think I can be of any help" or to look for the earliest possible moment to break contact with you. As with all psychological resistances, treat them with compassion and understanding. If appropriate, reflect what you feel to be the real feelings behind such reluctance. But at no time should you force involvement.

Techniques

The single most important thing to keep in mind at this stage is to remember that you are working in a *brief* counseling model. In chapter 4 we outlined categories of techniques appropriate for this type of counseling. The most common mistake in such counseling is to try to go beyond the guidelines we have outlined. Allowing transference to develop, interacting in a completely nondirective way, or introducing such techniques as implosion *are not* appropriate strategies. You must decide which techniques are most appropriate for a particular client given the nature of his crisis and the number of sessions you will have to work with him (always easier said than done). This can be a trial-and-error process, but the break for consultation can serve to minimize your mistakes. A good supervisor will be able to see some of the issues that you cannot because of your proximity to the case. As an additional backup you will want to check with your client (and occasionally his environmental resources) to make sure that everyone involved is working under the same basis of understanding. You are not asking for permission or approval but are informing the client and at the same time enlisting his support in order to proceed.

To Work With or Refer a Client?

During the course of the first session you will ask yourself if it is appropriate to work with a client or if he should be referred to another agency. To answer this accurately there are two important issues to consider: (1) do you have the clinical skills and agency resources necessary to meet his problems? and (2) can you or another resource implement the plans necessary to solve these problems?

There is no one so dangerous in a counseling situation as a counselor who is unable or unwilling to recognize and accept his counseling limitations. Such an attitude is directly injurious to the vulnerable client and can cause more harm than good. You may set in motion any number of counterproductive problems such as overdependency, excessive guilt and shame, or despair. The opportunity to act out your own unconscious conflicts through the client is always present, but it becomes particularly dangerous when the client is suicidal. Close supervision, formal therapy, and continuing education are all necessary if this is to be avoided. It requires from you a motivation to face such personal deficits and take action to correct them. Additionally, you run the risk of legal litigation if you have implied that you are more clinically skilled than you really are (Cohen 1979). Therefore be extremely realistic about your level of skill and do not hesitate to refer a client to someone who is better qualified. If you are unsure of your qualifications, check with a supervisor, colleagues, or an administrator. It is no sign of weakness to make such an admission. If you decide you are unable to counsel a client, do not apologize for it. State matter-of-factly that another counselor or agency will be better in this instance than you would. Do not be defensive about the matter or make the client feel his problems are too much for you. As is always the case in such situations, a fine balance between self-disclosure and candor is called for.

A second equally important consideration is your training and experience. There is no such thing as a universal counselor. If you have been trained as an alcoholism counselor, then you have little business working with nonalcoholics who are abusing their children. If you are not skilled in sexual-assault counseling, make sure you bring qualified counselors immediately into such cases. The situations that call for special expertise are endless. If, on the other hand, you are the only resource person in your community available to provide crisis-intervention services, you may not have any choice. But please set up as many safeguards as are humanly possible. If you must, pay for consultation with someone who knows more than you do. If face-to-face meetings are not possible, use the telephone. If you or your agency cannot afford to pay for consultation, barter. This form of backup is crucial when you are the first and sometimes only one contacted by suicidal persons.

It is essential that from the beginning you consider what is the best resource available to each client. If it is you, fine. If not, search for a better resource. An effective counseling-intervention plan requires that you have up-to-date knowledge of available community resources. You will want to know about public and private services, what the going rates are, and what types of clients you can refer to these services. Just as you must know your own level of skill, you will want to know the skill levels of your referral sources.

You will also need to know if this client has insurance that covers mental-health counseling, and if so, which practitioner(s) does it cover? If not, will the referral agency accept the client on a sliding-scale basis?

Is there a waiting list at the referral agency, how long is it, and is there any way to get around it in a crisis?

One of the sixteen basic questions asked that you recognize how the environmental supports will accept your proposed treatment plan. This applies to the referral process as well. Will the environmental supports help financially and if necessary provide transportation or child-care if you refer the client to another resource? Finally, you should know the peculiarities of the referral source. Will the referral source provide feedback about whether or not the client came to his appointment or will nothing be said because of agency policy? Is a lengthy report required from you or is a concise telephone report sufficient?

All these are important concerns that affect your success or failure in trying to match clinical skills with client needs. Agency policies and individual practioners' subtleties must be considered at this stage of the treatment plan. Even referring your client to someone within your own agency or professional group requires the same attention to detail.

Implementing Your Treatment Plan

Most clinicians, as "people who care," would like to think that client needs transcend politics and the art of compromise. But in inter- and intra-agency dealings, this is simply not the case. To the extent that you recognize this you will be far more effective in doing your work. Knowing what type of clients are likely to be accepted by which agencies can be just as important as making a correct diagnosis or a timely interpretation.

Another reality is that like it or not there are certain types of clients who are harder to refer. How to deal with this situation when it arises is a matter of individual conscience. Some colleagues have falsified a diagnosis to get a client referred. They have justified their action on the grounds that it was best for the client. Perhaps; but we take a different tack. We suggest frankness and candor from the outset even though the referral source may reject the client. To do otherwise sets in motion a series of events that ultimately play havoc with the client. The referral source may terminate the client prematurely or send him to someone else, which may fail because the client knows he is being shuffled around. Although you may make a placement by falsifying information for a referral, this method will not be in the client's best interest nor in yours. You will not be able to mislead your colleagues for very long before it catches up with you.

Counselor–Client Alliance

Any treatment plan that overlooks or minimizes the significance of the two-part process in crisis work weakens the likelihood of its success.

Although techniques and accurate diagnosis are important, knowledge of agency policies and community resources invaluable, and your level and type of skill indispensable, if you ignore the two-person counselor-client alliance, you will end up without a client, and your carefully reasoned plan and techniques will be useless.

Client Motivation

As we stated in chapter 2, your client must recognize that he needs help and must be willing to invest something of himself in the process to get it. He must also have some confidence in you and your ability to help. At the outset of the counseling process he may be ambivalent or want your assistance. But this should not deter you. His resistance may be largely a product of his crisis state or the result of some misconceptions he has about counseling. Timely interpretation, reflection of feeling, and education will help you remove some of these hindrances.

Perhaps the most difficult clients are those who are not self-referred and do not want to be there in the first place. They will communicate this verbally and by their behavior. If you perceive this to be the case, you have several options. If it is an institutional referral, for example from probation officer or juvenile court, contacting the referral source is absolutely essential. Without this contact you have no way of knowing precisely why your client is there. He may say, for example, that he is depressed and has thoughts of ending his life. This may be true, but he may be using this presentation to avoid imprisonment or revocation of parole. Unless you are highly skilled and have extensive experience with this client population, you will not be able to pick this out in a single session. If the client is indeed suicidal, you must then make the clinical decision of how to work with him. If on the other hand his suicidal declaration is a maneuver to avoid other serious consequences, your referral source may be able to tell you this. Chapter 13 on adolescent suicide also deals with the reluctant, "I don't want to be here" client. It is sufficient to remark here that in crisis counseling you do not have much time to deal with the reluctant client. However, if during your assessment you detect that depression and suicide potential are masked behind antisocial behavior, your treatment would be very much the same as it would be for any other depressed client. Confrontation and clarification of the client's reluctance is the strategy of choice.

If this does not produce a workable counseling alliance, then you must enlist the support of family and friends. To ignore these sources of social support is to do a disservice to your client. Not only might you jeopardize *his* safety and welfare, but in the event of a suicide attempt he could kill innocent people in an automobile accident or some other form of violent death. The family members and friends can provide valuable information about your client's state of mind when he is unable or unwilling to do so himself. He may have told them many times over what he will not tell you. Much valuable information about your client's motivation will be provided by answering the first question of the sixteen basic questions. Having a clear understanding of the factors related to why your client has come for counseling will contribute greatly to your ability to formulate an effective counseling plan.

Counselor's Feelings

There is no single way to characterize the kinds of feelings that are related to success in the counseling process. There are some general guidelines, however, and these should be followed scrupulously. On the extremes of the continuum, beware of too much dislike or too much positive feeling for the client. If you find yourself giving too much positive or negative thought to your client you have probably exceeded these guidelines, and you should consult with your supervisor about this. If the issues can be resolved at this level, the case should then progress smoothly. If they cannot, referral is the proper course of action. As we mentioned in the sections on countertransference (chapters 1 and 2), there are any number of pitfalls to keep in mind. Review these issues and maintain an appreciation of the part they play in the counseling process.

Verbalizing Your Plan

Everything we have discussed so far has described a thought process, an internal dialogue of questions and answers. In counseling you may have revealed bits and pieces of what you have been thinking by such nonverbal cues as smiles, nods, grimaces, and the like. But in the main all of your formulations have been made silently. Now comes the time to formally propose your solutions in the form of a recommended treatment plan. You must tell your client what you think. It matters little whether you present your plan ten minutes into the interview or ten minutes before the hour is over. What matters is that you have allowed sufficient time to pass to have a clear picture of the facts of the case. You must also leave enough time to discuss fully what you propose and why. It is inappropriate to simply impose your plan without allowing time for discussion. To accomplish this you may have to interrupt your client before he has completed his story. In such instances, you must use your clinical judgment. Always explain why you are interrupting and be prepared to help him make the transition.

We recommend that prior to your presentation you offer a summary. This summary should include the major themes that have emerged in steps 2 and 3 of the deductive model. You should also include a restatement of the client's feelings as you perceive them. Be very careful at this stage not to introduce new ideas or to overwhelm your client with information. We repeat, *do not overload him*. Be cautious and remain focused on the key issues in such a way that you do not unnecessarily increase his anxiety. Your summary should be short and to the point.

Your summary sets the stage for and leads into your rationale for the counseling plan. Your ideas must flow logically from your client's presentation to your conceptualization of what needs to be done. It is important to check your thinking with your client to reduce the chance of error and misunderstanding. After you have presented your plan, you will want to have the client summarize to be sure that your proposed solutions are acceptable and appropriate. This process is a continuation of the counseling alliance. It reinforces in a most meaningful way the fact that client and counselor are joint participants, partners in resolving the crisis.

In the case of a recommended suicide contract it is best to leave enough time for the client to absorb the meaning and significance of the agreement. Under no circumstances should he feel pressured or rushed at this stage. Signing such a commitment without intellectually and emotionally accepting its real meaning renders it almost worthless. We have included examples of suicide contracts in appendix E. As you will note there is ample space for specific additions to fit your client's needs.

Your treatment plan must be, above all else, realistic. It is relatively easy to create the ideal plan in the comfort and safety of the office. Proposing and implementing a plan that works outside the office is often another matter. You will have opportunities during subsequent sessions to assess how effective your plan has been. Throughout the counseling process the plan will be modified and amended according to the client's progress. There are any number of unforeseen variables that could interfere with what you have planned. This orientation will provide both you and your client whatever flexibility the situation may dictate. In addition, telephone contact between sessions can serve as another opportunity to check and ensure that your plan is adequate. Such flexibility is both a technique and a goal. It protects both parties in the alliance from feeling they have failed if the plan does not work.

Summary

The counseling and treatment plan follows steps 1, 2, and 3 of the deductive model. Being clear about the difference between acute and chronic issues and focusing on the latter is paramount. The decision to work with or refer your client depends on the nature and severity of his problems, your level of training and types of skills, the availability of other resources, you client's motivation, and your feelings about your client and his problems. The client-counselor alliance is central to the effectiveness of the treatment plan. The plan must, above all else, be realistic and geared to the major concerns of your client. Flexibility should be inherent in the techniques and the goals of any counseling intervention.

References

Allinsmith, W., and Goethals, G. "Cultural Factors in Mental Health: Anthropological Perspective." *Review of Educational Research* 26 (1956):429–450.

Caplan, G. *An Approach to Community Mental Health*. New York: Grune and Stratton, 1961.

Cohen, R. *Malpractice: A Guide For Mental Health Professionals*. New York: Free Press, 1979.

Cohen, S. and Walder, L. "An Experimental Analog Derived from Crisis Theory." *American Journal Orthopsychiatry*. 41 (1971):822–829.

Getz, W., Wiesen, A., Sue, S., and Ayers, A. *Fundamentals of Crisis Counseling*. Lexington, Massachusetts: Lexington Books, 1974.

Jahoda, M. *Current Concepts of Positive Mental Health*. New York: Basic Books, 1958.

Maslow, A. *Toward a Psychology of Being*. Third ed. Princeton, New Jersey: Van Nostrand, 1968.

Parad, H., ed. *Crisis Intervention: Selected Readings*. New York: Family Service Associates of America, 1965.

9 The Middle Phase of Counseling: Part I

The middle phase, beginning with the second session, is the core of crisis counseling. It is the time in the counseling process when, as counselor, you must be prepared to be more than a good listener. Your effectiveness in the middle phase of crisis work and in the office in general will be determined by: your knowledge of effective treatment techniques, your ability to set realistic counseling goals, your ability to establish and maintain a counseling alliance, and your ability to know when, how, and to whom to refer your client when your short-term work is completed (Wolberg 1980; Strupp 1973).

The second and subsequent sessions may be begun with one of several approaches. Before you enter the session you may want to review the events and themes of your first session by going over your notes or by simply remembering what transpired. We suggest writing down the major themes and issues that arose in the first session by using steps 3 and 4 of the deductive model (major themes and treatment plan). This review will help you to decide how to begin and will help you keep in mind what you want to accomplish during the interview.

How to Open the Session

How to begin will depend on a number of factors: the tone of the previous session, the type of relationship you have established with the client, how the last session ended, what themes emerged, and perhaps most importantly, what direction your client wishes to follow. Keeping all these issues in mind, you have several choices. You may begin with either open- or closed-ended techniques depending on what you think is best in the situation. In general it is best to begin with open-ended questions and then use closed-ended questions later as your client needs them or as you need very specific information. However, there are disadvantages in using open-ended questions with psychotic or particularly upset clients. Clients who are psychotic need more structure than open-ended questions offer in order to help them organize their thoughts. Very distressed clients may respond to an open-ended question like ''what would you like to talk about today'' with topics that are irrelevant.

What Is New? What Is Old?

As your client begins to talk about what has been going on since you last saw him, it is important to sort out what has changed and what has not. You will want to listen to what has happened in his environment (living situation, relationships, school, job). You will also want to note differences in the way your client is thinking and feeling. Reviewing the previous session before the start of the next helps you recognize changes in the client's status. As the client is talking, listen for any changes and listen for new facts and feelings that were not discussed previously. This new information may be something about the client's past, it may be something that was mentioned earlier but was not explored in depth, or it may be something that is happening currently that you did not know was going on. Often new information will emerge when discussing the outcome of the treatment plan, especially if the plan was not very successful. Figure 9–1 illustrates a way to organize old and new material using the deductive model. Note that this form allows for alterations in the treatment plan that may be dictated by changes in the client's status or by new information.

What Does the Client Recall about the Last Session?

At some point during the session you will want to find out what the client remembers about your previous session. What he remembers and what

1. Current Status of Client's Crisis
             Previous Interview   *This Interview*
      a . _____   _____
      b . _____   _____
      c . _____   _____
      d . _____   _____
2. Current Status of Crisis Prevention Plan
             Previous Interview   *This Interview*
      a . _____   _____
      b . _____   _____
      c . _____   _____
      d . _____   _____
3. New Information
      a . _____
      b . _____
      c . _____
      d . _____
4. Crisis Intervention Plan for Next Session
      a . _____
      b . _____
      c . _____
      d . _____

Figure 9–1. Format for Outlining Subsequent Interviews

he does not remember will give you much information regarding his psychological functioning and patterns. In some cases, you may decide to begin the session by asking what he remembers. Beginning the session in this manner is appropriate if the client was especially stressed or overwhelmed in the previous meeting. As he talks, listen to what he omits or does not appear to remember.

As the client tells you what he does remember, listen for distortions, which can take many forms. Some of the more common distortions are remembering only part of what was said or agreed upon; hearing the opposite of what was said; understanding you to have said something you did not say; misinterpreting what you said; and denying having said something he did say. Distortions usually occur in material that is highly emotionally charged and threatening.

Just as distortions are highly charged, so too are omissions. People forget things that happen in sessions because the material forgotten is painful or threatening. Omissions usually take two forms: repression (pushing the thoughts or feelings out of awareness and into the unconscious); and denial (believing that the event never happened when in fact it did). Examples of repression and denial are:

Counselor: Last time you said you were really angry at your husband
               just before you tried to kill yourself.
Client: That's funny, I don't remember either saying that or feeling
               that way. (*repression*)

                              Or

Client: Oh, I didn't say that. I would never say anything like that.
               (*denial*)

Whether you are dealing with distortion or omission, it is important to remember that there is a reason that the material has been altered or avoided.

There are other reasons material is left out. Repression and denial are unconscious processes. But sometimes clients will distort or omit as a result of a conscious decision. It is useful to consider the reasons for altered or omitted information as a continuum from ignorance of what is important psychologically to the defensive reactions of repression and denial. Some clients will not include information they remember because they do not feel it is important. It is necessary to educate these clients as to what information is significant, which may lead you to discuss what is expected of them in a counseling session. Later in this chapter we will cover techniques for dealing with material that is repressed or denied. Keep in mind, however, that not everything your client forgets is a result of a defensive reaction. There may be too much noise in the room, your telephone may be ringing in the middle of a discussion, or the client may have an allergic reaction to the flowers in your office; all of which may prevent him from concentrating.

It is important to define some guidelines as to what kinds of material can be dealt with in short-term counseling. It is best to follow two rules. First, do not try to uncover unconscious material unless it is directly relevant to the suicidal crisis. Second, do not try to resolve long-standing issues such as chronic unhappiness, twenty-year drug habits, or long-term rage. Acknowledge such problems; but if you try to address them you may end up making things worse for your client. Stick to issues that directly relate to the current crisis and to things that you can do something about relatively quickly.

Is the Client Better, Worse, or the Same?

In general there are three things that can happen to your client between appointments: he can get better, he can get worse, or he can remain the same. Let us explore these in detail and discuss what you can do in each case.

If the Client Reports that He Is Better

There are two aspects to consider when your client reports that he is better. On the one hand you want to ask yourself if he is really better and if so why. On the other hand, he may not really be better and may just claim to be so. What you should listen for are objective as well as subjective changes in the client's environment and attitude. Listen for reasons why he is feeling better. There should be some observable changes such as improved mood; there should also be more objective signs such as a report that he is sleeping better, eating better, is less irritable, that his work performance has improved or, most importantly, that he is feeling less suicidal.

You should not automatically accept a client's assessment that he is feeling better regardless of the reason and see it as a sign of progress. There are two major reasons why your client may report he feels better when he really does not: denial and "flight into health" (a special form of denial). Denial, as we have stated, is believing that something does not exist when in fact it does; in this case the client may deny feelings and thoughts of suicide, because those thoughts and feelings are very threatening. Flight into health is a form of denial that sometimes occurs early in counseling (Langs 1974). Oremland (1972) defines flight into health as "those rather sudden, global, massive repressions and suppressions of the pathological feelings, actions, and activities which characteristically occur very early in the therapy, sometimes even before the first appointment is kept" (pp. 64–65). In cases of flight into health it is usually difficult to discover what is going on because it occurs so early in counseling.

It is difficult to differentiate between denial in general and its special form, flight into health. Generally denial has less emotion associated with it and takes the form of simple statements such as "I'm not feeling suicidal any more," or "I'm OK now." Usually your client will be unwilling to talk at any length about his feelings or why he is no longer feeling suicidal. Further questioning is usually responded to with statements like "I'm just not [feeling suicidal], that's all." Denial is an unconscious process and your client really believes he is no longer suicidal. In flight into health, there is often more emotion associated with the information. Your client will usually praise you and repeatedly tell you how helpful and effective you have been in solving his problems. You will often hear such things as "I'm feeling so much better, you've been so helpful and kind in helping me, I don't know what I would have done without you, you saved my life." When asked what has changed to make things so much better, your client will usually respond without actually telling you that anything has changed, responses such as, "Oh, I just feel so much better having had someone to talk to and share my problems with," or "I've just changed my attitude about my problems, you helped me to see how unimportant they were." It is easy for a counselor to be flattered by these kinds of responses and to overlook the lack of depth of the explanation for improvement.

What do you do if you are dealing with denial or flight into health? Langs (1974) suggests that you take a reassuring and supportive stance in an attempt to allay your client's fears of counseling, and gently but firmly confront your client with the dangers of termination of counseling without any real changes. If you have not already gathered such information, listen specifically for major childhood traumas, especially those associated with trust and loss. With suicide more than with any other counseling issue, it is essential that you cover all issues and bases. If evidence suggests that your client is still in danger of killing himself even though he denies it, take all precautions necessary to make sure he will not be left alone.

If it becomes apparent that your client is consciously withholding information regarding suicidal thoughts, more firm confrontation is called for. You may take any one of several tacks in confronting him. A typical confrontation might be something like the following:

Client: I'm just not feeling suicidal anymore, that's all.
Counselor: That may be how you feel, but yesterday you said you
             really wanted to kill yourself. Now today you don't want
             to kill yourself. I don't understand. What's going on?
Client: I just feel better.
Counselor: I know, but why?

It is often difficult to tell the difference between unconscious denial
and conscious withholding of information. In general, if your client is
consciously withholding information, your confrontations will be met
with increasing resistance and anger on his part. If you are dealing with
unconscious denial, your client is more likely to respond as if he had no
idea why you said what you did.

In addition to possible denial or withholding, you must consider that
it *is* possible for your client to get better after one session; that he will
no longer be suicidal at the next session. The crucial question is why.
Has something changed for the better in his environment? Has the reason
for your client's suicidal thoughts or actions changed for the better?
Common sense here will help you a lot. Would you feel better if you
were in his position? If so, then you may be more sure that your client
is no longer suicidal. However, it is a good idea to continue to be cautious.
Check out with him, in detail, how things have changed, and especially
how his thoughts and feelings have changed. Reflect on the information
you received in the previous session. Does the information he is giving
you now make sense when viewed in light of the last session?

It is quite possible for a client who looks so confused and so disor-
ganized in the first session that you would consider him to be psychotic
to come back twenty-four hours later looking relaxed, coherent, and
competent. This happens when the stress a person is under is so great
that he becomes immobilized. Often in a first session you see a person
who has been under a great deal of stress for a fairly long period of time
with few environmental supports. If your client has experienced this, the
opportunity to talk about his distress with an interested, caring person
will bring enough relief to allow him to organize his thoughts and pull
himself together in a short period of time.

If your client is truly better, you will want to help him understand
how he has been able to accomplish this. Whatever it is that has helped
him, urge him to take as much credit for this as possible. Help him
internalize the problem-solving skills. Accept your own role in this helping process but remember that you only facilitated your client's ability
to help himself. In actuality he did most of the work. Now that he appears
to have weathered the storm he needs to feel a sense of success and
mastery.

If indeed the client is no longer suicidal you can begin exploring alternative treatment options. Keep in mind that your ultimate goals in short-term treatment are (1) to help reduce your client's suicidal feelings and (2) to refer him on to longer-term treatment (Patterson et al. 1977). It is often advisable to use the fact that the client is feeling better because of your help to facilitate the referral process. Point out to your client that treatment has been successful so far and that he can continue to grow and change with further help. The danger here is that the client who is feeling better may no longer see the need for treatment. If this happens, it is advisable not to push for an outside referral, but to suggest that he may want to come back and see you again sometime in the future.

If the Client Reports that Things Are the Same

When your client returns for a session and states that his situation is pretty much the same you should listen for several possible explanations. Was the previous treatment plan inadequate? Were there unforeseen circumstances that affected the plan? Were there things the client did not tell you the first time that made the plan inoperable? If so, was the withholding of information conscious or unconscious? Are things really the same or has he misperceived and distorted the situation such that he feels nothing has changed? At this point it is best to start from the beginning and revise your treatment plan. Be sure to find out if anything you suggested has provided relief; if so, include it in your new plan. At this stage, treatment plans often do not work because they try to do too much. You may find it necessary therefore to reduce the scope of your plan. It may also be necessary to help the client recognize that some small changes have already taken place. Often a client will expect you to have the power to fix any human problem immediately. When he finds that this is not happening he loses sight of changes that have taken place.

If the Client Reports that Things Are Worse

If your client returns for a session reporting that things are worse, do not panic. Things may in fact not be as bad as he reports. It may be that they are only perceived that way, and some more work on your part is all that is required. But in the event that your client is right, here are some ways to approach the situation. First, ask many of the same questions you would ask if your client reported that things were the same. Was the treatment plan adequate? Did something happen between appointments that undermined the plan? And so on. Your questions should help you to understand what went wrong and point to a way of correcting it. If your client has become seriously suicidal consider such alternatives as partial or complete hospitalization, more frequent sessions, or immediate referral to a more experienced counselor. Just because you may have ruled these alternatives out in the first session does not mean that you have to forget them altogether. Most of these options are available at all times. Assess the client's situation using the suicidal- and mental-status exam mentioned in chapter 6 and do not hesitate to hospitalize him if necessary.

Another factor that may contribute to a client's feelings that things are worse can be antidepressant medication. If your original treatment plan included a referral to a physician for medications, there are several things to be alert for. Do not discuss at length whether the drugs are or are not working or are otherwise affecting the client. Since you are not a medical expert you will have no way of knowing. Sidestep the issue and consult with the client's doctor and have your client do the same thing. Once you find out the facts, you will have any number of options to pursue, including confrontation, reassurance, education, and others. Do not offer advice in such matters unless you really know what you are talking about and you understand the consequences of the complaint in the context of the counseling situation. If you are interested in knowing more about medications, their effects, side effects, and other information, we suggest the following books: the current edition of *The Physicians' Desk Reference* (PDR) (Oradell, N.J: Medical Economics, Inc.); N.S. Kline, S.F. Alexander, and A. Chamberlain, *Psychotropic Drugs* (Oradell, N.J.: Medical Economics, Inc., 1974); and L. Valzelli, *Psychopharmacology*, (Flushing, N.Y.: Spectrum Publications, 1973).

Remember, some clients would rather take a pill than talk things out in order to feel better. And when this does not work immediately, you are likely to hear about it in one way or another, for instance a complaint that all things are worse.

Summary

In preparation for the middle sessions review your recollection and notes of previous appointments. Keep in mind the key issues, begin the interview in an open-ended manner, and listen first to what is on your client's mind. As he talks, look for indications of change and of the effectiveness of the treatment plan. Listen also for distortions and omissions of what has gone on in previous sessions. Later in the interview gather whatever additional information you need to determine whether things are better, the same, or worse than they were at the time of the previous session. This assessment will be the basis for modifying the counseling plan.

References

Langs, R. *The Technique of Psychoanalytic Psychotherapy*. Vol. II. New York: Jason Aronson, 1974.

Oremland, J. "Transference Cure and Flight into Health." *International Journal of Psychoanalytic Psychotherapy* 1 (1972):61–75.

Patterson, V., Levene, H., and Berger, L. "A One-Year Follow-Up of Two Forms of Brief Psychotherapy." *American Journal of Psychotherapy* 31 (1977):76–82.

Strupp, H. "On the Basic Ingredients of Psychotherapy." *Journal of Counseling and Clinical Psychology* 41 (1973):1–18.

Wolberg, L. *Handbook of Short-Term Psychotherapy*. New York: Thieme-Stratton, 1980.

Suggested Readings

Budman, S., ed. *Forms of Brief Therapy*. New York: The Guilford Press, 1981.

Davanloo, H., ed. *Short-Term Dynamic Psychotherapy*. New York: Jason Aronson, 1980.

Langs, R. *Psychotherapy: A Basic Text*. New York: Jason Aronson, 1982.

Mason, A. and Grenacher, R. *Clinical Handbook of Anti-Psychotic Drug Therapy*. New York: Brunner/Mazel, 1980.

10 The Middle Phase of Counseling: Part II

Is the Session Flowing Smoothly?

As the middle sessions progress, there are several additional questions you will want to ask both yourself and your client. As he begins to talk, note how easily and freely he shares the information with you. See if you can detect any problems your client may be having in conveying information to you. One major source of difficulty that often arises is embarrassment about something that happened or was said in a previous session. Many times a client is brought to you soon after a suicide attempt and may still be toxic from a drug overdose, in a partial state of shock from a self-inflicted physical trauma, or extremely emotionally upset. At times like this, a client is likely to say or do something that he is later embarrassed about and would not have said had it been a less intense situation. The result is that your client remembers what was said or done and is afraid to talk for fear of having to confront that issue. In situations like this it is best to gently meet the issue head-on. If your client states that he is embarrassed, acknowledge the feelings by stating you can see how he could feel that way. Do not deny his feelings by stating something like "you shouldn't be embarrassed by that." If the source of the feeling is not central to the suicidal ideation you can state that it will not be necessary to pursue the matter unless he wants to. If it is central, state that you will have to talk about it at some point, but that you will not do so until he is ready. This gives him the choice and some control over when to talk about it.

If the client does not state that he feels embarrassed but information is not flowing freely, introduce the subject yourself. If you are not sure what the source of difficulty is, you might simply note to the client that there seems to be a block and you wonder what that might be. If the client does not respond, or if you suspect what the source of difficulty is, state what you think it is. For example, "It seems to be difficult for you to talk about this. I wonder if you don't feel embarrassed or ashamed about this whole situation, and that's what is holding things up."

Langs (1973) discusses silences and offers some general guidelines for dealing with them which we will summarize here. First of all, silences are both resistances and forms of expression that serve as gratifications and defenses. They are most often used by more severely disturbed clients who tend to have fragile egos and weak defenses, and by those who tend to act out. It is important for you to be patient and not react with anger or condemnation. Generally long silences are not productive. You must be prepared to be somewhat more active without talking too much. You should listen to anything the client does say in context of the silence and be prepared to translate into words what the silence appears to mean.

What do you do with someone who was suicidal the first time you saw him, but refuses to talk during the second session? In this case you will have to use all the resources available to you as well as your own common sense. If your client refuses to talk, first interview members of the family or support system and gather as much information as you can from them. Second, review what you know about the suicide attempt or ideation. How serious was the attempt or ideation? What has changed in the client's environment between sessions? Are the circumstances that brought about the suicidal feelings still present? What is the client's support system like? Are there individuals willing to stay with the client? If you have doubts, take no chances. If the first attempt was serious, the client's environment has not changed, and he is not willing to talk, do not hesitate to hospitalize him. Remember that people who use silence tend to act out their thoughts and feelings, and in a person who is suicidal, this is a deadly combination.

How Well is the Client Working Through His Crisis?

As you listen to your client in subsequent sessions, try to determine what changes are taking place and at what level they are taking place. For our purposes, the levels we refer to include cognitive, behavioral, and emotional levels. *Integration* means how a change in any one of these levels affects the other levels. For example, your client may intellectually (cognitively) understand the reasons for his suicide attempt, but that understanding will not affect him emotionally or behaviorally and will result in no observable changes. Ideally, cognitive understanding will lead to an emotional connection but frequently you will find cognitive understanding without emotional understanding and few subsequent behavioral changes. This pattern is fairly typical. When you are dealing with a crisis like a suicide attempt, however, the rate at which integration is attained can vary greatly. The anxiety that is produced during a crisis assists the person to integrate the changes that must be made to reduce the anxiety; but anxiety can also reinforce and strengthen the existing maladaptive defenses.

The most apparent test for integration, that of behavior change, will need to be monitored in subsequent sessions. Cognitive understanding followed by emotional understanding usually results in a period of silence while the full impact of the connection is realized, followed by some affective response like crying, laughing, or feelings of hurt. It is not realistic to expect your client to have a fully integrated understanding of his problems before he leaves you at the end of four or five sessions. If you can use your time to begin making those connections and to monitor the level of integration, you will have accomplished a great deal. Your knowledge of the level of integration of understanding will assist you in your assessment of the client's suicidal potential. In general, the greater the integration, the more likely that your client is out of danger.

Is There Enough New Information?

Pay close attention to the amount of redundancy in the information you are getting in the middle sessions. This refers not only to the subjects being brought up by your client, but also to the depth of information you are receiving. In the middle sessions many clients have no trouble bringing up new information that relates to a suicide attempt. However, there will be a portion of clients who will talk only about a very narrow range of subject matter. One of the reasons for this is the natural tendency for those in crisis to be preoccupied with the person or event that precipitated the crisis. A second reason will be reluctance to talk about possibly threatening material. Most often you will encounter this in a person who is unable to see his role in his crisis. He will often tend to direct all conversation toward another person or event and not to talk about himself or other relevant topics.

If part way through the session you find yourself with no more information than you had in the previous session, it is time to direct the conversation toward other topics. We suggest you begin by asking questions about such other relevant topics as your client's background, family, or support system, and inquire about feelings, thoughts, and fantasies. If your client responds by returning to the same topic, a statement about this followed by an interpretation is appropriate. For example, "You know, I've noticed that we always end up talking about your wife, and not about you. I think it's difficult for you to talk about what is going on inside of you, but I'd like to try. Tell me what you're feeling." It may be necessary to make this type of statement several times before your client begins to talk more about himself.

What Is the Counselor Not Hearing?

What you do not hear is based largely on your comfort level with your client and the topic matter being discussed. In general, the more discomfort you feel during a session, the more you are going to miss. We refer you back to Chapter 2 and the discussion of countertransference. If you are feeling discomfort you are probably not hearing all that you should be hearing. This should be a sign to you to take a few moments to reflect on why you feel uncomfortable and to take steps to listen even more closely.

How to Prepare for the Next Session

Toward the end of any middle session, you will begin to make some decisions about the next session, such as, will there by a next session? If there will be, when should it be, and what does your client want? Whether to terminate counseling depends mostly on how well your client is doing and on his feelings. If the person is no longer suicidal and his life is back to normal, your work is done and further sessions are not necessary. However, use caution. We feel that anytime someone considers suicide seriously, important changes need to be made in his life. Those changes can best be addressed in longer-term counseling. You can use your influence to effect a proper referral and to promote the idea of long-term counseling. We would suggest in most cases at least three sessions with any client who has made a suicide attempt or had serious suicidal ideation. This will give you a larger sample of behavior over time and a better idea of how your client is functioning.

If your client is not doing well, the next appointment should be set as soon as possible, not longer than two days away. If your client is functioning fairly well, you may want to give him up to a week before the next appointment. This will give the client a chance to better implement the treatment plan and get feedback on how it is working. Keeping in mind that weekends can be particularly trying, it is best to schedule appointments on Friday and Monday if possible. All of these decisions need to be made in conjunction with your client's wants and needs, and with the basic question of whether he will return. Treat any hesitancy to return on your client's part directly and take a firm stand on the importance of his next session.

Review of the Session

Before you end the interview it is best to review the session with your client. Highlight the major issues discussed in the session and conclude with a review of the treatment plan. Be sure to include the client's feelings in your review. If done skillfully, this review can tie together many apparently unrelated issues and provide a new way of looking at things for the client. We suggest pulling all this information together in a summary whenever possible.

Another method is to have the client review the session in order to check on his understanding of the treatment plan. If you do this, listen carefully for omissions and distortions and note them. After he has completed his summary, correct any major distortions you have heard. You will especially want to correct any misunderstandings regarding things you have said. When all business is finished, terminate the session, making sure the client knows your next appointment time and has phone numbers he can call in an emergency.

Special Situations

The Client Does Not Return

What do you do if your suicidal client does not return? First, it is important for you to try to get in touch with him by phone. If he is home, find out why he did not come back, without making him too defensive. If he appears to be all right, you can then spend some time talking with him and use the opportunity as something of a substitute for an in-person session. If he is not all right, do what you can to get him in to see you. If there is any doubt about his safety and you judge him to be fairly suicidal, do not hesitate to use the police, medic units, flying squads, or designated mental-health specialists to reach out to him.

If you are unable to reach him, go back over the previous session to find some clue that may explain his actions. Was there someone to watch him? Was that person reliable? In assessing the situation, keep in mind that you have basically two alternatives. The first is to wait a while longer and continue to try to reach him by phone or to call other places where he may be. The second alternative is to call the police or a friend and have them check the person's residence. Which you decide on will depend on your assessment of the situation. If there is any doubt, we suggest you call the police and have them check the residence. It is better to be wrong and risk a little embarrassment than to take the chance that the person will die.

The Client Is Very Early or Very Late

There are some valid reasons for a client to be early or late—accidents, unexpected traffic jams, misunderstanding on the part of the person's source of transportation, dependence on and adherence to bus schedules, and so on. Listen to the validity of the conscious reasons while formulating other possible explanations. In general, if the client is early he is likely to be in more distress and anxious to begin his next session. If he is late, there is a good chance that there is some resistance to counseling and it should be viewed and dealt with in the way we suggested earlier. Whatever the overt reason, keep in mind that you are probably the most important person in his life right now and counseling should be the top priority for him.

The Client Insists on Being Hospitalized: Bringing in the Support Systems

Occasionally you will see clients who are suicidal and come in with the stated goal of being put in the hospital. Often these are persons who have either had some prior experience with psychiatric hospitalization or have some fantasies about hospitalization. Clients who want to be hospitalized are often demanding, childish, and tend to exert great pressure to be taken care of. It is important not to be overwhelmed by such clients but to assess carefully past history with hospitals, suicidal history, and their fantasies about hospitalization. You may feel a great deal of pressure to act immediately with such a client. This is a mistake. We believe that hospitalization, while appropriate in many cases, should be used only as a last resort (Mendel and Green 1967; Mendel and Rapport 1969).

Associated with the client's demand to be hospitalized in the middle sessions is the situation in which the family or support group has "had enough." If your initial treatment plan included the family or other supporting persons who are no longer willing to participate, this will be perceived by the client as desertion or abandonment and he will often request hospitalization. If you have not already included the support-system individuals in your counseling sessions, now is the time to do so. It is important to ask your client's permission to bring in these others, and to agree on what specific topics will be covered. If your client is adamant about not bringing others into the session, then do not. Usually, however, it is not difficult to get the client's permission to bring them in, and frequently it is requested by the client.

Once you have your client's family and/or friends in your office, it is important to find out if indeed they are unwilling to help with the proposed treatment plan. Do not assume that your client has accurately perceived their unwillingness to help. Often in times of stress people will badly misperceive others' words and actions. If this is the case, facilitate the correction of the distortion by acting as interpreter between the parties involved. This is where good active-listening skills are useful. If the supporting individuals do not want to participate, find out why. Frequently what you will hear is that the support-system individuals have gone through this kind of thing many times before, or that they have been going through this for a long period of time and no longer see the use of continuing their support.

When you hear things like this, it is important to find out what is different this time. Sometimes not being willing to continue in the same pattern is a healthy sign for the support group, however, it may produce a crisis for your client. This situation presents one of the most difficult decisions a counselor may have to face and will call on all your clinical skills to resolve. We suggest several alternatives. First, work with the support-system persons to try and come to a healthy resolution or alternative. Negotiate a workable solution with both sides, one they can agree on. Remind each side that you are providing a short-term solution, and this is a beginning to that solution rather than an end in itself. Second, try to persuade the support group to hold on a little longer. Convince them, if possible, that if they follow your plan things will be better. Use your position of authority to your advantage by stating things definitely and with confidence. Clarify that you want to work with them and that if they can cooperate just a little longer, things can be different. Finally, if the family or other support system is unable to participate further, hospitalizaton or partial hospitalization may be your only alternative.

If your client refuses to participate in a family session or one that involves the support group, you have several alternatives. You may wish to emphasize that he can best help himself by involving his family. If he refuses this offer, ask him to offer alternative solutions and suggestions of what to do. It may be possible that he will come up with a workable solution that does not include the family or hospitalization. However, if one cannot be found, we suggest you see the family alone (with the client's permission) to work out a solution with them. Remind your client that you will keep confidential all that is relevant to working out a solution while he is out of the room. In working with the family, it is best to present your client's feelings briefly and concisely and compare them with the feelings of the family.

A final note about hospitalization. If a person comes to you wanting to be hospitalized but is not an appropriate candidate for it, you will have to say no. This can be a very difficult things to do. The client will usually get angry and emphasize how suicidal he really is. This needs to be recognized as a manipulation and confronted as such. You can state to your client that you are willing to help but you are not willing to hospitalize him as it is not in his best interest. If the person is willing to stay and work on your terms, do so. If he is not, you should be prepared for him to walk out. In such instances you can never be sure that the person is not going to kill himself. But you can reduce the odds of such an event through careful initial assessment. We have also found that such clients usually go from hospital to hospital or from agency to agency until they find someone to hospitalize them rather than actually taking their lives. But check with your supervisor before you reach the decision to deny hospitalization.

The Seductive Client

In short-term counseling, the first response to sexually seductive behaviors should be no response at all. This has several advantages. First, it shows your tolerance without criticism, and allows your client the opportunity to examine his behavior. Second, it gives you a chance to gather your thoughts and avoid an impulsively angry or otherwise defensive reaction. Finally, an accepting silence helps foster your relationship with your client and shows your ability to constructively handle difficult issues. Keep in mind the short-term nature of your work with your client; one incident of seductive behavior that does not reoccur or interfere with treatment may need to be addressed only with silence.

Seduction takes forms other than sexual ones. Such things as gifts, devious fee arrangements, inappropriate requests, or attempts to get you to do something you would not normally do as a counselor are all forms of seduction. The seductive client is probably not fully aware of the nature and quality of his behavior. In general, this style is related to long-standing, characteristic patterns of behavior that are fixed aspects of the client's personality. For this reason a direct comment that confronts or interprets his seductive behavior will be experienced as an unjustified personal attack or insult. We recommend that you *do not* interpret or confront seductive behavior but use the technique of implicit limit-setting. This is communicated in your tolerant attitude in combination with firm adherence to the ground rules and limits of your role as a counselor. This stance will be reassuring to your client and will best serve the goals and objectives of short-term counseling.

Summary

Success in the middle phase of counseling requires attention to the counseling *process*. Is the flow of information smooth? Does your client's sense of shame and guilt interfere with his ability to discuss his thoughts and feelings? Do you see evidence of change in what he reports? Does such change appear to be well-integrated and internalized? Is progress marked by new information and a deeper level of understanding? Your assessment of these issues forms the basis for the feedback you give your client in your review and summary and is also the basis for further planning.

A number of special issues may be encountered in the middle phase of counseling. Your client may be late or he may not return at all. He may be silent, confused and upset, or seductive. He and his family may demand his hospitalization. Each of these situations puts pressure on you and requires direct and active intervention.

References

Langs, R. *The Technique of Psychoanalytic Psychotherapy*. Vol. I. New York: Jason Aronson, 1973.

Mendel, W. and Green, G. *The Therapeutic Management of Psychological Illness*. New York: Basic Books, 1967.

Mendel, W., and Rapport, S. "Determinants of the Decision for Psychiatric Hospitalization." *Archives of General Psychiatry* 20 (1969):321–327.

Suggested Readings

Ackerman, N. *The Psychodynamics of Family Life*. New York: Basic Books, 1958.

Bowen, M. *Family Therapy in Clinical Practice*. New York: Jason Aronson, 1978.

Minuchin, S. *Families and Family Therapy*. Cambridge, Massachusetts: Harvard University Press, 1974.

Zuk, G. *Family Therapy: A Triadic Approach*. New York: Behavioral Publications, 1971.

11 The Termination of Counseling

The treatment plan and counseling contract negotiated in the first session should include an explicit discussion of the duration of counseling. This ensures that the subject of termination is an integral part of each session, not treated as a separate issue and postponed until the end. This gives your client time to adjust to the idea, so that it does not come as a surprise. Addressing it before the last visit also gives you time to deal with the client's feelings toward you as well as feelings of loss, rejection, anger, abandonment, and dependency, issues that often arise when short-term counseling has been successful. When you talk about these themes, you lower the risk of having your client skip the final session. In addition you reduce the chance that his suicidal feelings will return at the time of counseling termination, and this increases the probability for follow-through on your referral. (Wolberg 1980).

The Client's Feelings

One mistake that most counselors in crisis work make with regard to termination is underestimating their own importance to the client, and therefore not taking the termination process seriously enough. Remember, you have stirred intense feelings in the client. For a brief period of time, you have empathically entered into your client's depression, his desperation, his rage, and his suicidal thoughts. We suggest to you that your importance has been second to none during this time in his life. Now this phase will come to an end. Though you have actively planned for your client to internalize some of the coping skills you have fostered, there is no real guarantee that this has been enough. Nor are you assured that his emotional stability will be retained for more than a few weeks after you have said good-bye. How the client's feelings are handled in the final session can be vital to the outcome of short-term treatment as well as to the referral process and to the eventual outcome of long-term counseling.

Positive, Negative, and Neutral Feelings

In general, it is best to allow your client's positive feelings to develop and continue, even if the feelings and good qualities attributed to you make you uncomfortable or in your opinion have no basis in fact. It is usually best not to disturb those positive feelings either by interpreting them as transference or by denying that those characteristics are true. In other words, simply let your client compliment you and let it go at that.

It is important that you listen for and be prepared to deal with negative feelings in a different way than you would positive ones. In the first place they are likely to be expressed indirectly and very subtly. Client behavior such as coming late for an appointment, not coming at all, getting appointment times confused, or other similar behaviors are examples of indirect expressions of anger. Freudian slips and statements like "I forgot my checkbook. Can I mail you the money?" are further indications that your client is angry about termination of counseling. Because of the disguised nature of negative feelings about termination, you should consider taking a rather active, interpretive stance; you should be rather forward in suggesting that your client may be angry with you for now having to say good-bye. If you meet with some defensiveness at the suggestion, do not be surprised. It is always difficult to confront anger with someone who has helped you and you will need to normalize this with him. This can in part be accomplished through education and by the manner in which you tell him that it is all right to be angry with you.

Anger often protects us from other, more threatening feelings such as abandonment, loss and helplessness. Whether you will be able to interpret these deeper feelings is doubtful. As a matter of fact, we suggest that in crisis counseling you do not even try. We do, however, want you to recognize the existence of deeper feelings since they underlie client feelings expressed in the termination phase. The anger mentioned previously is probably the deepest level you should work with; even then you are working with very delicate and complicated material. In light of this, you should be very cautious in how far you push your interpretation of a client's anger. It may be too threatening given your client's history of dealing with such emotionally charged feelings. Dealing with such anger involves considerable sensitivity, timing, and tactfulness. On the one hand, you have been charged with bringing the interview to a successful close. As part of that responsibility, you are being asked to say good-bye in a healthy and growth-promoting way. Your client, on the other hand, is giving every indication by his mood and behavior that this is not what he wants to deal with. Hence you are faced with a clinical dilemma. Solving it is as much an art as it is a science. By now, you should know your client well. You know how he has dealt with previous losses (you found this out when he talked about his history of relationships and you can predict that the way he said good-bye to other significant people will be the same way he says good-bye to you).

Most often your client's feelings about you and his counseling experience in general may appear to be neutral. In addition, your client may react to your relationship as if he were uninvolved. Certainly not all clients will form strong attachments to you. In such instances, termination may involve little discussion, and your client may have no trouble saying good-bye. He may express little or no gratitude, and he may leave your office for the last time with little fanfare. This type of situation arises if clients have formed little or no attachment to others and have a bland history of termination and dealing with loss. With such clients, making a big issue of termination is unnecessary and usually counterproductive. After what we have just said about your importance, it may come as a shock that to some clients you may be no more than a passing figure.

In summary, the feelings that arise in your client at termination will vary depending on the type of relationship, the client's past history with terminations and loss, the length of treatment, and the manner in which you handle the termination.

The Counselor's Feelings

Many of the feelings that arise in your client may also arise in you at termination. Feelings of loss, abandonment, anger, and fear, are all common during this phase of your work. You will be in a better position to deal with these feelings if you pay attention to certain issues. First, if things have gone well with a particular client, you may feel reluctant to give up this source of reward and validation of you as a good counselor. You can avoid these kinds of feelings by making use of consultation time with your supervisor or colleagues. In addition you can seek gratification and validation of your personal worth in other areas of your life. This could include outside activities and relationships, sports, and hobbies. It is also useful to arrange your clinical involvement in such a way that you are working with several cases at any given time. This will reduce the chance of overinvolvement with one case, and increase the likelihood of making a healthy and appropriate termination.

On the other hand, if things are not going well for you and you are aware of it, you may be tempted to either terminate too early or hang on too long to try and make things better. Again, by adhering to the original number of sessions you contracted for and by making use of your supervisor and/or colleagues, you can help avoid these problems. Likewise, it is important to know you have outside activities and relationships that are supportive and that provide personal gratification and validation. If all of your identity is tied up in being a good counselor, and counseling is your exclusive source of reinforcement, any treatment failure will be extremely difficult for you to deal with.

Finally, termination may bring into focus other personal issues that have not adequately been resolved. A careful examination of your own history of dealing with termination of relationships and loss is an important first step. Since most countertransference issues are by definition unconscious and therefore out of your awareness, you may not realize the complexity of the issues until after the fact.

Collusion of Client and Counselor

Client-counselor collusion may arise at any point in counseling but it seems to arise most frequently around termination time. One issue we want to address is the attempt to continue the relationship beyond termination, as a friend, business-partner, or the like. We feel that once the client-counselor relationship has been concluded it should stay that way. We do not advocate the practice of after-hours socializing with clients, nor do we feel it proper to engage in joint business ventures, vacations, or the like with former clients. The original treatment contract was only to help the client through his crisis, and extensions such as these are simply ways of denying the contract is over. The transference or countertransference issue may be met with some resistance and rationalization on both sides, but the rule stands. You did not meet as friends or business-partners, and it is unprofessional to conclude your treatment contract that way. In brief therapy you do not have the skill nor the time to resolve such complex issues as introjection, internalization or incorporation (Hartman 1958; Loewald 1973).

As a counselor you must be clear about the boundaries and limits of the relationship you have with your client. It is neither friendship nor is it one of equality. It is by definition a relationship in which one is trained to help another. This does not include extending the therapeutic relationship beyond the office. From a technical point of view we would say that after-hours activities prolong the client's wish for inappropriate gratification. This delays the frustration necessary for psychological growth and leaves the client stuck in childhood phases rather than leading him in the direction of adulthood (Winnicott 1953; Segal 1964).

Special Considerations at Termination

Not every situation can be anticipated nor spelled out for you. The complexities and individual differences are myriad. There are, however, points of discussion that emerge repeatedly when it comes time to say good-bye. We will briefly cover four of them.

When Clients Do Not Come to the Last Appointment

When this happens we recommend you call him to find out why. If you reach him, be sensitive in the way you raise the issue. Do not blame or criticize him for not remembering the appointment time. Rather, remember your clinical responsibilities and the conscious or unconscious reasons he forgot the last session. Take the extra time and with your client's permission explore the matter with him.

The healthy way to end the relationship is to talk things out rather than act them out. If the client is unavailable, we suggest you make several attempts later that day or the next to contact him. If this proves unsuccessful and you are sure he is avoiding you and not trying to end his life, let it drop.

Receiving Gifts

In short-term counseling the dangers of not accepting a client's good-bye gift far outweigh the complications of accepting the gift. Saying no in such a situation may cause bruised feelings that will likely be interpreted as rejection of him rather than rejection of the gift. A client's gift is an extension of himself. If you say no to the offering, you are essentially saying no to his person. In clinical terms, you will understand that it is a magical way of keeping in touch with you after the relationship is ended. But there is not time to interpret this, unless it has emerged as part of the earlier issues of ongoing therapy. Though it may be controversial, it is probably best to say thank-you and accept gifts from clients at termination. Common sense dictates that sexual favors, expensive gifts, and the like are quite inappropriate and should always be refused.

New Problems

As a general rule, clients who store up new problems until the last session are trying to manipulate you so as not to have to say good-bye. It is imperative therefore that you adhere to your treatment plan and stick with the issue of ending the crisis contact. Be gentle but firm and state, "we will have to stop now." If you have referred the client elsewhere you can suggest he bring this issue before the next counselor. Interpretation in this instance is likely to be a waste of time if the client is conscious of what he is doing. If you sense the broaching of new problems is unconscious, a tying-together comment is appropriate, for example, "We've spent much of this session saying good-bye. Now this new information. It sounds like you're having a hard time with that. But we will have to stop here." It may sound cruel to be so firm, but such a stance is necessary for the client's growth.

Eruption of Old Problems

In all likelihood clients who are experiencing a setback with the eruption of some old material will introduce it at the beginning of the last session. Once you have determined that the client's concerns are real, you must be prepared to take the appropriate action. If the flare-up is serious enough, you may have to revise your original plan and offer additional sessions. If that does not appear to be necessary, you may have to extend the current interview a bit longer. If you sense this to be the case and you have another appointment, be prepared to excuse yourself temporarily and ask the next person to wait. If the current problem(s) get too sticky, do not hesitate to call in a supervisor or colleague to assist you. For whatever reason, your current client may not be able to handle termination in any other way. At one level we would suggest that the client's unconscious motivation is to hold on to you. And if interpretation to this point is fruitless and the eruption of problems is too severe, you might have to see him for an additional interview. An accurate diagnosis and treatment plan will serve as something of a hedge against this event. But because of the vulnerabilities of many of the clients you see, they may not always be able to conform to your original expectations.

Client Summarization

Early in this final session we strongly recommend that you ask your client to review what he has received from these sessions. This is not an attempt to put him on the spot. It serves two therapeutic purposes. In the first place, the responsibility for the outcome of these sessions is shared. Second, it is a check on how much internalization has actually taken place. By introducing this subject early in the interview, you will have some idea of what to focus on for the remainder of the clinical hour. If your client expresses a misunderstanding of key treatment concepts or goals, you can offer a correction or clarification of what you meant. If your client is accurate in his recall, you will have an opportunity to reinforce his perceptions and hence strengthen his internalization of problem-solving skills.

A structured summarization such as this sets much of the tone for the final session. You follow the lead of your client, much as you have in earlier sessions. You demonstrate a consistency of approach that is rare in his life, particularly since it is geared toward improving his ability to care for himself. And organizing your summary around his recall prevents you from introducing extraneous and irrelevant material.

Time to Say Good-bye

There is no one way to say good-bye. The most common expressions are a handshake, a smile, some friendly words. But regardless of the method it should be sincere and appropriate to your style of ending the relationship. There may be a wish to set aside the client and counselor roles at this time, but resist it. Actions such as inappropriate self-disclosure, joking, and small talk, as well as excessive physical contact, are not helpful and may impede any further counseling in the future. If you have paid close attention at the outset to the myriad of issues involved in the termination of counseling, this experience can be a positive one. Saying good-bye is as natural a process as saying hello, and in many ways it is just as important that you address it with the same care you gave to your original introduction.

Summary

The manner in which you handle the termination of counseling is vital to the overall outcome of crisis work. Your feelings and your client's feelings both play a part in this process, and it is necessary for you to be prepared to recognize and deal with them. Anger, loss, desertion, and abandonment are key feelings to look for. You should also recognize such special issues as collusion, gifts, new problems, and eruption of old problems. Finally, we talked about several ways to say good-bye.

References

Getz, W., Wiesen, A., Sue, S., and Ayers, A. *Fundamentals of Crisis Counseling.* Lexington, Mass.: Lexington Books, 1974.

Hartman, H. *Ego Psychology and the Problem of Adaptation.* New York: International Universities Press, 1958.

Loewald, H. "On Internalization." *International Journal of Psychoanalysis* 54(1973): 9–15.

Segal, H. *Introduction to the Work of Melanie Klein.* New York: Basic Books, 1964.

Winnicott, D. "Transitional Objects and Transitional Phenomena." *International Journal of Psychoanalysis* 54(1953): 17–25.
Wolberg, L. *Handbook of Short-Term Psychotherapy*. New York: Thieme-Stratton, 1980.

**Part III
Special Topics**

12 When a Client Commits Suicide

There is a high probability that at some time during your counseling career one of your clients will commit suicide. In crisis work the probabilities are even higher given the clinical population you work with. This is one of the harsh realities of suicide counseling. And it is best that you understand it now. The death of a client has far-reaching implications for all survivors. And unless they are addressed properly you become ineffective at a time when you need to be at your best. This is no easy task. It requires a very special kind of skill that is difficult to convey in the pages of a textbook. No academic preparation fully prepares us to deal with such an event. We make no pretense to be able to give you more than a set of guidelines should a suicide occur.

The emotional impact of a client's suicide can be compared to being struck in the solar plexus when you least expect it. Everything comes to a momentary halt and for a time you are stunned and disoriented. You struggle for breath and as that returns you try to figure out what happened. Feelings of failure and puzzlement can become devastating handicaps unless understood and resolved. Not only can this ruin a promising clinician, but it also leaves the former client's survivors equally vulnerable because you are unable to help them cope as you should. In either case the original tragedy becomes compounded and much of what the client has unconsciously wished for comes true. We will first consider the impact a suicide can have on the client's relatives and friends, then the impact it can have on you. We realize that many of the principles governing the successful resolution of such an event apply to both parties. But there are differences as well, and the effects will be felt by all survivors in a unique and individual way.

Effects on Relatives and Friends

There are many psychological issues that are likely to be raised in relatives and friends when someone they know or are related to commits suicide. Myths and old wives' tales are likely to come to mind even if they are never verbalized. Worries about heredity, eternal damnation, and social stigma often surface. Though you may never have complete access to this material, you would be wise to remember that it does exist and is likely to create anger, confusion, guilt, shame, and fear in survivors. This is a delicate situation, because unless one of these persons considers himself to be a client of yours, you theoretically have little access to him. In reality, you should offer your services. But remember you walk a fine line and must therefore be extremely sensitive to this lack of a "consent to services" contract. Of course, you offer yourself in a voluntary way and only intervene if asked to.

Unless a person has formally declared himself to be your client, you do not know who they are nor how they may react to what you say. In an earlier chapter we commented on distortion and the role it played in some lives. Your comments, though well intentioned, could easily be misunderstood in such a trauma-filled moment. Without a therapeutic relationship you leave yourself open to all manner of problems that are unlikely to be ever resolved. In such a circumstance it is often wise to simply say nothing. And if there is the slightest possibility of a lawsuit in the near future, you may wish to remain silent for your own protection as well.

We are not, however, trying to direct you away from counseling survivors. We simply want to alert you to the complexities that exist even before you say a word of guidance or condolence. Unless you have more than a single contact with a survivor, we suggest limiting yourself to making supportive grief-work comments and not much more. If a survivor asks to see you as a client then you may go beyond this point. But unless this happens, it is best to stand on the sidelines and keep fairly quiet.

Clinical Considerations When Survivors Are Your Clients

Each survivor will react to the news of a client's death in somewhat individualized ways (Wilkinson 1982; Resnik 1969). Lindemann (1944) in his classic work on survivors of the Coconut Grove fire observed the following sequence of reactions: "disorganization and tension with disruption to bodily and thought processes; preoccupation with and rumination about the past; and attempts to mobilize resources and to adjust to the situation." (cited in Getz et al. 1974, p. 9).

Although the Wilkinson and Lindemann studies do not deal with death by suicide, the core elements are the same regardless of the cause of death. You should have little trouble adapting their findings and principles to your specific work. The extent to which the survivors in these studies returned to their previous levels of coping depended on the success with which each person did the "grief work"; that is, achieved an emancipation from the person who had died, readjusted to the environment in which the person had lived, and was able to form new relationships (Parad 1965). Although it may be difficult for you to determine in a single contact if your survivors pattern themselves after these guidelines, you will nevertheless receive some inkling based on what they say and do and what you may have learned about them from your former client. It is from this information that you take your cues as to the appropriate interventions to make. If the survivor appears receptive to the idea of grieving, then by all means help him in this task. But do not delve too deeply if there is little opportunity to connect him to a resource that can follow through with what you have initiated.

In many ways the most effective intervention—assuming the survivor will let you—is to check on his environmental supports. Foremost among these is his pastor or rabbi. If possible contact these persons who will then be able to provide immediate and follow-up services. Lacking such a resource, you may have to inquire about someone else—a neighbor, a former employer, or a distant cousin—anyone who may have some perspective about this whole situation and who can be supportive.

As Lindemann (1944) and others have observed, survivors are likely to show great resistance to experiencing the feelings of grief. In many ways our culture does little to support them when they do show grief. Most people do not feel comfortable when they observe someone crying uncontrollably; it stirs a sense of helplessness and psychological vulnerability. Feeling threatened, we try and deal with these fears by moving away from the object of threat or by trying to stifle the person who is causing the discomfort. Fearful of losing control, we try to hush the griever directly or indirectly. In either case we convey the message that full expression of such anguish is to be limited and stopped as quickly as possible. There are exceptions to this, or course, but in the main we expect the survivors to grieve in private and rather quietly. Therefore, it is likely that survivors will respond with considerable reluctance to your suggestions of grieving. If this is the case, back off. Allow them their defenses even though you may think their adaptation is unhealthy. Unless you have a treatment contract, there is nothing else you really can do.

Clinical Considerations When Survivors May Become Your Clients

Given the nature of the circumstances surrounding such a trauma, survivors may not be organized enough nor possess the ego strength to formally request that they become your clients. Some will be able to recognize their distress and ask for help, but this is unusual. Generally those in crisis turn to a non-mental-health person for comfort and support (Getz 1975) or they will try to work it out by themselves. But for those who do ask for help or who seem to be leaning in that direction here are some things to keep in mind. If you sense that a survivor is in great anguish and could benefit from several sessions, but who has not directly asked you for help, be sensitive to how you propose your services. You might say, "Would it help to talk with me?" or, "If you like, you can come and talk with me. I have some time." or, "If I can be of any help, don't hesitate to let me know."

However the person responds to your gentle invitation, continue to treat him and his situation carefully. Even if he gives you permission to counsel him, proceed carefully. In one sense you have intruded into his grief process. You have inserted yourself into something that is both public and private. Though your motives are professional, it is nevertheless an intrusion. Ask yourself continuously how you might be communicating when you present your offer. With great care ask the survivor how he feels about it. If you perceive too much ambivalence, it is best to back away. Even though the survivor may have given his tacit approval for you to help him, remember what it is like to work with an ambivalent client who is *not* in crisis. Then multiply this by a factor of five for one who is. This uncertainty and the possibility your motives may be misconstrued are two of the major reasons we caution a conservative approach with such survivors.

In the event you feel a more direct approach is indicated, pay particular attention to the enormous influence you exert in such a situation. Treat this knowledge with great respect and sensitivity. You have the power to sway someone; to direct him into a situation that may not be in his best interest, regardless of your motives. You may influence someone who is ambivalent; someone who wants and does not want to ask for help. Unless you recognize these two-way feelings you can end up with a weakly motivated client who may feel manipulated and resentful for having been talked into seeing you. It may be, however, that the survivor has always been able to respond to a more direct approach, someone who has a history of taking orders and profits from such an approach. You must be a very skilled clinician in order to recognize such personal dynamics. And unless you do, it is risky to take anything more than a conservative stance under such delicate circumstances. The vast majority of survivors will not be so difficult to diagnose. They will either say yes or no to your invitation.

Clinical Issues with Survivors Who Become Your Clients

Although no two survivors will respond exactly alike, they are nevertheless likely to share some reactions. If you can anticipate and listen for them, you will be in a stronger position to help the survivor master his feeling about the client's death. These feelings include guilt because of thoughts he had about the former client; anger at some or all of the key people involved with the client including himself, the former client, and you the counselor; a desire for reparation, (the wish to repair and repay because of these thoughts and feelings); and finally, a constant state of bewilderment as to why this death really happened. Not all of these feelings will appear in every survivor. And when they appear, you may not be successful in resolving them. You will find that these themes occur over and over again. With experience and very good supervision you will know what to do when they appear.

Unconscious Wishes

For some relatives and friends the client's death represents the fulfillment of an unconscious wish toward the client. This is more likely to be the case if the client had repeatedly made suicide gestures than if it was a sudden and singular attempt. The survivors of a chronic suicide attempter are exhausted and frustrated by the many previous attempts. They may have seen little hope of being able to help. When they had tried to help, the client may have turned their caring efforts into something sour and futile with each repeated attempt. Survivors may have gotten angry, said "what's the use" and thus psychologically turned away from your former client. They may have had enough of late-night telephone conversations; enough long talks; enough of offering a shoulder to cry on; enough of referrals to see a "shrink." And all for what? The client did not seem to change. The survivors probably had heard enough depressing stories to last them a lifetime. They may have said to themselves, "I just wish he would go away," or "I'm so sick of hearing how depressed he is. Sometimes I just wish he would go away." These and other similar thoughts are disguised wishes that the client would indeed commit suicide and thus solve their own conflicts and feelings of helplessness in the situation.

Few people have enough ego strength to admit such feelings and then deal with them in a confrontive and healthy way. What the relatives are more likely to do is to push such thoughts out of their minds and then reprimand themselves for thinking such things. The feelings that accompany such unacceptable ideas then become repressed. The individuals may be able to function more effectively at a conscious level when such ideas are repressed and forgotten, but if the person they have directed these thoughts at does indeed die, there will be all sorts of problems to face. The survivors will feel guilt for somehow having contributed to the deceased's death. They will feel ashamed and privately ask themselves, "How could I have had such a thought?" Self-punishment will begin almost immediately and if it is not dealt with in a therapeutic way it will linger. Denial will set in. And then there will be anger, sometimes obvious, as seen in the facial muscles and attitude; sometimes subtle, as in angry dreams or cross comments for no apparent reason. However the survivors' feelings are expressed there is sure to be some negative lingering effect. To secretly wish for someone's death and then to have it happen, is not easily dealt with. Successful resolution of these feelings, if such a thing is to happen, requires that you and the survivors observe several important principles. They are (1) understanding the normalcy of angry feelings, (2) recognizing the difference between normal and neurotic shame and guilt, and (3) understanding past crises in the light of the present one.

Angry Feelings

The Angry Book (Rubin 1969) was written because the author felt there was a great deal of confusion and misinformation about this subject as a normal human emotion. Because of this, he felt the price paid was incalculable in terms of poor mental and physical health and destroyed interpersonal relationships. It is his belief that recognizing anger for what it is will give us the mastery we seek in order to prevent the worst expressions of it. In order to accomplish this we must first understand anger and then through insight and eventual acceptance we will be able to work through many of the resistances we have to this part of the personality.

We all want to be liked and accepted; this is universal. This desire serves as the basis for much of our behavior. We are taught at many levels that in order to be approved of we had better not show or express too much anger, and apologize for anger we do show. We know that in the extremes unbridled anger creates chaos, while unrecognized anger leaves us defenseless. Rubin deals with the many types of anger between these extremes in such a way as to create a realistic and accepting attitude about anger. You too will need to convey a similar attitude to your former clients' survivors. Showing that their feelings are normal is one way to accomplish this. Another way is to educate your client through very carefully chosen and softly spoken words.

Anger is essentially a psychological defense. It serves to protect us from feelings and conflicts that would otherwise overwhelm and immobilize us. Anger allows us to do our jobs, interact with our families and friends, and in general meet the demands of daily living. To tamper with this defense too much is a risky intervention—particularly when there are only a few sessions in which to help survivors integrate your words and meanings. In our opinion it is best to let survivors retain some portion of this defense, using such reassurances as "it's all right to feel angry." Stripping a survivor of his anger defense without being able to follow up in long-term counseling is not in his best interest. Even with normalization, education, and reassurance, you must be prepared to deal with some measure of guilt and shame that will surely accompany your comments. Crisis counseling is not designed to accommodate anything more than a rather superficial level of integration and incorporation. If you interpret anger in an attempt to dig deeper into the psyche, you may uncover more material than you can deal with in a constructive way. Your goal is to return the survivor to his precrisis level of functioning. To that end you must judge the depth of your interpretations and comments. You may have no other choice but to leave the issue of anger at a superficial level, ending up with a client who is somewhat angry at the relative or friend who took his own life, but nevertheless functioning effectively.

Normal versus Neurotic Guilt and Shame

It is commonplace for guilt and shame to be considered one and the same. Although both may be evoked by the same action such as breaking a rule of some kind, they are in fact separate and in some ways quite different. Lewis (1971) makes the following distinctions. Shame is primarily experienced as a deficiency and inadequacy in one's self, usually in the whole self and not just in some part of the self. It is an acutely painful experience and it involves a sense of failure and inability to live up to personal standards and ideals. Shame is a relatively wordless state. It is often played out in mental imagery; one part of the self wrestles with another part. Hostile feelings are directed against the self, causing something of a paralysis of action. The individual feels small and "just wants to crawl into a hole." Humiliated fury accompanies shame, but is expressed only after repair to the injury of the self. The repair work—the healing process—is intrapsychic. The individual repairs his own self-image, improves his own self-esteem, tells himself he is better than what he feels. Guilt is similar in some ways but different in others. Guilt is about real failures of real events and not about mental pictures. Like shame, guilt may be felt as acute and painful, almost to the point of despair. This can lead in a circuitous way to shame and the two may become intertwined and are sometimes impossible to separate. Guilt pushes us to make amends for our actions, and in some cases these actions go beyond the rational. Indignation rather than fury accompanies guilt, expressed by correcting the person or thing that occasioned the guilt in the first place.

You will be dealing with both guilt and shame in survivors and must therefore pay careful attention to the extent and accessibility for correction of these phenomena. Denial is the most common defense for shame while guilt tends to be defended by rationalization and isolation of thoughts. In both instances you are working with very complicated and sensitive issues that require a skilled and educated approach if you are to help. Normalizing and reassuring comments are the best interventions in the short term, along with helping survivors to talk about their feeling state. Ventilation in a nonjudgmental setting with a neutral listener has marvelous healing and restorative properties. If there is a time for you to comment on what seems to be a conflicting issue, you may choose to say something, but only if it will help the survivor better understand his psychological position.

Helping survivors through the acute stage of their shock and grief is your primary task. To accomplish this you should be prepared to make use of every brief-counseling technique available, which in many instances means that you simply encourage them to talk about what they are thinking and feeling. You observe their reactions, and from this offer supportive comments clarifying their feelings or ask them to tell you more, whichever seems most appropriate. Since you may have no more than a single session, you cannot expect to achieve much more than some type of paranormalization of these feelings. You want to prevent, if you can, the survivor's slipping into irrational guilt and shame.

Neurotic or excessive feelings that accompany guilt and shame cannot be resolved in such a short time, but with your timely intervention they may be mitigated. Under the circumstances, perhaps the best you can do is set the stage so that at a later date the survivor may work out these conflicts in his own way. Returning such a client to his previous state of functioning is complicated and perhaps technically impossible, since you have little baseline data to work with in the first place. For this reason if for no other, listening and then reflecting feelings with a nonjudgmental attitude is one of your strongest interventions. Anything more must be based on solid clinical evidence and substantial expertise.

Past and Present Crises

As Kahlis et al. (1961) have noted, present crisis events sometimes reactivate previously unresolved issues. In the event such a situation has occurred with a survivor, your task is to recognize you are dealing with two or more superimposed events and to determine the survivor's accessibility to interpretive work. Your approach is based on a combination of facts and impressions: (1) the survivor/client's motivation and ability to do this work; (2) the type of counseling contract you have with him; (3) the type of working alliance you have with one another; (4) your clinical-skills level; and (5) your survivor/client's resources.

In the event that these factors are favorable, you may want to suggest several sessions rather than a single one, because one interview is simply not enough to be very helpful. You cannot expect to probe and uncover such unconscious material and have your client digest and integrate everything in one hour. Try to contract with him for a series of sessions. Do this openly and honestly, explaining how restricted you are to help given the limits of your time. Emotional rather than simple intellectual understanding takes time and the survivor will need to reflect and evaluate what goes on in your office and integrate it with how he is functioning in the real world. Out of this process he will be able to dismantle the respective conflicts and contain them in their proper perspective, emerging from the crisis in a healthier and less vulnerable state.

There is no hocus-pocus in this work. It is demanding and requires all your skills as well as a firm treatment contract from your survivor/client. Lacking this type of commitment, you should not dig any deeper than you may already have. Reluctance to continue on the client's part is his right and it must be respected. If you can not secure a "contract to counsel" at this time, then at least make sure you keep the door open for him to return at some future time. It may be that he is not yet ready for counseling or that you are not the best counselor for him to work with on this matter. Whatever the resistance, deal with it gently. Reassure him that he can always call you if he feels the need and that you will help him get in touch with someone else if that would help. Do not take his rejection personally as it well may have more to do with intrapsychic processes than anything you have said or done.

Impact of a Client's Suicide on the Counselor

Much of what we have written in this chapter is applicable in certain ways to you the counselor should one of your clients commit suicide. You will be faced with the options of dealing with the event in direct or indirect ways. If you decide to face the situation squarely, it means you will have to do the grief work mentioned earlier. You will be affected by some disruption of thought and there will be the expected preoccupation with and rumination over what happened. Depending on the depth of the relationship you had with the client you will surely feel some degree of shock, anger, sadness, and puzzlement about him, about your role in this event, and its impact on your present and future functioning. Shame, guilt, embarrassment, and fear will likewise accompany the news of a client's death, and depending on your ego and environmental strengths it can have a significant present and future impact on you.

Just as for other survivors, this event is likely to stir up all manner of feelings in you. There will be issues that have not been resolved from previously felt failures and disappointments. Ghosts of feelings that you thought had been relegated to the past and forgotten once again creep back into your thoughts. Issues and conflicts that you thought had been solved also return for a brief scrutiny before they are laid to rest once again. Even with the support of your colleagues, friends, and family you will have moments when you feel utterly alone in all of this. Throughout this grieving process and for as long as it takes to resolve the conflicts, we urge you to stay in close touch with your own thoughts and feelings and share them with your professional intimates (Holden in press). A certain portion of the resolution of feelings and thoughts will be accomplished when you are by yourself. But this will be facilitated and enhanced enormously by the support you receive from others, particularly if they have suffered through the same experience (Kolodny et al. 1979). Although no academic prose can fully prepare you to deal with such an event, we offer the following ideas.

The Big Question: A Partial Answer

More than any other question, you are likely to be haunted by "Could I have prevented this suicide?" It will recur frequently and just as frequently must be confronted by you. Keeping perspective in this situation is difficult, and if you try to deal with this question solely by yourself, the outcome can be catastrophic. Just as you have asked your survivor/clients to come to the office to share guilt, anger, shame, and all the other feeling states, you must share your feelings with others. Shame and guilt can become oppressive and interfere with your clinical abilities for the present as well as the future.

An emotionally crippled counselor can become one who is unconsciously cared for by his clients. They somehow sense that you cannot accept their problems and conflicts and they hold back in order to spare you. They are then cast in the role of taking care of you without really understanding how or why this is happening, and the resulting conflicts add mysteriously to their many other problems. They may handle this by acting out the conflicts and not continuing counseling with you or by sinking into a deeper depression because of having to carry your conflicts as well as their own. All of this can at least be minimized if not avoided if you will pay careful attention to some helpful principles.

Marshall (1980) talks about agency policies that can be followed when a client commits suicide and these questions arise. First the client's chart is to be reviewed and all recorded material analyzed as to the facts of the case. Second, a list of all staff involved is compiled and meetings are held to discuss the situation. Third, the acting supervisor seeks sources of outside information to compile a more thorough picture of just what happened. (In the case example reported, this involved law-enforcement personnel and relatives who were directly involved with the former client. These people were of invaluable help in separating fact from fiction, information which was then relayed to the agency staff for incorporation into the overall understanding of the case.) Finally, adequate time is given the staff to come to terms with the information and a formal report is made to the whole agency, staff and administrators alike.

Following this process, everyone involved should have worked through the grief process well enough to be able to return to their previous level of functioning. Marshall described several phases she observed as the staff worked through their conflicts. The first one was the "resuscitation phase." This encompassed anger, distress, and questions of responsibility. The second phase was the "rehabilitation phase," in which handling new information, resolving guilt, and grieving was done. The final stage was the "renewal phase," in which new learning had taken place along with a willingness to continue counseling other clients.

Angry Feelings

Crisis counselors are not noted for their ability to recognize how frustrating it is when their best-laid treatment plans go awry. Treatment failure may be rationalized with statements like "What more can you expect, given his many problems?" But this or a similar explanation does not address the underlying anger that is to be expected in such cases. Nor does it help you, the clinician, face the very human side of this work. Just as you help other survivors to come to grips with their anger toward the deceased, so too must you deal with your own anger. Do not feel it is unprofessional to harbor such feelings. Professionalism has nothing to do with it. As a feeling and reflective person you are affected by such an event and to deny this is a mistake. It is your responsibility to implement all the counseling skills you have and turn them to yourself in order to function effectively in what you are trained to do. Your other clients cannot wait while you ignore the realities of what you feel. They will not improve with a robot for a counselor. They may get better if they see you as a compassionate personality who is not unaffected by life's events, but who possesses the skills necessary to master them. From this experiential base you model for them how to handle such a situation. If you need to express anger, do so with your support group. This will show that you are congruent and believe in the advice you offer to others.

Countertransference

Another major issue is one of unconscious motives. Did you have a secret wish that your client would die? Was there a part of you that hated this client so much that you hoped he would end his life? If so, was this fantasy conveyed to him in such a manner that he became aware of it and acted it out? These questions are not unreasonable under the circumstances. Your unconscious is a storehouse of conflicts, wishes, and fantasies that appear in unusual and often unpredictable ways. Although you can never know for sure when or how they may express themselves during your counseling career, you can be sure that they are there, seeking expression of some kind (Racker 1968).

Because of the intensity of suicidal counseling, all kinds of feelings can be aroused in you and these feelings must be contained if you are to maximize your effectiveness. You should understand that your client's inner world at times is similar in many ways to yours. The fact that you accept the parts of yourself that wish destruction and devastation on others without acting on them is a significant aspect of what makes you different from him.

Perhaps you had such destructive thoughts. If so, did you project them in some fashion that may have contributed to this awful event? You will answer this as you go through the process of unraveling fact from fiction and separating contained wishes from acted-out impulses. If peer support and counseling do not help, select a competent therapist and become the client yourself. This action should not only prove to be invaluable in the current crisis, but also will help you improve your performance in all aspects of your clinical and personal life.

Other Questions

You may find yourself struggling with a series of questions, some of which are rational, some of which are not. "Does this mean I'm a failure as a counselor?'' is one of them. No single event such as this should affect you to the extent that you feel your career is a failure. If it does you have exceeded the boundaries of normal guilt and shame and have become hobbled by excesses of these feelings.

"Should I ever work with another suicidal client again?'' is to be answered with a resounding *Yes!* As a matter of fact you may be especially capable with clients having gone through this experience.

"Will this ruin my career and reputation?'' If your professional and lay community is narrow-minded to the point of seeking a scapegoat, it might. But if you have followed all the steps to document that there was no negligence on your part, you can effectively combat whatever community criticism may be directed at you, and in the process establish the fact that your reputation stands very solid indeed.

"Should I attend the funeral?'' and "Should I insist on helping the former client's family work through this experience?'' You should emphatically answer *no!* to both questions and be prepared to examine your motives for proposing such questions in the first place. Perhaps it is out of a deep feeling of helplessness that you are proposing such overcompensation. If this is the case, ask yourself, "Whose needs am I really trying to address?''

Legal Issues

From a psychological point of view there is nothing quite like having the facts in hand to help resolve your apprehension about responsibility in a client's suicide. To accomplish this you should keep meticulous records of all your clients, but particularly of those who are depressed and suicidal. Apart from the mental and emotional benefits of this practice, there are considerable legal implications as well. No clinician likes the thought of being served a subpoena as a defendant in a lawsuit over alleged malpractice. But this could happen, particularly if your client commits suicide while under your care. In his book *Malpractice: A Guide for Mental Health Professionals,* Cohen (1979) writes that no one wins once the gavel falls in the courtroom when a lawsuit is on the docket. He addresses the specific issue of counseling with suicide-prone clients. He states that a complete and accurate recordkeeping system is a must. Your records should include a complete history of your client, notes on his suicidal or homicidal gestures, as well as any suicidal ideations he may report. You should also include all evaluations from other professionals and what they have said about your client. Your notes should be concise. You should include the reason(s) for termination of counseling. Cohen believes that well-kept records may mean the difference—if you are called into

court—between a court judgment for or against you. Further, he states
that a clinician fumbling and trying to make sense of his notes is viewed
quite negatively by the court. Slawson (1970) agrees that good records
are the keystone in a defendant's case.

Do not be defensive about collecting and recording this type of legal
information. It does not matter that you are innocent of any or all charges
brought against you. Almost anyone can sue you for alleged malpractice
regardless of your guilt or innocence, and you should be prepared to
protect yourself in such cases. Cohen gives a checklist for this purpose.
He includes practicing within your competence, being familiar with the
literature, solid recordkeeping practices, providing and receiving good
supervision, obtaining insurance, and understanding the issue of confidentiality. Although we are not trying to alarm you unnecessarily, you
should follow these precautions when working with suicidal clients in
order to legally protect yourself.

Summary

When a client commits suicide it sets in motion many clinical and sometimes legal issues. It affects relatives, friends, business associates, and
counselors. No one who was affiliated with the deceased escapes some
impact. Helping the survivors adjust to this event requires considerable
skill. Such feelings as guilt, shame, anger, embarrassment, and fear have
to be faced and resolved in a healthy way so that the excesses of these
feelings do not spill over and cripple either you or the other survivors.
A framework for resolving the counselor's feelings was offered, as well
as guidelines to protect you in the event of a lawsuit.

References

Cohen, R. *Malpractice: A Guide for Mental Health Professionals*. New
    York: Free Press, 1979.
Getz, W., Wiesen, A., Sue, S., and Ayers, A. *Fundamentals of Crisis
    Counseling*. Lexington, Mass.: Lexington Books, 1974.
Getz, W., Fujita, B., and Allen, D. "The Use of Paraprofessionals in
    Crisis Counseling: Evaluation of an Innovative Program." *American
    Journal of Community Psychology* 3 (1975):135–144.
Holden, L. "Therapist Response to Patient Suicide: Professional and
    Personal." *Psychiatry Digest* (in press).
Kahlis, B., Harris, H., Prestwood, R., and Freeman, L. "Precipitating

Stress as a Focus in Psychotherapy." *Archives of General Psychiatry* 5 (1961):219–226.

Kolodny, S., Binder, R., Bronstein, A., and Friend, R. "The Working Through of Patients' Suicides by Four Therapists." *Suicide and Life-Threatening Behavior* 9 (1979):33–46.

Lewis, H. *Shame and Guilt in Neurosis.* New York: International Universities Press, 1971.

Lindemann, E. "Symptomatology and Management of Acute Grief." *American Journal of Psychiatry* 101 (1944):141–148.

Marshall, K. "When a Patient Commits Suicide." *Suicide and Life-Threatening Behavior* 10 (1980):29–40.

Parad, H., ed. *Crisis Intervention: Selected Readings.* New York: Family Service Association of America, 1965.

Racker, H. *Transference and Countertransference.* New York: International Universities Press, 1968.

Resnik, H. "Psychological Resynthesis: A Clinical Approach to the Survivors of a Death by Suicide." *International Psychiatry Clinics* 6 (1969):213–224.

Rubin, T. *The Angry Book.* New York: Collier Books, 1969.

Slawson, P. "Psychiatric Malpractice: A Regional Incidence Study." American Journal of Psychiatry 126 (1970):136–139.

Wilkenson, C. "Haunted by the Sky Walk Disaster." *New York Times,* July 6, 1982.

Suggested Reading

Litman, R. "When Patients Commit Suicide." *American Journal of Psychotherapy* 19 (1965):570–576.

13 Adolescent Suicide

More and more teenagers are killing themselves today than ever before. The increase in the rate of suicide in adolescents has far outdistanced the national average. Today twice as many teenagers are killing themselves as ten years ago. We would like to discuss some possible reasons for this and describe treatment strategies for dealing with suicidal adolescents.

Why Do Adolescents Kill Themselves?

There are, of course, many individual reasons why teenagers kill themselves. The reasons usually fit into three general categories: developmental issues, family-interaction issues, and societal influences.

Developmental Issues

In order to fully understand adolescent suicide, it is essential to understand adolescent development. The account given here will be necessarily brief, but will touch on the major issues confronting teenagers as they go through adolescence. The three major tasks of adolescence are separation, individuation, and psychosexual development.

Separation is a recurring theme throughout human development, starting with birth and ending with the death of a parent, child, or loved one. In adolescence, separation has to do with the eventual physical and psychological separation from parents. Bloom (1980) identifies adolescent separation as a five-stage process. In the first stage, the adolescent must gain control over the impulse to remain attached to his parents. Here, the child has ambivalent feelings about separating. At the same time there is confusion about identity; the childhood identity begins to give way to an unknown adult identity. The second stage involves the cognitive realization of the separation. During this period the adolescent begins to make known to himself, his parents, and the world that the separation process is taking place. The child begins to stay away from home for longer periods of time, take on more responsibility, make more decisions, and focuses more on relationships outside the home. The third stage relates to the emotional response to the separation. This phase of the separation process is of primary importance in our discussion of suicide, for here feelings of guilt, anger, ambivalence, and depression come into play. Bloom points out that the way in which these feelings have been dealt with in the past will in large part influence how they are handled during adolescence. The fourth stage concerns identity. Identity formation has to do with the discovery and development of an individuality separate from parents. Adolescents begin to develop their own ideals, morals, and values. They also begin to provide important gratifications for themselves rather than relying on parents for those gratifications. The fifth and final stage is the process of ending the parent-child relationship and developing a new relationship with parents based on relative equality. In this process, the child begins to accept the parents as individuals who have strengths and weaknesses just as all people do.

The process of separation is not necessarily smooth. Blos (1962) points out that "adolescence is a process of regressive and progressive movements appearing and alternating at shorter and longer intervals" (p. 11). Much of this progression and regression has to do with the ambivalent feelings that adolescents face during this period. The most pervasive feelings have to do with loss and guilt about the separation. Feelings of loss include loss of parents, loss of childhood, loss of the feelings of mastery over childhood tasks, and loss of control of self, including loss of control of growth, identity, feelings, and impulses. These kinds of losses can lead to what Seligman (1975) called learned helplessness. Seligman describes helplessness as the feeling that one cannot influence one's environment regardless of one's actions. A classic example is the experience of living through a natural disaster such as a flash-flood or tornado. In this example no individual action makes any difference in the outcome of the situation. The results of feeling helpless are periods of inactivity, indecisiveness, and depression. Seligman points out that those people who have a history of having more control over their lives show less depression and helplessness. Similarly, Bowlby (1973) describes three stages that children go through when separated from their parents: protest, despair, and detachment. In the first stage the child protests the separation using behaviors designed to reunite the child with the parent. The second stage is characterized by sadness, unresponsiveness, and distance, signifying the process of coming to grips with the loss. The final stage is the process of working through the loss and a gradual return to normal patterns of behavior and openness to new relationships.

The point is that the process of separation is an inherent part of the adolescent growth process and is normally characterized by feelings of loss and depression. Because of this inherent depression, the likelihood of suicidal ideation is increased. This normal depression is not necessarily enough to cause an adolescent to become suicidal, but can easily contribute to such feelings especially if the adolescent has not had prior experiences of success or control in his life.

Individuation is the process of discovering and developing who you are as a person as separate from your parents. Individuation or identity development differs from the process of identification, though they both go on during adolescence as well as earlier and later. Identification is an intermediate process on the way to identity. It is usually temporary and in its simplest form is a characteristic or belief that is held by one person (child) because it is a characteristic or belief held by another (parent or significant other). For example, a small child will say he believes that stealing is bad because his mother said it is, not because it is a part of his moral code. Adolescents will often begin walking and talking like a favorite coach or other significant person. Identity, however, is an internalized part of an individual, and is part of his own belief system or personal characteristics. The process of gaining identity is one of forming identifications with various people and incorporating some of those identifications into the self while discarding others.

Adolescents try various identifications, often ones completely opposed to the values of the parents, keeping those identifications that fit the individual. These are eventually combined into a unique identity. The problem that can arise is an inability to arrive at an identity. Erikson (1950) calls this identity-versus-role confusion. Most adolescents are able to arrive at at least a partial identity by the end of adolescence, but in the process there is a time when the individual's identity is not set and is in a state of flux. The period of time when identity is not at least partially formed can be a time of great confusion and loss. This confusion and loss can add to the feelings of loss and depression the child is feeling about separation and increase the risk of suicide. In order to combat this loss of identity, adolescents will form various identifications. These identifications are often very intense and often very contrary to parental values. They can be seen as an attempt to separate from parents and to get help in the identity-forming process.

Psychosexual development is the final major task of adolescence. During adolescence there is a rapid influx of sex and growth hormones and a resultant development and growth of primary and secondary sex characteristics. Along with these developments comes a development in sexual identity. The influx of hormones contributes to the rise of new feelings and sexual impulses. Initially these impulses are fairly generalized and give rise to both homosexual and heterosexual feelings. These diverse feelings create fears and confusion about sexual identity, thus adding to an already confused sense of self. In addition to the fears and confusion, there is often guilt associated with sexual wishes and urges. Since sex is a difficult topic for adolescents to talk to anyone about, these feelings often cannot be expressed in healthy ways and are kept inside, where they cause more fears and guilt.

There is much more to adolescent development than is mentioned here, but it is not the purpose of this book to provide a complete summary of adolescent development. Separation, individuation, and psychosexual development are the major tasks in adolescent development, and are issues that often give rise to feelings of depression and thoughts about suicide in adolescents. Let us next look at a second contributing factor in adolescent suicide, the family.

Family Dynamics

Whether or not you decide to work individually or within the family context, it is important to understand the role and reaction of the family in teenage suicide.

Just as individuals go through developmental stages, so do families. In families with adolescents, the most common developmental issue the family faces is separation. The whole family, not just the adolescent, is struggling with the issue of separation. Separation is a natural part of family development and many families handle the issue very well. However, in many other cases separation becomes an issue the family has difficulty adapting to.

The family as a unit has several purposes, the most important of which are to provide protection for the members; to provide continuity of ideals, morals, and customs; and to allow for change. There is also a strong drive within the family or any system to maintain what it already has, or in other words to maintain homeostasis. This means that each family has a balance that it strives to maintain and that it takes steps to regain that balance if it is upset. For the most part, families are able to change and adapt to upsets in the balance by allowing for changes in their internal boundaries and balances. However, there are instances when, because of rigidity or lack of interpersonal boundaries, families are unable to adapt or appropriately react to internal changes. When this happens, there are many kinds of reactions the individuals within the family can have, one of which is depression and suicide.

How does this work? How can separation troubles either for the parent or the child result in the child's suicide attempt? A typical example follows.

W., a sixteen-year-old male, was brought to the emergency room of
a local hospital by his parents after attempting suicide by taking an
overdose of sleeping medication. During the interview, the counselor
learned that W. had two older brothers, age nineteen and twenty-one,
both living at home. It became clear during the interview with the
parents that the three boys were the center of their attention and pride.
Virtually any conversation the parents had was centered on one of the
boys, especially W. W. had the feeling that if he and his brothers were
to leave home and separate from their parents the parents would have
nothing to do and nothing to talk about. He was afraid that if he and
his brothers were not around, his parents' relationship would deteriorate
and end in separation or divorce. Since W. was the youngest, and would
be the last to leave the home, he felt the burden of holding his parents'
marriage together. He saw no way of every being able to go out on his
own. The only way out he saw was suicide. The counselor intervened
by pointing this out to the family, and over time worked with the parents
and W. by having the parents prove to W. and his brothers that they
would be all right if they eventually separated. Through this process
the parents found new things they could do together that did not include
W. and his brothers.

In this example, separation was hindered both by the perception W. had
about his parents and by the parents' reaction to separation attempts by
the older boys, who were also having difficulty with separation.

Families usually get into trouble when they do too much of what they
do best, namely nurturing and protecting. The example of L. points this
out clearly.

L. was a nineteen-year-old girl and an only child. Her parents, both
well educated, provided virtually everything L. wanted as well as un-
limited attention. The family prided itself in having no secrets from
each other and in doing things together all the time. One day for no
apparent reason L. attempted to take her life by slitting her wrists with
a razor blade. At the hospital, the family was seen by a counselor, who
learned that L. had been feeling depressed for about six months, but
had not let her parents know this. She took some pride in the fact that
this was the only secret she had been able to keep from her parents.
The counselor also noted that the parents talked to and generally treated
L. as they would a small child. L.'s parents' initial reaction was to
blame a new (L.'s first) boyfriend, and to forbid L. to see him again.
The counselor worked with the family and L. individually to help them
understand her need to begin to build a life of her own, which she did
by enrolling in a college several hundred miles away from her parents.

Here is a family in which the boundaries between the individual members
and between parents and child were virtually nonexistent. Indeed, L. and
her mother sounded exactly alike and took great pains to dress alike as
well. The job of the counselor was to create boundaries between the
parents and L., and to help the family to develop separate interests.

In other situations, boundaries can be too rigid.

J., a thirteen-year-old boy, came to the attention of the authorities after he had attempted to jump out of a fifth-story apartment window. As the story unfolded, J. was the oldest of four children and lived with his divorced mother. J. was in charge of getting the younger children up and off to school as well as being responsible for their lunches and dinners. J. very seldom saw his mother, who worked two jobs in an attempt to make ends meet. J. was seen by his teachers as a quiet boy with few friends, but who worked hard and did well in school. On weekends J. was in charge of looking after his brothers and sister while his mother worked a weekend job. J. stated that he hated looking after his brothers and sister and tried hard to please his mother, who he felt was very critical of him. J. had not seen his father in over five years, and neither he nor his mother knew where his father was. The counselor worked with the family, and helped J.'s mother to see the need to be supportive of J. and to create time to spend with her children. The counselor also helped the mother and J. to talk with each other, and showed the mother how to communicate without seeming critical.

In this situation, the boundaries between mother and children are too rigid, and the counselor's job is to adjust those boundaries to ones appropriate for a thirteen-year-old. While separation was not a direct issue in this last case, the counselor anticipated that it might be a problem in the future, helped the mother to recognize separation issues, and gave suggestions about dealing with them in an appropriate way.

The basic job of the counselor in working with a family is to note the patterns of interaction within the family, discover which patterns are hurting the functioning of the family, and help the family to gain an equilibrium that will be more functional than before. This is done by recognizing where the boundaries exist or do not exist and either creating boundaries where none exist or breaking them down where they should not exist or where they are too rigid.

There are many good books out on family therapy, some of which are included in the suggested reading list at the end of this chapter.

Societal Influences

There is little solid research to connect the various societal changes with the rise in teenage suicide in a conclusive way. However, there are several societal trends that appear to relate to the rise in suicide among teenagers.

First, it appears that as the divorce rate rises, so does the teenage suicide rate. It is not unreasonable to assume a relationship exists between the breakdown of family structures and teenage problems. As the feelings that children have about their parents' divorces become better known, we see that guilt, uncertainty, fear, and anger play a large part in their lives. Many children have no ways to express and understand these feelings. As they grow, they carry with them the feelings that they were to blame for the divorce or that somehow they could have prevented their parents' separation. In addition, the relative stability they have experienced is often taken away from them. Money becomes more of a worry for them and their parents, and often they are shuffled back and forth between parents for holidays and vacations. The result for some is a perceived lack of attention and feelings of helplessness in many areas of their lives. These feelings often lead to depression and suicide attempts.

A second contributing factor appears to be the number of choices for and expectations of young people today. Our society is no longer structured so that sons do what their fathers did, and daughters are no longer expected to be housewives and mothers. The opportunities for education and jobs are much wider than ever before, and young people are expected to choose their careers from this broad spectrum at an earlier age. Not only are the choices for careers broader, but so also are the choices in behavior. The access to world events through ever-more-sophisticated mass media provides more information and models for behavior. Young people can watch an actual murder or riot or see people from other countries act and react to various world events by watching television or listening to the radio. This kind of information provides youth with more choices and models for action. The peer group has been extended from the immediate neighborhood and school to a virtually worldwide group, thereby increasing pressure for a wider range of behavior.

The pressure to succeed is well documented. Suicide among college students ranks second only to accident as the major cause of death in this population. The competitiveness of colleges and internal and external pressure to succeed is often overwhelming for many adolescents, and when they are faced with possible failure, many see suicide as the only way out.

There are many other possible societal influences that may contribute to the rise in suicide among teenagers. Such things as growing world unrest and the threat of nuclear war, dissatisfaction with schools and their ability to meet adolescents needs, and economic pressures and growing despair among the adult population are contributing factors we have heard in working with adolescents.

One final societal influence that bears special recognition is the effect of drugs and alcohol on adolescents. We live in a drug-oriented society, and the addictive use of prescription drugs, alcohol, caffeine, and nicotine is widespread. In addition, drugs such as marijuana and cocaine are widespread in their use among teenagers (although marijuana use appears to be dropping). The abuse of drugs may be a contributing factor in teenage depression and suicide, and is something to assess in working with depressed teenagers. Keep in mind, however, that cause and effect are difficult to determine. In other words, it is almost impossible to determine if abusing drugs causes depression or if depression influences adolescents to use drugs.

Depression in Adolescents

Assessment of depression in adolescents is often difficult because, prior to age sixteen or seventeen, adolescents are not likely to display the traditional adult signs of depression. (Weiner, from Adelson 1980). Weiner identifies two major reasons why this is so. First, developmental tasks such as biological changes, identity formation, separation, and peer relations pose such threats to self-esteem that adolescents find it difficult to admit or display self-critical attitudes about being a competent person and therefore do not display the gloom and helplessness usually associated with adult depression. Second, adolescents are at a developmental stage where they are still more inclined toward acting upon rather than thinking about internal processes.

Weiner goes on to state that younger adolescents usually express depression through fatigue, hypochondriasis, and difficulty in concentrating. One or all of these signs may be present. He points out that these symptoms are usually ascribed to other causes. Fatigue is ascribed to rapid growth, hypochondriasis to normal attention to changes in the body, and concentration difficulty to lack of interest or learning disabilities. Although these can be contributing factors, the possibility of an underlying depression cannot be ignored.

In many adolescents the actual signs of depression are not seen so much as are the attempts to ward off the depression. McCoy (1982) identifies fifteen different possible signs of hidden or masked depression in adolescents. These include dysphoric moods, changes in eating and sleeping habits, social isolation, sudden change in normal behavior, acting-out behavior (running away, conflicts at home, cutting classes, sexual promiscuity, shoplifting, and so on), hyperactivity, excessive self-criticism, extreme passivity, psychosomatic complaints, substance abuse, risk-taking behavior, accidents, school problems, sexual acting out (especially in girls), and suicidal talk or behavior. Weiner (1980) adds to this list temper tantrums, stealing, and other defiant, rebellious, antisocial, and delinquent acts.

Some of these symptoms are also characteristic of the sociopathic adolescent. Weiner (1980) states that depressive behavior differs from sociopathic behavior in three ways. First, depressive behaviors are usually uncharacteristic of the adolescent based on previous behavior; second, the onset of depressive behavior can usually be traced to a specific event or series of events, usually entailing a loss; and third, it tends to be carried out in such a way so as to ensure getting caught or observed. These kinds of behaviors can usually be interpreted as attempts to communicate or as cries for help.

As adolescents mature, they tend to become more introspective and thoughtful and therefore more able to think about themselves and be more self-critical. As a result, they become more likely to express depression in more traditional, adult ways. However, as Weiner (1980) points out, there is still a tendency for older adolescents to express depression indirectly through such things as drug abuse, sexual promiscuity, alienation, and suicide attempts. He goes on to point out that adolescents dealing with underlying depression often seek out others with similar feelings and form unconventional, antiestablishment groups. The main purpose of these groups for many is to avoid being and feeling alone, inadequate, or unimportant. All these things need to be kept in mind when assessing depression and suicide potential in adolescents.

Establishing a Counseling Relationship

Perhaps more than any other age group, adolescents tend to be resistant to outside help in spite of their behavioral cries for help. The individual reasons for this vary, but the developmental issues of separation and individuation are fairly constant for all adolescents. The counseling situation requires an individual to some extent to establish a bond and become closer to another individual. The developmental tasks of separation and individuation require the adolescent to pull away from adults and break bonds with parents and parental figures (as the counselor seems, at least initially). In many ways the counseling process works against the normal separation process that is required of adolescents.

In establishing a relationship with an adolescent, it is important to keep the need for separation in mind, and conduct the initial portion of the first session as unintrusively as possible. In our experience, one of the best ways to do this is to avoid, as much as possible, asking questions. Questions tend to be intrusive, and in many instances require the adolescent to disclose information before he is ready.

What we suggest if the adolescent is resistant to help or does not want to be there, is beginning with an empathic statement that reflects your guess as to how the adolescent feels about being there. Technically, this is an appropriate use of your own countertransference feelings to establish rapport. Specifically, first make constant observations of the adolescent as he enters your office. Watch especially facial expressions, clarity of eyes, eye contact, posture, and overall appropriateness. Second, pay attention to the feelings these observations produce in you. If the adolescent appears sullen, angry, or hostile, that may produce feelings of dread, fear, or not wanting to be there in you. Very often we find that the feelings that are produced in us are similar or the same as those the adolescent is experiencing. Third, use your feelings to make a guess as to what the adolescent is feeling. Often our first utterance to an adolescent will be a statement about how we imagine the adolescent feels about being in our office. This approach has several advantages. First, it addresses the resistance issue from the very beginning and puts it up front where it can be interpreted or dealt with. Second, it avoids the use of intrusive questions and protects the adolescent's autonomy by not requiring a response. Third, it lets the adolescent know that you are different from other adults, and different from their probable fantasy about "shrinks." Finally, it sets the stage for the kind of work you want to do with this person. It lets him know that you are trying to understand how he feels and that you are going to talk differently with him than anyone else has. An example of a possible opening statement with an adolescent follows.

> (Adolescent enters office looking at floor, arms crossed and frown on his face. As he sits, he slouches down into the chair, looking away from the counselor). (Counselor thinks to himself, "This kid looks angry and like he is going to be tough to work with. I hate these kinds of interviews because it seems like a lot of extra work. Also, what will I do if he won't talk? He tried to kill himself, and I'm scared I won't be able to assess him properly.")

Counselor: (to client) Well Jay, I don't know for sure how you're feeling about being here, but I suspect you're a little scared and a lot angry about having to talk to me.

Client: (Silence)

Counselor: You know, there is no way I can or am going to try to make you talk. But the reality of the situation is that we are stuck here together, and I need to find out some things. I don't know if you have any problems or not, but I know there are some people out there who think you have a problem, and I guess that means you have at least one problem, them.

Client: What do you want to know?

Counselor: I'd like to start by talking about how you feel about being here.

In this example, the counselor used his own feelings to make a guess as to how the client might be feeling. In addition, the counselor did not allow Jay's silence to go on too long, which we find is not productive in initial sessions with adolescents. Instead, the counselor used the time to point out the reality of the situation while attempting to join in an alliance with the adolescent.

Other issues we feel are important to address at some point in the initial interview with an adolescent are trust and confidentiality. It is important to explain to the adolescent that what you and he talk about is confidential, with the understanding that you will do what is necessary to keep him from killing himself. At some point the issue of trust also needs to be addressed. It is necessary to state that while trust is important in your relationship, you expect to have to earn that trust. In the meantime he will need to trust you somewhat when you say you will never lie to him and that you will protect his confidentiality.

We do not mean to imply that all adolescents are resistant to counseling. In fact, it is just as likely that the adolescent will welcome the help you are trying to give. However, be cautious in the beginning and watch for issues concerning intrusiveness, trust, and not being understood.

Treatment of Suicidal Behavior

The treatment of suicidal behavior in adolescents is both different from and similar to that of adults. The same basic techniques of interviewing, listening, and counseling apply. The differences in developmental and family issues are noteworthy and need to be considered. It is also important to treat older adolescents differently than younger adolescents. (The distinction between older and younger adolescents is difficult, since we are dealing with developmental issues rather than discrete age ranges. For general reference, younger adolescents will be defined as age twelve to fifteen, older adolescents as age fifteen to twenty).

From a conceptual standpoint, it is useful to understand adolescent suicide attempts as problem-solving attempts. Seen in this way, the idea of teenage suicide becomes less threatening to you and provides you with a framework that includes helping the adolescent solve the problem in another way. We feel that a problem-solving approach should be primary and an insight-oriented approach secondary in crisis-counseling situations. By using this approach, you reduce the chance of regression in the adolescent and increase the chance of getting him functioning more quickly, which is the immediate goal.

The need to get the teenager functioning quickly is related to the developmental issue of control. Adolescent suicide attempters have high control needs, usually because of feelings of being out of control or having no control in their lives. A suicide attempt can often be seen as a way of regaining some control over themselves and their lives. In this light, finding some way to help the adolescent regain more appropriate control in his life is imperative.

To help a teenager regain control, it is usually important to look at the developmental stage of the family as well as at the event that precipitated the crisis. As we stated earlier, the most common developmental stage and issue in families with adolescents is that of separation and individuation. Often the child feels trapped and unable to separate from the family while at the same time he does not feel he is part of the family. The precipitating event is usually connected to the larger issues, expressed in such things as not being able to see certain friends, stay out past a certain hour, or do certain things the peer group is doing. In these cases working out solutions with the child and his parents is the quickest, most effective way of helping him regain some control. The following case illustrates this point.

> R., a fifteen-year-old boy, was brought to the emergency room of a large county hospital after ingesting twenty to thirty pills he had found in his stepmother's medicine chest. In the counselor's office, R., a bright, articulate boy, stated that he felt apart from his father and stepmother and rarely talked at any length with them, but was expected to anticipate what they expected of him. Further, he felt as though they were extremely strict about allowing him to attend functions at his high school because they were afraid he would get drunk, something they had caught him at once before. The precipitating event occurred when he had asked about getting his driver's license after his upcoming birthday and his parents refused because they feared he might drink and drive. Over the course of six sessions, the counselor was able to help negotiate a mutually agreeable amount of freedom to go to school functions and use the car. In the sessions the counselor worked individually with R. as well as with R. and his parents. The counselor spent her time with R. helping him to identify what he wanted and showing him how to negotiate for those things. In the joint sessions, when it came time for the negotiations the counselor let R. take the lead in negotiating for himself rather than doing it for him, helping only when things got off track or when an impasse was reached.

In this example, the counselor worked with R. individually at times because of the separation issues. By working individually and within the family context, the counselor was able to emphasize the separation and individuation issues as well as R.'s feelings of not being part of the family. After some separation issues were settled, R. and his family were referred for ongoing therapy.

The example of R. brings up the issue of who you work with when an adolescent attempts suicide. There are several considerations that go into this decision. The first consideration has to do with the age of the child. Generally, younger adolescents should be seen in the context of the family because separation, while an issue, is not as intense an issue as it is for older adolescents. Older adolescents should be seen in a combination of individual and family counseling with emphasis on individual counseling. This emphasizes the importance of separation and the need of older adolescents to work on autonomy issues. The second consideration is one of family dynamics. If the family is extremely enmeshed or close to one another (Minuchin 1974) it is likely you will only succeed in effectively treating the adolescent if you see the whole family. At the other end of the spectrum are families who have little to do with each other, who do not communicate, and who are not interested in participating in counseling. In these cases, you may have no choice but to work with the adolescent individually. Rarely does one family fit into one of these categories or the other. Often you will find elements of each within the same family, and will have to assess what the situation is to determine who is willing to participate.

A third consideration is client preference. Some adolescents refuse to be involved in counseling with their parents. In these cases it may be necessary to see the parents separately from the adolescent. In cases like this, it is important to respect the confidentality of each side, especially of the adolescent. Although this arrangement does not usually allow you to form an especially good relationship with the adolescent, it may be necessary under the circumstances. When possible, separate counselors for the child and the parents should be arranged. You need permission from both sides for the counselors to talk to one another.

A final consideration is that of counselor preference. Since there are many schools of thought and varying levels of experience and training among counselors it is difficult to say which approach is best. Followers of the psychoanalytic school of thought would usually prefer to see the adolescent individually while suggesting the parents seek help from another counselor. Followers of the family-therapy approach would almost always see the entire family or the family and various subsets of the family individually. We feel the counselor should feel comfortable in whatever method he chooses and should choose a method that emphasizes his strengths and reflects his training. However, we also feel that beginning counselors, especially those working on a short-term basis, should work to develop both family and individual skills and be able to conceptualize accordingly.

Another issue counselors may face in working with suicidal adolescents is that of parental denial. Frequently, when an adolescent makes a suicide attempt that does not appear to be serious, the parental reaction will be one of "it really wasn't serious," or "she's just trying to get attention.'' If this is allowed to go on, with little or no help given, the child gets a message of "try harder next time.'' How the first attempt is handled sets the stage for the future. It is best to put forth effort to change things after the first attempt rather than after the second or fifth attempt. If you meet with parental denial, it is necessary to confront it very directly and insist on counseling until the conditions that produced the suicidal behavior are corrected. (This applies to the adolescent's denial as well.) The following example demonstrates the handling of parental denial.

A. was seen by a counselor after the fourteen-year-old girl tried to kill herself by taking five or six aspirin. A.'s parents were reluctant to bring her in as they felt she was trying to manipulate them into letting her stay out later on school nights, and did so only at the insistence of their family doctor. The counselor saw A. as a very depressed and impulsive person and suggested that some ongoing counseling for A. and her parents was in order. The parents objected, stating that the attempt was not that serious and that treatment was too expensive. The counselor pointed out that often one suicide attempt leads to another, usually more serious attempt, and it is best to correct the problem rather than take a chance on another attempt. A's parents stated they would think about it and call the counselor later. The counselor said he would call the parents in two days to see what they had decided. When the counselor called the parents stated that things were much better and that they didn't think counseling was necessary. The counselor expressed regret at their decision and suggested some things to watch for in the future that might help them anticipate another suicide attempt. In doing so, the counselor fairly accurately predicted A.'s increasing difficulty at being able to concentrate and her related inability to function at school, as well as her eventual running away from home after a fight with her parents. After the running-away incident, the parents could no longer avoid the fact that there were difficulties at home and the family entered counseling.

A more extreme example is the case of C., a seventeen-year-old boy.

C. and his parents were seen by a counselor in the emergency room of a metropolitan hospital after he had attempted to slit his wrists with a razor. No major arteries were severed in the attempt but his wounds required over thirty stitches. The counselor assessed C. as being extremely depressed and extremely suicidal, and recommended he be admitted to the hospital. C.'s parents rejected the idea immediately and said they would handle their own family problems. The counselor presented information regarding adolescent suicide and expressed her extreme concern for C. After forty-five minutes of trying to persuade C.'s parents, the counselor was still unable to change their minds. Seeing no other options, the counselor explained to the parents about involuntary commitment and stated she was going ahead with it. This made C.'s parents extremely angry and they threatened to take C. from the emergency room immediately. The counselor responded by stating that if they did, not only would she call the hospital security guard, but she would also contact the appropriate child-protection agency and report the parents. C.'s parents were furious, but saw that they had no alternative and allowed C., who wanted treatment, to be admitted to the hospital.

This example, though extreme, illustrates, as does the first, the counselor's use of increasing confrontation as the situations require. Note that in both cases, especially the second, the counselor used only as much threat as was necessary to get treatment for the adolescent.

Number and Frequency of Sessions

As with adults, the number and frequency of sessions will vary from case to case. The issues we discussed in determining these decisions for adults also apply to adolescents. In addition, there are some additional factors that need consideration with adolescents. Because of the fragile nature of counselor/adolescent relationships the number of sessions indicated may differ from what is necessary for adults. Keep in mind that the major task of adolescence is separation. In a counseling relationship you are asking an adolescent to get closer to you and trust you. Movement in this direction is contrary to the developmental task of adolescence. This is not to say that relationships cannot be formed with adolescents. Quite the contrary. Some of the most intense relationships you form with clients will be with adolescents. Because of all that is necessary in order for an adolescent to form a therapeutic relationship with you, it is important not to terminate that relationship too early. If you are able to form a good relationship with an adolescent, you may need to add one or two or more sessions to talk about termination and referral. We feel that under these circumstances you should spend at least six or seven sessions working with an adolescent, paying particular attention in the last sessions to termination issues.

If your situation is not such that you can see a client for six or seven sessions, we suggest that you make every attempt to refer your adolescent clients after not more than two sessions. You should avoid developing a strong relationship with an adolescent without the opportunity to talk about termination.

Summary

In assessing and treating adolescent suicide, you should be aware of the developmental issues, family dynamics, and societal influences that affect teenagers in today's world. The adolescent should not be seen as a little adult, but as an individual with separate needs and who deals with different issues. The context in which you choose to see suicidal adolescents will depend on the willingness of the family to participate, the age of the adolescent, the preferences of the adolescent, and the preferences and skills of the counselor. All suicide attempts made by adolescents should be taken seriously, and every effort should be made to see that the adolescent receives the treatment he needs after any kind of self-destructive attempt.

References

Bloom, M. *Adolescent/Parental Separation*. New York: Gardner Press, 1980.

Blos, P. *On Adolescence: A Psychoanalytic Interpretation*. New York: Free Press of Glencoe, 1962.

Bowlby, J. *Attachment and Loss*. Vol. II, "Separation." New York: Basic Books, 1973.

Erikson, E. *Childhood and Society*. New York: W.W. Norton, 1950.

McCoy, K. *Coping with Teenage Depression: A Parent's Guide*. New York: New American Library, 1982.

Minuchin, S. *Families and Family Therapy*. Cambridge, Mass.: Harvard University Press, 1974.

Seligman, M. *Helplessness: On Depression, Development and Death*. San Francisco: Freeman, 1975.

Weiner, I. "Psychopathology in Adolescents." In *Handbook of Adolescent Psychology,* ed. J. Adelson. New York: Wiley and Sons, 1980.

Suggested Readings

Andolfi, M. *Family Therapy, an Interactional Approach*. New York: Plenum Press, 1979.

Blos, P. *The Adolescent Passage: Developmental Issues*. New York: International Universities Press, 1979.

Bowen, M. *Family Therapy in Clinical Practice*. New York: Jason Aronson, 1978.

Haley, J. *Leaving Home: The Therapy of Disturbed Young People*. New York: McGraw-Hill, 1980.

Lamb, D. *Psychotherapy with Adolescent Girls*. San Francisco: Jossey Bass, 1981.

Madanes, C. *Strategic Family Therapy*. San Francisco: Jossey Bass, 1981.

Minuchin, S., Rosman, B., and Baker, L. *Psychosomatic Families*. Cambridge, Mass.: Harvard University Press, 1978.

Stanton, M., et al. *The Family Therapy of Drug Abuse and Addiction*. New York: Guildford Press, 1982.

Part IV
Case Studies

This section is designed to serve as a teaching and training instrument. It will provide you with an opportunity to put into practice some of the principles and concepts you have learned in the previous sections. We have included three case examples that represent a spectrum of suicidal situations that required counseling intervention. They were chosen because they represent many of the crucial issues inherent in all suicidal cases. They have been edited to protect the identities of the clients, but the material is accurate.

In all cases we have provided you with an opportunity to review some of what you have been exposed to earlier by filling in the blank pages just as if you were the counselor. As a further aid we have inserted some of the counselor's thoughts in brackets to recreate for you the emotional experience of what it was like in the office. We have also interspersed our own comments throughout the cases to include remarks on matters of theory and technique as they relate to the clinical material and the counseling process. The commentary following each case summarizes our assessment of the counselor's performance and provides some follow-up information about what happened to the client.

The consultation format for handling all cases was as follows. The counselor would excuse himself prior to the end of the interview to discuss the case with the supervisor. This process ordinarily took about five minutes. We have recreated those discussions in order to illustrate the value of consultation in general and in our model in particular. The counselor would then return to the interview, attempting to integrate this information into the body of the counseling session. This break provided the counselor with an opportunity to clarify his perceptions and to double-check his treatment plan. Since the cases always carry the threat of death, we felt it was both proper and therapeutically sound to institute this practice of consultation, which in fact has always proven useful and correct.

14 "I Don't Understand Why the Gun Didn't Go Off"

Mr. Davis is age thirty-two, Caucasian, married seven years, father of two children (a boy age six, and a girl age five), and has been separated from his family for the past month. Currently he is living alone in a rented apartment across town from his home. He is employed as a delivery man for a bread company, for which he has worked for the past three years. Mr. Davis walks into a mental-health clinic on Friday afternoon, saying that he is very upset and wants to talk with someone.

Mr. Davis is about 5 feet 10 inches and weighs approximately 165 pounds. He looks tired and has a rather heavy five-o'clock-shadow beard. He is dressed in gray work clothes, and it appears he has come to the clinic from work.

Upon introduction to the counselor, he appears tired and his smile seems forced. His handshake is weak, and he avoids the counselor's eyes in order to stare down and away from the greeting. As he enters the counselor's office, he asks where he should sit. Upon getting comfortable he slumps forward and stares at his hands.

Counselor: Tell me how you happened to come here this afternoon?
Client: Well, I have to try and get my head straight and I'm trying to get back with my wife. What can I do to try and reach her?

[Should I answer that question now? I don't think so. It's too early. Just wait.]

Counselor: What is the situation with your wife?
Client: Well, she filed for divorce and probably I could handle the situation a lot easier if there was a man involved or with me if there was a woman or something. But over the course of the years something went wrong with her. She doesn't have the love for me and she is not happy and so it would probably be best to get a divorce. All I can think of and all I want is (starts to cry) . . . getting back with her. (Pause) . . . I can't think about, maybe we won't get back together. I can't get it out of my mind. (Pause) . . . All I can think of is getting back with her, wanting her, getting back and saving our marriage. I can't think that maybe we won't get back. Maybe I should be thinking about other things. (Pause) What am I going to do if this happens? It's driving me up the wall. (Pause) . . . I'm doing crazy things.

181

[He says that all he wants is to get back together. Does that narrow my treatment options? And then he says he's doing crazy things. I'd better follow that up.]

Counselor: What kind of crazy things are you doing?
Client: I get in super depressed moods . . . I really go down. (Pause) I have tried to take my life and it wasn't a sympathy thing either. Something went wrong and that is why I'm here today.

[Oh! Oh! Let's find out about that statement right now.]

Counselor: Tell me how you tried to take your life.
Client: With a gun. I know there was a shell in there. When I pulled down on the trigger . . . twice . . . it didn't go off. It was a 30–06 and believe me it was loaded. But I don't know why it didn't fire. (Pause) If I would have gone out and popped pills or something like that it would have been a sympathy thing more or less. You know a normal person has a better chance of pulling through something like that a hell of a lot better than with a gun.
Counselor: Why don't you tell me what happened right from the beginning?
Client: Well, I was living in an apartment after we separated and I wanted to move back into the house so the other evening after work . . . I had had a few beers . . . and started driving home. I just started feeling "What's the use?" And by the time I got to the house I just had hit the bottom. Then later that night, it was a hell of a thing that had to happen because maybe if there was a chance that we were getting back together, what I did probably didn't help things much. (Pause) We've been married for seven years and I have never laid a hand on her, but that particular night . . . I don't know, my mind just snapped. She's laying on the couch and I went over to her and started beating her up. And I have never done this before.
Counselor: You said she was laying on the couch and your mind snapped?
Client: By that time I had been drinking a lot; of course there always is alcohol involved. I don't really know. I just wanted to hurt her I guess. But I'm not positive what made me fly off like that.

[He's impulsive, a drinker, and with a gun he could be very dangerous. I'm a bit nervous and I've not heard everything yet. Besides I don't like guys who beat up their wives. I'd better watch myself so as not to sound judgmental or reject this guy because of my own feelings.]

Counselor: What do you remember feeling and thinking at that time?
Client: I'm thinking at the time that she was hurting me; she had just been tearing me up and I had to hurt her. After I was doing it. It just stopped, just like that.
Counselor: What did you do?
Client: I was hitting her. I was beating her mostly around the

head. She had a couple little cuts where I was hitting her. (Pause) First she started screaming; then I think she was just scared. I know she was and she said, "Can we talk?" First she said, "Now there is no chance." Then she says, "Can we talk?" and I don't know if it was the fear that I seen in her eyes or the blood that I seen. But I just stopped.

Counselor: And then?

Client: And then? I comforted her as well as I could. I held her and talked and tried to comfort her.

Counselor: And how did you feel right then?

Client: I felt right at the time. I kept thinking in my mind that I really didn't feel that bad about it because it was the first time since we had been separated that I could hold her and give her protection and comfort her. It looked like she was accepting it but I don't think she really was. (Pause)

[Good grief! That's a pretty primitive way to maintain a relationship. Not much insight here and not the type of therapy to use with him. I'd better be pretty straightforward with whatever I suggest. But I still need to hear more.]

Counselor: I didn't get everything you said when you were talking about the gun that had the shell in it. Would you tell me again please?

Client: Well, as I was driving over to the house, I just kept getting more and more depressed. And by the time I got there I just felt like, "What good is there to live without my wife and the kids?" I pulled halfway down the driveway. I put the rifle right up here (pointing to his chin) and I pulled the trigger twice. But it didn't go off.

[Whew! Can you imagine what it would have been like for his wife or the cops to find him if the gun had fired? That's grizzly. That's a horrible scene. Thank God the gun didn't fire. But look at his intention. He really wanted to punish her and the kids too. But I doubt if he's aware of any of that material. And I don't have enough contact with him to get into that just yet. Maybe later. Maybe during a second or third session.]

Counselor: What did you hear when you pulled the trigger?

Client: That's what I can't understand. I felt I didn't hear the pin click but I know I reached down on it because to do it I had to do it fast. Because if I sat there and thought about it and put my finger on the trigger gradually, I probably wouldn't have been able to pull down on it. I didn't hear the pin click that I can recall but the safety was off and the trigger should have moved easily.

[He seems to know a lot about guns. I'm feeling more sensitive and afraid about his potential for danger. I feel some tension in myself.]

Counselor: It didn't move?

Client: I'm sure it did. It felt like it moved but I don't know for sure.

Counselor: Where is the gun now?
Client: I don't have it. It's over at the neighbors'. They took it
             and I haven't asked for it back.

[That's good. Oh is that good. I'd better reinforce that immediately.]

(A clinical comment: the counselor should have asked him about more
guns at home or in his possession.)

Counselor: How did the neighbors get it?
Client: He went out to the car and got it. Like I say after I did
             that and it didn't go off, I think my wife's girlfriend came
             over to the car and evidently enough time passed when she
             came over that it was out of my system. But I don't know
             for sure.
Counselor: What don't you know for sure?
Client: I don't know why it didn't go off. I'm glad it didn't now,
             I guess. But it's like the neighbor said, "That should tell
             you something."
Counselor: What does it tell you?
Client: That evidently I shouldn't. That isn't the way to do it, to
             solve the problem.

[Reinforce that. It would sure help a lot if he had some kind of internalization system to hold onto rather than the chance of the gun mis-
firing.]

Counselor: You're right! Now what kind of ways could you solve the
             problems?
Client: I don't know. . . . The only way I feel right now that
             I can see is by getting back together.
Counselor: Are there any other . . .
Client: No. Ever since we have separated that's the only thing
             that my mind has focused on. It's the only way my mind
             has worked; getting back together. I love my wife. I love
             my kids. I don't want to lose them. (Pause)

[Well, so much for my comment about alternative ways. But that's what
he said a while ago and he's not about to entertain anything else yet—
if ever. So I'd better drop that idea for now. He looks very pained and
upset.]

Counselor: It sounds pretty painful.
Client: Yes it is . . . (tears begin to form) I know life has to go
             on, but so far I can't take the other life. That is what's
             getting me down. I don't know. . . . My friends figure
             that there is no chance; that I have lost her. They say to
             start going out and having a good time and thinking about
             what you are going to do in your future. They say that it
             is good to talk to people. I guess it is good to talk to
             people, but at times I can talk to people and still leave
             depressed.

Counselor: Do you have any relatives in the area?
Client: Well, yeah, I've got two sisters and we get along fine.
            But none of us are really close. Not super super close you
            know.
Counselor: And what kind of contact have you had with them lately?
Client: I haven't had any contact with them this weekend yet. I've
            been out to one of my sisters who told me to come over
            when I get in these depressed moods or whatever. But one
            thing she said that I don't like, that I don't think is neat
            at all was "I'm glad you beat up Joan," she said. "Maybe
            she can see that you can get emotional too." And that's
            not being fair to Joan; to show that I can be emotional or
            something like that. That's not the way to go.

[With that kind of a comment from a sister, I can see where he's coming
from in relationshp to females. She sure must have some kind of an
axe to grind. And not the best kind of support. But good for him to at
least intellectually recognize that he must control his angry impulses.
Actually what he's probably saying is if "I beat her up I won't get her
back." Don't be overly optimistic. In Rotter's terms he is an exter-
nalizer, he feels forces and people outside of himself control him, rather
than having a sense of internal control. He's a reactor rather than an
initiator.]

Counselor: What do you do when you get in a down mood?
Client: Oh, sometimes I call her. Sometimes I go over there and
            drink a few beers. But that's bad 'cause I can get really
            depressed that way. I've been at work and been hit with
            a bad depression too. In fact one day I got hit just before
            I started to take off in my truck and I sat down and prayed
            and I came out of it. I felt relieved for a while so I guess
            I can have it any place.

[This guy sounds unstable and chaotic the more I listen to him. Should
I consider commitment if he won't come into the hospital voluntarily?
I don't know. But I'd better talk with my supervisor before this guy
leaves the office. What's this about praying? Ah, but of course. He's
been telling me all along that he turns to outside sources. So yes, prayer
would indeed help him. Will I be able to use this as a treatment strategy?
I sure hope so. So far all he's got is beer and prayers and that's not
enough.]

Counselor: And when you pray, that helps?
Client: That did help . . . that day anyway. I felt real relieved
            all day and I don't remember if I got depressed after I got
            off work.
Counselor: What else helps?
Client: When I see the kids I'm never down. Even when I see my
            wife I never get down I don't think; not when I was around
            them.

[Now that's a nice turning point. The first time I asked him he said
nothing helped. Now this. The kids and his attachment to them will be
very valuable if push gets to shove about him staying alive. I can use

the kids and the fact that they need him as a suicide deterrent. It's dangerous, however, because I'll be using a mixture of guilt and shame to keep him alive and that's risky. But I may not have much else to work with. And he may decide that he'll have to kill the kids and wife so that he'll be reunited with them all. Now that's a terrible thought, but it's also a real possibility. I'd better be very careful.]

Counselor: What kind of things don't help?
Client: Going out for a few beers . . . that's when I start thinking and I get depressed. I want to get back together but maybe we're not going to get back together. I start building things up in my mind; like she's gonna ask me to come back home tonight and then it doesn't materialize.

[Now the last place he should be going to is a bar. That's where everyone else who's lonely and depressed goes. And besides that they start crying in their beers and then it's all downhill from there. I wonder if I could get him to church. It might tie in with strengthening his prayer response. And if he finds the right pastor that could be another resource as well. Let's wait and see.]

Counselor: What happens then?
Client: I don't know what kind of feeling you call it; just terrible inside. At times it feels like there is nothing in there except, except . . . eating at it, eating at it. Then like that one time, once before I felt crazy and thought crazy things.
Counselor: What kind of things did you think?
Client: About my life. (Pause) I just thought about it. That night I wasn't around nobody. I just thought about it but I didn't do it.
Counselor: What did you think?
Client: The same thing; if I can't have my family . . . but then I couldn't go through with it; doing myself in that particular night.
Counselor: How were you thinking of doing it that time?
Client: The same way, with the rifle. That night it didn't seem so critical as it was this last time.
Counselor: What was the difference?
Client: I don't know to be honest with you. Maybe it was because I was going over to the house and by going over there and seeing her and this and that; it seemed more like it was over.
Counselor: It was more final then?
Client: Yes, just like when I get my papers.
Counselor: Papers?
Client: Divorce papers.

[Oh good grief! His potential for acting out of impulse just went up again. But wait a minute. They've been chronically unhappy; therefore, is this just another play on her part to passively/aggressively needle him? Has this happened before? If so, is this as big a deal as I first thought? I don't know. Settle down and get some more facts. Is this the precipitating event that set him off to come in tonight? I'll bet so.]

Counselor: Tell me what it would be like.
Client: I don't know until I get them. I can't tell you what it's
            going to be like . . . there is no way that I can imagine
            how I am going to feel. I know I dread getting them
            . . . (Long pause) . . . She has filed . . . she has said
            . . . she's lost it; there is nobody else involved. Her love
            for me, she is not happy and she can't see any point living
            with someone if you're not happy . . . this is something
            that has built up over the years, small things . . . like
            . . . lack of communication, but we never really hassled.
Counselor: Argued you mean?
Client: Yeah, because I'm a holder-in; I don't like to argue.
            (Pause)

[Not verbally anyway, but maybe this is another area in which I can
be helpful and thus defuse him. Maybe I can get him to use ventilation
and sharing in a counseling situation as an alternative. Maybe that's
my focus. I should explain that people who hold in blow up and get
out of control. And talking with a counselor would be better than having
to use a gun or his fists.]

Counselor: And how long have you been separated?
Client: About a month. She went down and filed the day I left
            because she is on welfare and in order to do that you have
            to file. She's not taking me to the cleaner's or anything.
            In fact, I was to pay the bills and she was staying at the
            house. She was going to pay the rent and utilities and since
            she's on welfare, I'm not required to pay child support
            until the house is sold. (Pause) She definitely wants out
            now but then she made the statement "that three months
            is a long time" and her mind could change. I went over
            to the house that night after I had talked to a friend and
            they thought I was being too good about the divorce; I
            wasn't fighting her enough. They said that I was making
            it too easy for her and they said, "you're crazy; you should
            have her pay for it, she's the one who wants it, have her
            pay for it." So I started thinking about it and I thought
            "well that's right. Why should I pay for something I don't
            want?" So I went over there all hot under the collar and
            I told her that I wasn't going to pay for something I didn't
            want. This was her thing. And she says, "Oh, I know
            who you've been talking to." She says I don't want to
            hear about who's going to pay for the divorce. And she
            says, "In three months you might decide *you* want the
            divorce." Three months is a long time and things can
            change in three months. And she said a few other things,
            you know. Everything she said made so much sense to me
            that I really left in a good frame of mind. They had a
            hopeful sound to me and I guess that's what made the
            difference. Some people I don't like to talk to because I
            get depressed. They won't tell me hopeful things; they just
            say realistic things like, "What could happen if you don't

get back?'' and "Don't get your hopes up" and this sort
of thing. Talking to someone who tells me to forget her
starts getting me down and if I went out and drank a few
beers by myself it would put me down faster. (Pause) But
then I had to fly off the handle and go crazy there for a
second and that may have just wrecked any chance I had
. . .

[More wonderful friends! But more examples of how he reacts to people,
which is his style. I'd diagnose him as passive-dependent, maybe passive-aggressive. His wife's comments could be a double bind (simultaneously giving an accepting and a rejecting message that leaves it
impossible for the recipient to be right). Or it could be that she'll tell
anything for fear of her life. It could also be that her husband will only
hear what he wants to hear which is "we'll get back together." Should
I get his permission to talk with his wife? I'll talk that over with my
supervisor.]

Counselor: Do you feel like you blew it?
Client: I really think I could have. I know I have to get my head
              straightened out too but I am reaching, hoping that I can
              find help and try to work something out with my wife. Of
              course that's not what you are here for. But like I say I
              do have to get in a better frame of mind. I can't go on like
              this forever, it's going to break me down. I don't want to
              have any more episodes like the other night. You know,
              it still scares me that I have these super-depressed moods.
              I will flip out because I can't continue having them I don't
              think.

[When he says "I'm not here to give him answers," I think he's trying
to manipulate me. But not consciously, so I'd better leave it alone for
right now. I'm not sure at this point that he'll accept much of anything
I say about healthy ways to begin dealing with this crisis. I think he's
so dependent that unless a treatment plan involves his wife and a reconciliation, he'll reject everything, and probably lump me in with everyone else he sees as not being supportive of him. So let's get back to
the state and history of his depressed moods.]

Counselor: How many times have you had these kind of moods where
              you want to take your life?
Client: Just a few times. I know of two. I told you of the most
              recent one. The first time I couldn't have gone through
              with it. I didn't have the guts. I wasn't so bad off like this
              last one.
Counselor: How far did you go the first time?
Client: I had the gun out and everything. I don't know what made
              me decide not to. (Pause) And that's why I know the round
              was in there the second time . . . I didn't check it when
              I got over to the house but I left a round in there. And I
              don't know of anybody who could have taken it out.
              (Pause)
Counselor: How do you feel right now about taking your life?

Client: Right now? No I wouldn't. I'm not going home tonight
              and do myself in.

[OK, Mr. Davis, if you really mean this, then let me switch gears and
see what your plans are to care for yourself tonight and through the
weekend. Your affect seems to be less flat and your mood seems less
depressed. But I've got to check out your safeguards.]

Counselor: What are your plans for tonight?
Client: I don't know. I might go to the apartment and then go
              over to a neighbor's if they are still up.
Counselor: Can you stay there?
Client: Oh, I wouldn't want to impose on them. I'm not going
              to flip out tonight I don't think. I feel good.
Counselor: What are you going to do if you start to feel bad?
Client: That's something else. I don't know, weather the storm
              I guess.
Counselor: What's going to help you weather the storm?
Client: Going to sleep; that would be the thing that would help
              the most.
Counselor: Anything else?
Client: Getting on the telephone to call someone. I could call my
              niece in Bellingham [sixty-five miles north from where he
              lives.] She's a good one for me to talk to because she
              always gives me good feelings. Then there is a couple
              south of me that I can talk with. And then I could call the
              Smiths; the people would come right over if I need them
              to.
Counselor: Or you could always call here.
Client: I forgot about that. I wasn't even thinking about that.

[It's nice to hear that he's got more support than I originally thought
he had. But his last statement confirms how angry he is with me—
probably for not siding with him. As I think about it maybe it's better
not to call his wife. It's a calculated risk because if he's too angry with
me he could pull another gun-to-the-head routine. I'd better look for
an opening here to consult.]

Counselor: What do you see ahead for yourself over the weekend?
Client: Oh I think I'm going to be all right. Staying away from
              booze is the big thing. I may have a beer with the neighbor
              one night if I watch a football game. (Pause)
Counselor: Mr. Davis, I want to discuss your case with my supervisor.
              If it's OK with you I would like you to wait here and I'll
              be back in about five minutes.
Client: That's fine. I'm OK.

The counselor steps out of the office for consultation. What would
you say to your supervisor about this case? Before you read what actually
took place, fill out the consultation model (figure 14–1), compare it with
the counselor's presentation that follows.

Name	Age	Marital Status

If Significant: Nationality, Race, Religion
Living Where
With Whom
Came to Agency for What Reason
Brought by
Referred by   Family Dr.

Counselor's statement of the problem(s) and the dynamics involved including a
mental status and suicidal status plus a proposed treatment plan.

Figure 14–1. Consultation Model

Consultation Discussion

In a recreated dialogue with the supervisor here is the way the consultation
was handled.

Counselor: Mr. Davis, age thirty-two, separated one month, father
of two kids, ages five and six, employed as a bakery
driver, drove himself here because he felt suicidal. He
made a recent suicide attempt with a 30–06 rifle that failed
he says because the gun did not fire. This event occurred
four days ago in the driveway at the house of his separated
wife. He claims to have had several beers prior to the
attempt. When the gun failed to discharge, he made no
further attempt and sat in the car until his neighbor came
over to talk with him. The neighbor took the gun. A little
later the client went into his house, got into an argument
with his wife and allegedly assaulted her, but apparently
no charges are pending. Although the facts show his dan-
gerousness, my impression is that he is manipulative and
passive-dependent. But because the method of the attempt, I'm nervous about letting him go. I would like to
get him into a hospital.

Supervisor: OK. that gives me an overall impression, but now give
me a mental status.

Counselor: He's about 5 feet 10 inches, approximately 165 pounds,
dressed in work denims. At first appearance he looked
tired but that's less so now. His motor behavior was originally slow but now is more normal. His speech was also
slow but normal now. He's oriented in person, place, and
time. He originally showed a depressed mood with some
flatness or affect. But by the time I took the consultation
break these features appeared to be gone. There was no
evidence of a thought disorder.

Supervisor: First get a clinical picture of his depression: weight, and
sleep and eating disturbances. Then, does his depression
interfere with his work performance? Also, is he an al-

coholic? And does he have another gun? If I were to ask you the five W questions what would you say?

Counselor: The *who* would be his wife and kids and the neighbors. I don't know exactly how obvious he was in letting all these people know that he was in the driveway or how unusual it might have been that he was there at the time he was. It was shortly after work so it was still daylight and he likely would have been noticed. I'm also not sure how long he was there before he put the gun to his head. The *what* scares me quite a bit because it was a gun, and it apparently was loaded. What puzzles me is why the weapon didn't go off. And he can't or won't shed any light on this either. The *when* was after a few beers and that's always a bad combination with a weapon. The *where* was the driveway and he parked in such a way so as to be discovered. The *why now*; that's a good question. I'm not sure what he was thinking earlier in the day or what was going through his mind while he was having those few beers. But that seems to be his chronic pattern. He's not usually—if ever—in touch with the precipitating events that set him off. Or if he is, he's not telling me about it. It's obvious he's feeling abandoned and mad as hell, but he won't own up to this rage and it seems pretty well disguised by him. I'm not sure this denial can be touched; for sure not in this session. His opening and almost closing words to me were that all he wanted was to get back with his wife and that any suggestions to the contrary would be rejected out of hand. And it seems to me that this attempt was part of his way of demanding a reconciliation. However, after beating her up I don't know. Not having talked to her it's hard to say. But he doesn't seem to be too upset about this, strange as that may sound.

Supervisor: How homicidal is he?

Counselor: I didn't get around to that.

Supervisor: Has he been in counseling before? If so, what did he learn? How long ago? How many sessions? Who was the counselor? What was he getting counseling for?

Counselor: I didn't ask that either.

Supervisor: Depending on the answers to some of these questions you might want to offer voluntary hospitalization. If he won't go for that then set up a follow-up appointment for Monday. But be sure you keep in touch with him by telephone on Saturday and Sunday. Part of your treatment plan, in case he won't be hospitalized, would be to reinforce prayer as a viable alternative to beer and wife-beating. If you see him to be primarily a manipulator who pushes other people's buttons in order to satisfy his dependency needs, would you contact his wife?

Counselor: No. Not at this time. I want to stay as neutral as possible and just focus on the immediate situation. Calling his wife might play right into his manipulative ideas—and hers as well since I don't really know what's going on with her. And besides, I don't have enough of a grasp of the case

to know what the consequences of that type of intervention
would be. I don't know how either one would use it. My
feeling is that it will be misinterpreted and thus misused,
which will simply compound an already chronic problem.

Supervisor: Do you think he'll come back for a follow-up?
Counselor: I don't know. But I'll sure try. I'd better get back.

The counselor returns to the office to find Mr. Davis looking much
better. His posture is relaxed. His eyes are brighter and upon seeing the
counselor, he breaks into a rather warm smile.

Counselor: Thanks for being so patient. Sorry I took so long.
Client: That's OK. I'm feeling fine and besides (chuckling) it's
keeping me out of the bars tonight.

[A sense of humor here and his mood and affect have really changed
since he first came in. Has ventilation brought all this about? Or is it
really a flight into health and when he leaves tonight, he'll blow his
head off? No, I don't think so. He's different now. More relaxed.
Positive transference? Something. It's hard to put my finger on it.]

Counselor: Mr. Davis there are several areas I would like to ask you
questions about. Do you mind?
Client: No! No! Go ahead.
Counselor: Tell me: have you had any weight loss in the past month?
Client: No, not really. For a while there I wasn't interested too
much in food. But I'm back on the feed again.
Counselor: How about difficulties getting to sleep and then staying
asleep?
Client: With a few beers, I just fall right off. Sometimes the TV
wakes me up but then I turn it off and go to bed.
Counselor: Have your super-depressed moods interfered with your
work?
Client: Not much. Just sometimes when I've finished my route.
I get to thinking . . . like I said, and it's hard then.
Counselor: Tell me more about your drinking.
Client: Well like I said, I stop off at a tavern, the Rat Hole, and
have a few beers. I might shoot a game of pool but then
that's about it. I just had to find something to do rather
than stare at those four walls, so this place is close and
it's kinda friendly so I started going there.
Counselor: OK. Let me then ask you some questions about your recent
suicide attempt, may I?

[As I mention this he doesn't seem fazed. Doesn't bat an eye. Holds
my gaze.]

Client: Sure, what else do you want to know?
Counselor: Do you have another gun?
Client: Nope! I gave the Smiths my only one. And they said
they'll keep it for me until I get my head straight.
Counselor: Good! Good to hear that! Again, can you explain why the
gun didn't go off?

Client: Nothing more than what I've already told you.

[Even though I've got to ask these questions, I get the feeling that Mr. Davis is getting tired and about ready to go home.]

Counselor: Just a couple more questions sir. I appreciate your time and cooperation. Have you ever felt you might lose complete control of yourself and really do harm to your wife . . . like maybe kill her?

Client: (Shaking his head) No. No. I still love her a lot and I couldn't do that no matter what she did. Besides there's the kids. Nope. Couldn't do that.

[He's really closing down—right before my eyes. And I want to ask him about his homicidal impulse while hitting his wife, but I don't think that will get me anywhere today. I'd better bring this session to a close pretty quickly otherwise he's gone.]

Counselor: Before I stepped out to talk with my supervisor we were talking about plans for your weekend. Now just to make sure you're going to be all right, let me first ask how you would feel about coming into a hospital for a few days?

Client: I don't like the idea, particularly.

Counselor: Tell me why?

Client: It makes me feel like I'm crazy . . . I don't like the idea. (Long pause)

[Well so much for that idea and he's not commitable either so that's out. Let's go then with what we've got and keep our fingers crossed.]

Counselor: OK, what we have got to decide is what you are going to do tonight and for the next couple of days, and there are several things that you *can* do. There is staying home and if you get down, getting someone to help you get over it . . . calling someone, going over to see your neighbor, calling your niece or your friends, or calling me.

Client: If things seem bad . . . I could call my niece . . . or probably Jim would even come over, and spend the night. Jim is the guy who lives next door. He has said that if I ever felt I needed someone to talk to to come over.

Counselor: Would you go over?

Counselor: If I run into where I really felt I needed to talk to somebody else to talk something out, I could count on him . . . but there is a thing that I keep getting back to, all the time about, you know . . . trying to find things to save my marriage and not just my mind . . .

[Stubborn, stubborn, stubborn. In spite of his passivity he holds on to this one theme like a bulldog. But darn it, it's a chronic problem. There's not much I can do about it in this session anyway. I don't have any alliance with him, not really. If I side with him I become a part of the entanglement in the long-standing issues of his life and marriage. But if I don't, he'll probably tell me to take a hike. But, will he kill himself if I don't side with him? Aaargh!!]

(Authors' comment: One way out of this "Catch–22" situation would be to say something like, "I've noticed as you describe people's reaction to your problems that if they are positive, you become positive. If they are negative you get depressed. It must feel like to go back and forth from one person's ideas to another. But that won't help you make up your mind about what's best. Therefore, what I'd like to do is help you with that confusion. I'll be neutral and help you look at both sides. What do you think about that?" This intervention at least clarifies the counselor's position and gets this very dogmatic issue in the open. Now it may be that Mr. Davis's mind is already so set that he would reject this position. But it affords you the opportunity of working in the present with what was formerly a preconscious issue. It is interpretative in that it addresses his externalization problems. It is educative about the counseling process and the role of the counselor. And lastly it offers something to the client in the way of structure and a clear statement that you want to help in a professional and nonjudgmental way.)

Counselor: May I suggest several things to tide you over the weekend? Number one, I'd like to call you tomorrow evening and see how you're doing.

Client: Yeah! That's fine. What time?

Counselor: How about 6:30?

Client: Let's see, where am I going to be? Yeah! You can get me at the apartment.

Counselor: I also want you to come back and see me Monday after work at 4:30.

Client: 4:30? OK.

Counselor: Then the last thing. I want you to remember what helped you the last time you were super-depressed. (Counselor pauses and looks squarely at Mr. Davis) Prayer!

Client: Yeah! You're right. You know you're right. Hey, this has been helpful. (Pause) But do I always do all the talking? Not that I'm unhappy to talk and I feel good when I do. But it helps when I get suggestions. Ah—well—I should get going . . . unless you have anything more?

Counselor: No, Mr. Davis. But let me remind you 1) I'll call you tomorrow, 2) prayer and 3) I'll see you here Monday at 4:30.

Client: Sure! He shakes the counselor's hand and leaves with something of a smile on his face.

[I'm exhausted. I don't think I got everything through to him. So this is one I'll probably end up sweating out. Just don't kill yourself.]

Follow-Up

In telephone calls to Mr. Davis the next night, he was not at home. The counselor tried several times throughout the evening to no avail, and indeed the counselor sweated it out. There were moments when the counselor fantasized Mr. Davis lying dead in the front seat of his car somewhere. There were also thoughts that perhaps he had assaulted his wife and then killed her and the kids and finally himself, or that he had killed himself on his wife's front steps. As the counselor thought this through, he considered calling the wife but quickly realized that this was his countertransference brought about because he was unsettled about the way he had handled the session. Any contact with the wife was highly inappropriate. The counselor considered calling the police precinct in that neighborhood and asking in a disguised way if there had been any catastrophe. But he ruled this out for very much the same reasons as calling the wife. The counselor was left then with no other recourse than to bide his time and suffer the anxiety that perhaps he had contributed in a very direct way to someone's death.

Although this thought is very painful, particularly if you are the counselor, this is one of the realities you face when performing in this type of counseling setting. There are many instances in which we can and should do nothing. We must turn therefore to our colleagues, supervisors, and ultimately to ourselves to contain the anxiety accompanying such cases. Any other action such as contacting the police, his wife, or the tavern would be antitherapeutic and in many ways a violation of the counselor-client relationship. Additionally it must be remembered that in this case Mr. Davis indicated his anger at and resentment of the counselor who would not tell him what to do. Therefore, it would be quite in context for Mr. Davis not to be available as his way of acting out his anger at the counselor, to "make him sweat."

Not surprisingly, Mr. Davis could not be reached throughout the weekend. Nor did he make his follow-up appointment on Monday. The counselor was able, however, to reach him later that evening. Mr. Davis stated that he was doing all right and did not feel the need to come back. The counselor pressed him a bit and asked about his suicidal impulses and how he was managing himself. Mr. Davis replied that although he was still a bit upset he had talked with friends and was beginning to come to terms with the idea that it was going to be all over between him and his wife. The counselor reported that while Mr. Davis was saying this there was that flatness in his voice that he had heard in the earlier part of the session, and thus he was not at all convinced that his explanation about resolving the situation was very accurate. However, there was little more the counselor felt he could do since Mr. Davis sounded so firm in his explanation. Because of the serious nature of this case several additional follow-up calls were made. Though Mr. Davis expressed appreciation of the counselor's interest, he stated that he felt he had things well in hand and would not need any further counseling contacts. He concluded the final call by saying that if he did he would be sure and get back in touch. We had no further contact with Mr. Davis.

Case Commentary

We would assume that Mr. Davis felt that he did not get much from this one-time counseling session. Regardless of the fact that some of his requests were inappropriate, there were, however, several that were legitimate and they were never dealt with properly. In retrospect the counselor did not pay enough attention to establishing a positive relationship. He erred in not offering sufficient empathic statements, instead asking questions. He was at times too information-orientated. Mr. Davis probably did not feel understood by the counselor and was not given full opportunity to be appreciated in his current feeling state. The point here is that the counselor did not allow for enough ventilation to take place and thus offended his client. This added further to Mr. Davis's confusion, since he was already having a hard time telling the difference between the counselor and others he had turned to for assistance.

A second critical area was that the client received little insight into either the nature of his problem or its solution. The counselor did not offer any clarification or interpretation of the angry and hostile component of his suicide attempt. It would have been the key area to explore and the counselor overlooked it. For example, some type of educative approach might have been offered. This would have given Mr. Davis something to hold onto and thus prove valuable in follow-up contacts: "Mr. Davis, what do you understand about why people try and kill themselves?" From this point your client has something to focus on. And based on what he says in response, you have some direction with a very specific goal in mind. If he does not understand the angry elements in his gesture, then you could say something like, "Mr. Davis, everything you say about suicide has some element of truth to it. But the number-one issue behind suicide and suicide attempts is anger. The person is very mad and he's got to let it out, in this case by ending his life. What do you think of that?"

This very direct and focused approach would have great impact on Mr. Davis. It would be the kind of thing he could understand. It would be spoken in his blunt style and the point would be free of psychological jargon. The counselor would have conveyed that he knew somewhat how his client felt, and equally important, what caused these feelings and how they were connected to his dangerous actions. Further, this directive would allow the interview to stay focused on the events in the driveway and the subsequent assault on the wife. This might have engaged the client in a wide-ranging discussion of his suicidal and homicidal fantasies.

Finally, there was essentially no treatment plan. It is true that Mr. Davis was psychologically on his way out the door by the time the counselor returned from his consultation. But this was primary because the client felt cheated in not being understood or cared for. By the time a plan was offered, it was virtually useless because of the previously mentioned mistakes.

It must be remembered that these critical comments are made in retrospect. We were not dealing directly with Mr. Davis; we were comfortably outside with endless opportunities for perspective and reflection. It was only after reviewing the session that we were able to assess completely what the counselor should have done. As previously stated, our purpose is to use these cases as teaching and training exercises. The criticisms are never aimed at the person or character of the counselor. Rather, they represent our years of experience focused in hindsight. It is from such experiences that we can see a beginning clinician become a seasoned and skilled veteran. We would hope that these observations become internalized. A good practitioner would accept nothing less.

15 "My Mother—A Big Problem"

First Session

> Counselor: My name is Kay Shields, I'm a crisis counselor and I'm on at this particular hour. The phone might ring and I might have to consult with a telephone intake worker sometime during the hour. It is part of my function now and then. Before we stop with this interview I'll want to talk with my supervisor, if you don't mind.

Here is a classic example of a structured and proper introduction. The counselor is considerate, descriptive, and educational. She states who she is and what she does. She explains what the client can expect in case of an interruption, and instead of overloading her with details about the purpose or reason for the consultation break, she makes the statement and then sets about the interview.

> Client: OK
>
> Counselor: You called the center this morning. Do you want to tell me why you called?

Note the open-ended approach. Not exactly the way we had diagrammed it in an earlier chapter but quite effective with this client nevertheless.

> Client: Well, Dr. Tuelly, my physician, told me I should call as soon as possible and start getting some help. I went to him on Friday. My husband went before me and then he saw me and said I should get help as soon as I can because I need it before it gets too bad; help me solve some of my problems and sort out some of my fantasies. So I called this morning. My husband has been to a mental-health center and he's been trying to help me. There are just some things that you can't talk over with your husband, so I want somebody else to help me straighten it out.
>
> Counselor: OK. What do you need straightened out?

Repeating the client's own words lets her know that the counselor is emotionally and intellectually tuned-in. It also follows diagnostically. The client is very concrete, so the counselor is very concrete.

Client: Oh, inferiority complexes and things that, it's hard to describe them all. We're living with a woman that I take care of and it's very cramped and close quarters. I'm getting that resolved. It's things that I don't want to be that I have to be. Right now we have to be there because he is unemployed, he has been for a long time, and then we had to get married and he was very much in love with his ex-wife. She left him, which created some problems for me, 'cause we split up. I was pregnant, then we got married. Just a whole mess of things. (Big sigh) My mother is a big problem. I lost her two years ago, and I have not gotten over that at all. That's one of the big things. That's what started the whole thing. I started talking to her, and I just haven't gotten over it and I can't.

[Just before she mentioned her mother, she gave a big sigh and her face changed a bit. Sadness. There's something going on with her mother I'll bet.]

Counselor: You started talking to her?
Client: Since Thursday night. She always wanted me to have another child and I was told that I could never have one. Well, she died and now I have one and so I feel like I've disappointed her again because I didn't have one she could see.

[Talking with her dead mother! Like in psychotic? Is this woman hallucinating? Maybe I have a crazy lady here. But she doesn't look like it. I'd better ask some mental-status questions.]

Counselor: So, Thursday evening you talked to her?
Client: Yes.
Counselor: Was she there with you?
Client: She was, but she wasn't. It's like God is there with you. You don't see Him or hear Him, but He's there, and that's the way it was with her. I didn't see her or hear her, but she was there.
Counselor: You didn't feel her?
Client: Yeah, I felt her when I talked to her and asked her if she thought he was a good boy and I get real quiet and peaceful inside like she was there telling me it was all right, that he was a nice boy.
Counselor: She was talking to you then?
Client: Not actually a voice, but in a sense she was talking to me. I didn't hear her voice. I'd get quiet and peaceful and I'd know she was there and I know she was listening. I know she saw him. And she told me to have another one, but we can't afford another one. We don't want another one. My husband doesn't want another one. I'd like to have another one, but he doesn't. We can't afford another one, there's no room for one, there isn't enough room for the one we have now. If it wasn't for me taking care of this elderly woman, I don't know what we'd be doing because

you see, I was taking care of her before I met him and then I got pregnant and I married him. I couldn't leave her because I promised I'd stay with her.

[Well I'm a little more relieved. There are no visual, tactile, or auditory hallucinations. And she describes her mother's presence as peaceful and quiet. So OK, she's probably not actively psychotic. She doesn't feel like it either. But my heavens! Listen to all of this so far. And all these promises.]

Counselor: Who did you promise?

Client: I promised her and my mother and another person I thought a great deal of. I used to live with him, I did for ten years. He used to take care of her and he died of a malignant tumor in the brain, and I took care of him until the day he died and he made me promise to look after her and take care of her because she was all alone. She has a sister, but really she was all alone, so I promised him I would. And my mother also made me promise to take care of her, and I said I would, and I promised her, the woman I take care of. If Lloyd died, I promised her I'd take care of her, and with the baby it's such a hardship with my husband and the baby and the house that she lives in. It's so small, it's only a one-bedroom. My husband, the baby, and I are all in one room, we live in one room, we sleep in one room, and I think it's a little hard on the baby. We can't afford to move out, he's unemployed. He only has to pay his share of the expenses, so actually it's better for us living there, but it's creating hard problems for me.

[Enough! Enough already. What a load of information to remember. Just keep in mind what's acute and what's chronic. The long-standing problems I can't touch in this session even though I'm tempted. Now what are the ones I can help with?]

Counselor: What kind of problems for you?

Client: Well, he doesn't go to bed until midnight and he doesn't get up until ten o'clock and the baby goes to bed at eight and gets up at eight in the morning, so consequently I've got to take the baby to the kitchen, put him into a highchair and leave him set there for two hours so my husband can get some sleep. And I think it's too hard for the baby. And then if we want to watch TV or anything, the baby can't sleep because it's in the same room with us and I've tried keeping the baby awake later at night, but still he keeps waking up in the night and I don't get sleep. I'm tired all the time. The baby's fussy and cranky sometimes, most of the time he's pretty good. But it just seems like an impossible situation with all that and then my mother on top of it.

[And here she mentions mother again . . . I think this is what I'd better focus on. I can't forget all her other problems but I think her mother is the biggest one right now.]

Counselor: Your mother on top of it. You say it's a peaceful expe-
              rience and yet you're upset about it.

Client: Yes, because mother's dead and gone and I know you're
              not supposed to be talking to people like that, especially
              when your mind runs away with what you're talking about.

[Now that's good reality testing. And she seems genuine when she says it so I don't think she's trying to get me off the track. I feel like she really means it. But she says her mind runs away. What does she mean? The way she describes things with her mother there is a certain amount of normalcy given the situation. Lots of people feel the presence of a dead relative, for a while anyway. Should I normalize this with a comment now or should I wait a while? I think I'll wait until I have more information.]

Counselor: Your mind runs away with it?

Client: Yeah, I was saying that he was a beautiful child, and was
              she happy with him and then the next day I was thinking
              about it while I was doing dishes in the morning and right
              away I built it into the fact that she said I should have
              another child and the talk came into it, to have another
              one when I know we can't have another one. So my mind
              builds things. I know that it does, but I can't stop it, I
              can't seem to control it.

Counselor: But you know that while you're saying what you're saying?

Client: Yeah, I know why I'm doing it and why I'm saying it,
              but I just can't seem to sort things out and make them stay
              where they belong. They keep coming back and coming
              back. I can't find any rest or any peace from it.

Counselor: What keeps coming back?

Client: Well, the recurrence with my mother. I've got her dead,
              buried, dead, put away, and then two, three months later
              she pops back up again. I start all over again with this
              mother deal. I get my problems solved with my husband,
              or what I think are problems, they may not be problems
              as far as he's concerned, and then they're back again with
              his ex-wife and my feelings of inferiority as far as he's
              concerned. I know that's one of my big problems. I feel
              very inferior. And as I say, I trapped him with marriage
              by getting pregnant when he didn't want a child.

Counselor: You did it deliberately?

[Oops! That really sounded harsh. I hope she didn't take it the way it sounded. What am I saying? That's not like me.]

This is a good example of the counselor's countertransference about trapping men into marriage. She has some very strong feelings about this subject and for a moment displayed the unresolved side of it.

Client: No, I didn't do it deliberately. I was told I couldn't have
              any. It was sheer accident. I don't know how I ever carried
              this one because I already lost one.

Counselor: I see.

Client: At six weeks. I lose them at six weeks. And I'd already lost one at six weeks. So when I got pregnant the second time I didn't even worry about it, but then I didn't lose it, and when it was confirmed, I went to the doctor and then I came home and called him up and told him that it was definite, I was pregnant. The first words he said were, "Jesus Christ, I don't want another kid." That's just what he said. And he didn't want him. So we decided not to get married. I didn't want to marry him, but then I decided I better. I loved him, I had better give the baby a name. He wanted to get married. He thought it was the right thing to do. So we did get married, to give the baby a name and try to raise it, try to make a marriage out of it. I don't know if I'm succeeding. (Pause)

Counselor: You look very upset.

Client: I am. (Starts to cry) It's getting to the point where I can't take much more. I'm being so confused by what I want and what I don't want, what is right and what is wrong, what is real and what is not real. I just have to straighten myself out. Because if I don't, I don't know what I'll do. (Pause—stops crying) I almost took an overdose of Librium the other night, about a week ago. I had a full prescription. I went to the bathroom and poured about half of them into my hand just got them up there and thought about my baby and I put them back.

[The baby. The baby. That's what stopped her. File that away for later.]

Counselor: What happened the other night to make you go into the bathroom and do that?

Client: I was just going in to get ready for bed. I always take a Librium and a birth-control pill just before I go to bed. And nothing had happened, in fact we had been watching TV and it was a nice quiet evening and I just went into the bathroom and saw them.

[No precipitating event. No triggering mechanism. And no awareness of feelings or thoughts that may have set this whole thing off. Poor impulse control is not good in a situation like this. That worries me.]

Counselor: Was that before or after you spoke with your mother?

Client: Before. And then, it's been longer than that, it's been; I saw Dr. Tuelly on the twenty-eighth, it was just before that, it was the night before that, it was the twenty-seventh of January that I was going to take the pills. That's when it was.

Counselor: Have you ever tried to take your life?

Client: No. I've thought about it many times, but I've never tried it.

Counselor: How have you thought of it?

Client: Well, we got into a big hassle about the baby, what I

wanted and what I didn't want before I married him. On
the way home I thought about how easy it would be just
to crash the car, and I would be gone, the baby would be
gone, and he'd be through with us. But I just couldn't
seem to do it. And then I hadn't thought about it again
until just recently. I just decided on those pills.

Counselor: How long have you been taking Librium?
Client: I started three years ago with the Librium, but I'm also
            taking Stelazine. I just started this weekend.
Counselor: How did you get it?
Client: My husband takes it. He has mental illness. He's a schiz-
            ophrenic. He has schizophrenia. He's been in here for
            treatments himself. So he takes Stelazine and he decided
            he'd try me on it and watch me and see how it would help.
            And it has helped; my fantasies haven't been as bad. In
            fact, I didn't fantasize at all this weekend. I was calmer,
            I didn't get excited or fly off the handle. Except today I
            got a little upset coming over here for the interview and
            things.

[Whoa! Wait a minute. Husband dealing out Stelazine! That's a major
tranquilizer. And he's a schizophrenic. Where did she get that diagnosis!
What kind of case do I have here? I am going to have to talk this over
with my supervisor! What's the dosage of that Stelazine? If it's 20 or
30 mg, I might have a case that's over my head. And I will check this
out with the psychiatrist.]

Counselor: Have you taken any medication today?
Client: Yes I did. I took one Stelazine this morning. I'm due for
            another one about four o'clock. He's had me on them
            every eight hours while I'm away. But I gained about three
            pounds this weekend on it and that's unusual for me be-
            cause I usually have to fight to keep what weight I have;
            I just want to keep losing. I have a good appetite, a terrific
            appetite, but I just can't seem to gain any weight.

[What in the world is the husband doing giving out medications this
way? He's no doctor. That's irresponsible. Or worse . . . is he trying
to overdose her as part of some kind of psychotic episode he's having?
And she's taking them. What's going on here? This could be a folie
à deux (shared paranoid disorder). And her judgment! I originally
thought she was better put-together than that. And he's schizophrenic!
What have I gotten into here? I can't handle a schizophrenic. Now wait
a minute—slow down. There's plenty of time left in the session. Take
it easy . . . don't panic. Just check out her mental status again. Easy
does it.]

Counselor: Fantasizing, can we go into that a little bit? You've de-
            scribed one kind of talk you've had with your mother
            where you felt she answered you but she didn't speak.
            You just thought you'd know what she was going to say.
            But were there other fantasies?
Client: Well, he made an application for work at a drugstore that

is supposed to open tomorrow. Well, we were talking about him getting the job and he turned the application in and the next morning I'm doing dishes and I think about him going to work there and my mind started thinking and the next thing I've got him running around with other women and I'm catching him and things like that.

Counselor: Do you know it's not real?

Client: Yeah, no I don't know because I don't know if he would run on me or not. I'm not sure if he would step out on me or not.

Counselor: Do you know that he didn't have the job, that it's just a fantasy?

Client: Yeah, I know that he doesn't have the job. It's just one thing that he could get the job and that he could meet this girl on the job and I could go to see him and the next thing I find him coming back from lunch with another girl. But I know he hasn't got the job.

[Sounding a little paranoid here. But it may be true. Who knows? I suppose anything is possible here.]

Counselor: Do you fantasize a lot?

Client: Well, yes, quite a bit.

Counselor: What else do you fantasize about?

Client: His ex-wife, the baby, and him. Because she wanted one and he wouldn't give her one and she left. That was her excuse for leaving and in June after the baby was born I had to take this woman I take care of into Seattle. While I was gone, he called his ex-wife and had her come over to visit with him and the baby. When I found out about it I could just see him taking the baby away from me and going back to her, when I know he wouldn't do it because she's married now. And her constant calling him and him calling her didn't help matters either. But the other things mostly concerning him about what he would do or what he wouldn't do, building things way out of proportion. Like some little tiny thing he'll say: "Well, she's quite a sexy dame." And then I'm way off to where he doesn't even want to look at me or nothing and he doesn't want me. Like the other day, I don't know why I did it, but Friday when he went to see Dr. Tuelly, I didn't know he'd gone to see him, but he came back and told me that he'd been over to the clinic to see the doctor and that they wanted to talk to us, to talk to me, and right away I accused him and the doctor of wanting to take my baby away from me. That's the first thing that popped into my mind, that they wanted to take my baby away from me. Sometimes I think I don't deserve him. Because I haven't been that much of an angel in my lifetime. Things like that. Why should I think they want to take him away? They have no reason to. Unless they didn't think I was well enough to handle him.

Counselor: Do you think you're well enough to handle him?
Client: Yes, I do. I'm well enough to handle him as long as
             . . . I wouldn't do anything to hurt him. That's the last
             thing I'd do is to hurt my baby.
Counselor: You sound like you're very fond of him.

Here's a red flag and the counselor did not pick it up. The counselor did
not say anything about the client hurting the child. She simply asked
about if she was well enough to handle him. The client's defensive answer
would lead a more experienced person to speculate that she was indeed
afraid of hurting the baby. In retrospect, this hypothesis would tie in with
her earlier expressed fears of loss of control when she talked about wanting
to crash the car. But since the counselor missed this point, she joins the
client in denial and avoidance; skirting what is by now one of the central
underlying issues to this woman's suicidal potential—anger.

Client: I am. He's a beautiful boy. So healthy. So lucky to have
             such a healthy baby. So lucky to have him, almost didn't.
             I was in labor, well, in the hospital, for twenty-four hours,
             before they gave me a shot to induce hard labor and when
             they did he lost his heartbeat. I was lucky I had him at
             all. After carrying him and being told I couldn't have any
             and almost losing him, that was quite a shock, but I'm so
             happy I have him, I don't want to give him up, I don't
             want to lose him in any way.

If the counselor had originally picked up on the anger and loss-of-control
themes, she then would be able to see how the client's heated denial of
wanting to lose the child was her defense. The counselor's blind spot and
not being able to investigate the client's unconscious wish to kill the baby
may well have been because of countertransference that prevented her
from asking the appropriate question, both here and earlier in the interview.

Counselor: Are you afraid you might lose the baby?
Client: Well, I had the idea that when the ex-wife came over,
             they were sharing part of him; and she shouldn't have any
             part to share of him because he is not hers. Not any part
             of hers. I think that's where my problem started, really
             started.
Counselor: What about talking to your mother? Have you done that
             before this last occurrence?
Client: No, that's the first time I've ever done that.

A very good job here in returning to the issue of mother. Notice also
how the counselor is looking to see if this issue is chronic or acute. It

would be unusual if this were the first time. But the client is consistent, and you must accept her claims at face value while dealing with her. But you should keep the issue of previous times open.

Counselor: A while ago I thought you said you buried her and then she came back four months later.

Client: Well, that means in the respect that I know she's dead, but then I'll get to talking and say it's mom and dad and I'll catch myself because I know she's dead and I have to keep correcting myself. I keep thinking of her as still alive and not dead. I was never home much and hadn't seen much of her before she died. I came out in '56, I moved out here, and I only saw her, it must have been six months at one time, and . . . I would say a month or two another time, until she died.

Counselor: So since she's been dead you have not conversed with her since this one time last week.

Client: Yes, that's all.

Counselor: But this particular fantasy bothers you more than some of the others.

Client: Yeah. Yeah, because mom is dead. I can understand fantasizing about someone who is alive, because the possibility is there. I can understand why I would do it, you know, if the person was alive, because there is always a possibility that the impossible can happen, but with a dead person . . .

Counselor: That bothers you more.

Client: Yeah. There is no possible way of her coming back or seeing him or talking to me because she's dead. That's why it bothered me so much. And then I haven't been able to control my temper. I flare at the least little thing and that's not right or normal for me. Usually I'm very easy-going, and the baby, I snap at the baby, I snap at my husband, I snap at the woman I take care of; I mean they just couldn't talk to me, I just snap right back at them.

Here is the confirmation we were looking for regarding her fears of losing control and expressing her real anger. In the crisis-counseling model it is not appropriate to seek out and then tell her the deeper motives for her rage. Rather, help her recognize that this is an issue in her life, but then give her coping skills to deal with it in the short term. In more technical terms, do not interpret the motives but clarify her feelings *in the present* with regard to all the events that are smothering her. One would speculate that her statement of "no possible way for mom to return" is expressing a profound sense of loss, accompanied by the wish that her mother would return. This would then give the client the approval she seeks, and by seeing the child, the mother in effect would be saying "you are acceptable." Another dynamic issue here is that the mother's return would magically assist the client in coping with all the daily problems she faces: husband, sick woman, small house, guilt, and so on.

Client:	I've been on Librium for several years, right after I lost this man I told you I had been living with.
Counselor:	He died?
Client:	He died. I took care of him, in fact I watched him die. It's horrible. It's something I hope nobody else has to see, to watch someone die. Then at the time he was dying, they called me and told me my mother was dying of cancer at the same time. And she was to be operated on and they didn't know if she would pull through the operation. Oh she did, she came through all right. She lived until November and I went back in October.
Counselor:	Back?
Client:	To where my mother was before she died.
Counselor:	Where?
Client:	Back to Wisconsin. I went back and I stayed back there for two weeks to help, because she was a heavy woman and the girls had her at home. They didn't want to put her in the hospital or nursing home. I wouldn't have let them anyway, and I went back to help. I was back there for two weeks and I left on a Thursday and she knew I was leaving and she begged me not to go, but I couldn't leave the woman I was taking care of for any length of time. I couldn't leave her for too long of a time, so I left on Thursday and my mother died on the next Tuesday morning. If I would have stayed . . . she wanted me to stay, but I didn't stay. It would have been easier for me if I would have stayed. (Starts to cry)
Counselor:	What would have made it easier for you if you would have stayed?
Client:	I wouldn't feel so guilty for running out on her. I feel like I run out on her and she run out on me.
Counselor:	When did she run out on you?
Client:	When she died. She didn't run out, she died; she couldn't help it.
Counselor:	Any more than you could help it?

Here is an example of how the counselor was corrected by the client. Wanting to put a cap on the client's guilt, the counselor tries to reassure her not to feel so guilty. The client sweeps this away in the next paragraph and continues to purge herself of the conflicts over not staying with her mother before she died:

Client:	No, I could have, I could have stayed, because I had asked the woman that I was taking care of if I could stay longer. She said yes I could. But I didn't think I could because I had to get back and settle out Lloyd's estate and take

care of her, because the other woman's husband who was taking care of Mary was in a nursing home. She had her share of problems and I didn't feel that I could leave her too much longer. I could have left her a little longer, and stayed until Momma died. (Pause) My mother very seldom asked me for anything. When she did, I didn't do it. She asked me to take care of Mary, and I'm doing it. She wanted me to stay when she was dying, but I couldn't stay. I couldn't watch her die either. I couldn't stay to watch her die. The day of the funeral I didn't even go to the graveside. We went out in a procession in the cars, but I got half way to the graveside and I couldn't go any further. I went back into the car. I couldn't stand to see them put her down in the ground. I went back the next day though to the cemetery after she was buried, covered over, but I couldn't that day.

[It's very clear to me that she's never fully grieved for her mother. I recognize that some of the guilt is pretty chronic and I'll save that for long-term counseling. What I can do is help her to see that her mother's death must be dealt with. But there's so much conflict I don't know how complete I'll be. I'll start by labeling what she's going through and tell her she's grieving.]

Counselor: It sounds very much like you're still grieving for your mother.
Client: I do miss my mother. I can see my little son growing up. I can see the pain I must have given her and the trouble I gave her because I was stubborn when I was younger, very stubborn. Mother had to be very hard with me. But later on before she died, she said to me, she said, "I didn't do right by you." She said she didn't do right by me and she said she was sorry.
Counselor: What did she mean?
Client: Well, soon as I was old enough, I didn't even get to finish high school. I had to go to work. I was working in a factory, a television factory, and I worked forty hours a week. I'd bring my check home, sign it over, hand it to her and she would give me $5.00. $2.50 was for my bus fare for the week and the other $2.50 I got to spend. And she didn't work with me like she did with the other girls, teach me how to cook or to sew. I could bake, and that's all she let me do was bake.

[What a family history! I feel so sorry for her! Wait a minute. Check that. Don't overidentify with this lady. I am me and she is who she is. She and I are different. I don't have these kinds of problems. But I can understand some of them because of my own background. But these are her problems and not mine. Now with that back in place let's get back to her. There are so many long-standing deficits that I can't touch. But by listening to some of them I'll be able to show her some empathy. But more than that I'll be able to do a better job with her. I can try and stay away from the deep holes and tell her as much, so that she doesn't

waste her time going over and over the same insurmountable problems.
If I can get her to long-term therapy, she can deal with them there.]

Counselor: Did you come from a large family?
Client: There was thirteen of us.
Counselor: And where are you?
Client: I'm second to the youngest. My sister that's four-and-one-
              half years younger than me, she got just about anything
              that she wanted. There was three of us girls at the end.
              My younger sister was the baby, and my older sister, she
              was so much of a lady she couldn't do anything, so I was
              the only one left that dad could take to the barn when we
              worked on the farm, and I always worked in the barn,
              helped dad on the farm. I was more of a tomboy than a
              girl. I think my mother thought that she didn't do right by
              me because as I got older she didn't help me learn how
              to manage money and run a house, things like she did the
              other girls. She didn't work with me at all, she just held
              me down. Then when I got married, it was just quite a
              step for me.

[So this is the pattern of how she got into such a rut taking care of
people.]

From a clinical point of view it is very helpful to gather this type of
historical background. It clarifies what the chronic problems are and what
the immediate issues are, and how the counselor is likely to be able to
separate them. You will get some idea of the success you are likely to
have based on what the history tells you, and as an added benefit you
will establish that much needed rapport we have spoken about so often.
Getting more history assumes that the information is readily accessible
and is not used as a defense to stay away from the current situation. If
so, then a few additional minutes can prove invaluable in the overall
treatment of the client's crisis.

Counselor: When you got married?
Client: Yeah, the first time I got married I was seventeen. She
              tried to talk me out of it, but I wouldn't, I was determined
              to get married. I think she realized then that I wasn't ready
              for marriage. I almost had a nervous breakdown then. I
              was working and I was married. They made me quit. The
              doctor made me quit. He said if I didn't I would have a
              nervous breakdown, so I quit work.
Counselor: How long were you married?
Client: About, let's see, four months. I was married about four
              months. I found out then that the only reason I got married
              was to get away from home, not because I loved him. If
              I were on my own, I wouldn't be under my mother's
              thumb. I found out it didn't work. Like throwing the frying
              pan into the fire, as the saying goes. It was worse, because

I couldn't cope with it. I didn't know how to run a house or how to cook or how to plan meals, things like that. And then work on top of it, I just couldn't cope with it.

[Oh! Oh! I've got to take a break here before the time runs out. Let's see what else I need. There's so much. I'd better find out about this medication; the psychiatrist will want specifics.]

Counselor: So basically you've been taking this Librium since your mother's death, just before your mother died?

This is an example of a poor transition question. Since the counselor was about to break for consultation anyway, she could have said this to the client and then asked the medication question. As it was, however, it did not seem to interrupt the flow of information, so perhaps we are being too picky in this instance. With another counselor who did not have such rapport and empathic understanding, the abrupt change could have been quite disruptive.

Client: Uh huh.
Counselor: What happens when you don't take it?
Client: Oh! I get so that I just shake. I get so nervous, and so tense, and I just have to take it. I just can't go without it. I go one day without it and I can't hold a cup of coffee in the morning. I don't drink coffee, I drink decaf because I don't want the caffeine in me, but I just can't hang on to anything, I get the shakes so bad. My nerves, if somebody dropped a fork I'd go straight through the roof. I'd just jump. My nerves are really on the edge, 'cause I've tried going down and going off of it. I went off of it for three days. I was such a nervous wreck, nobody could even look at me. I would just jump right through the ceiling and be snappy and short and quick, so I went back on it again.

[I wonder if this type of reaction is to be expected with someone who is on Librium? Something else I'll check out with Dr. De May.]

According to the *Physicians' Desk Reference* (1982) the usual daily dose of Librium for adults for "the relief of mild and moderate anxiety disorders and symptoms of anxiety" is "5 mg or 10 mg, 3 or 4 times daily." Under the heading Warnings; Physical and Psychological Dependence, the manufacturer states that "after extended therapy abrupt discontinuation should generally be avoided and a gradual tapering in dosage followed." Therefore it is quite possible that the client experienced her reaction because of the withdrawal of Librium. In all such cases involving medication, consultation with a physician is mandatory.

Counselor: How much do you take?
Client: I take three 10-milligram tablets a day. I was taking 10-milligram capsules.
Counselor: Do you know the dosage of Stelazine?
Client: Uh, 5 milligrams, I think. I'm not taking Librium and Stalazine together. I'm only taking the Stelazine now.
Counselor: I'd like to chat with my supervisor for just a minute. But before I do let me make sure I understand that what you've come to work on is to gain control of the fantasies, is that it?
Client: Uh huh.
Counselor: OK. If you'll pardon me I'll be back in a few minutes.

The counselor steps out of the office for consultation. What would you say to your supervisor about this case? Before you read what actually took place, fill out the Consultation Model (figure 15–1) then compare it with the counselor's presentation that follows.

Consultation Discussion

In this recreated dialogue we see how the counselor presented the case to her supervisor.

Counselor: Mrs. Jackson is a married woman in her mid-thirties who lives with her infant son, her husband, and an elderly woman she takes care of. She was referred by Dr. Tuelly, her family physician, whom she and her husband saw Friday to discuss her emotional problems. What is bothering her most right now is that recently she has been fantasizing that she is talking to her mother who died two years ago. She denies that these are hallucinations and realizes that there's something wrong with the way she's feeling. She is very guilty about her mother's death because she left her mother just before she died, even though

---

Name	Age	Marital Status
If Significant: Nationality, Race, Religion		
Living Where		
With Whom		
Came to Agency for What Reason		
Brought by		
Referred by	Family Dr.	

Counselor's statement of the problem(s) and the dynamics involved including a mental status and suicidal status plus a proposed treatment plan.

Figure 15–1. Consultation Model

her mother asked her to stay. I think she needs some help with the grief process. She's also had a lot of other losses in her life: she was married at seventeen for only four months, had a miscarriage of her first pregnancy, and was told she would lose her next baby; the baby's father didn't want him and threatened to abandon her, and a man she lived with and took care of for ten years died last July. She has a lot of fears that people will leave or be taken from her. She is afraid that her husband and his ex-wife will take her son. She was afraid last week that the doctor would take her son away from her. She also fantasizes that her husband will meet and go off with some other woman. But of all these losses her mother's death is the greatest. In the interview she is very tearful and upset, but able to pull herself together fairly quickly. She is oriented to person, place, and time, and denies hallucinations, though some of her fears sound delusional. There is no evidence of thought disorder. She reports suicidal ideation over a number of years. She thought seriously of wrecking her car while she was pregnant to kill herself and her unborn child because the father had rejected her. Last week she went to the bathroom, poured half a bottle of Librium into her hand, but stopped short of swallowing because she thought of her son. I don't think there was any clear precipitant for it.

Supervisor: Sounds like you've gotten a lot of information and have a good understanding of it. Seems like you have a good relationship with this woman too. What about vegetative signs of depression: sleep disturbance and weight loss?

Counselor: I didn't ask directly but I think that she hasn't lost weight. She takes Librium to help with sleep.

Supervisor: How much Librium does she take and when? Any other medications?

Counselor: She's taken Librium for over two years. She takes 10 milligrams three times a day. This past weekend she's taken some of her husband's 5-milligram Stelazine and says that it cuts down the fantasies and has calmed her down. She says he's a schizophrenic and has received treatment in the past.

Supervisor: What's her psychiatric history? Any previous counseling or any hospitalizations?

Counselor: I don't know.

Supervisor: Try to get to it. What do you want to do with this lady?

Counselor: I'd like to see her again next week. I have a good feel for this case and even though she has suicidal ideation, I don't think she'll do anything. We relate well, she talks easily with me, and doesn't seem to be hiding very much. I like her and think we have a good relationship going.

Supervisor: I agree. Double-check suicidal thoughts in the last few days, summarize what you've heard about her problems, tell her you think she needs to work out her feelings about her mother's death, and that you would like to help with that. Set up six sessions, twice a week. Also talk with Dr. De May [psychiatrist] now and find out if he can see

her for a few minutes after you see her. (Counselor does
this and Dr. De May agrees to review the medications,
if the client will come to his office in about five minutes.)

The counselor returns to the office. Mrs. Jackson greets her with a
warm smile.

Counselor: Thanks for waiting. I just want to talk with you for a few
             minutes longer.
Client: That's fine.
Counselor: Let me begin by asking you to summarize what we can
             focus on for the remainder of this session. And if you feel
             right about it, another session next week.
Client: I want to get enough self-confidence. I want to be helped
             to put everything back in perspective. It's come out of
             perspective with my mother and everything and I want
             help to put it back where it belongs.
Counselor: Out of perspective with mother, because you feel guilty
             about not being there when she died?
Client: Yes, and then feeling that she run out on me. I run out
             on her, it's not right, and I know it's not right, but I can't
             help myself put it where it belongs, and that's what I want
             some help with to help put it where it belongs, everything!
             My marriage, everything between my husband and me has
             got to be put back where it belongs. The way it belongs,
             and I need help with it. I can't do it alone. And there are
             just some things that I can't talk over with him, because
             it's not very good. You say things that you can't take
             back. You can take back your thoughts, but you can never
             take back your words, so you just don't want to talk to
             him about it.

Without being prompted this client has stated the precise goal that un-
derlies all short-term counseling. It is, to quote Mrs. Jackson, to "put
things back where they belong." It is returning the client to her precrisis
level of functioning. To go beyond this is to move into a different treatment model of counseling. And just as surely as you do that, the client
will terminate treatment. If the counselor is sensitive she will recognize
how the client has (1) set the treatment goals, (2) established the number
of visits, and (3) dictated the issue to be worked on. If there is an opportunity, the counselor may be able to get a word in about continued
treatment. But do not bet on it.

Counselor: What don't you want to talk to him about?
Client: Well, his ex-wife and things he's said to me, and things
             that hurt me that I can't talk to him about.
Counselor: What would you like to say to me about them?

This is just a beautiful way to bring the clinical material directly into the counseling relationship. Unfortunately it was a little late for use as a therapeutic method. What the counselor learned from it was a confirmation of the material the client wanted to deal with all along.

> Client: That isn't right now my biggest problem, I mean as far as he is concerned. I can pretty well set that back in place. It's my mother, it's this thing with my mother that has me shook up really bad.

Here the client helps the counselor understand once again the difference between acute and chronic problems, and reminds her that her mother is the focus for this and all subsequent crisis visits. Any spillover into other areas is incidental to the real work of her visits. Until such time as her mother is "back where she belongs," nothing much will be accomplished. Fortunately, the counselor has done a good job in making contact with the client so the client does not appear to be too upset at having to educate her counselor. More often than not clients will be happy to let counselors wander away from the real issues; it is their way of handling the real situation.

> Counselor: So in essence you're reasonably satisfied with the way things are in your marriage?
>
> Client: Well, I want to talk about that too, you know. But this mother thing is what's the biggest thing bugging me right now.
>
> Counselor: OK. I agree. I'd like to meet with you again next week so we can continue to focus on getting your mother back in place. Now because of the time and before we stop I want you to see our psychiatrist, Dr. De May. I want him to review your medications.
>
> Client: OK. I'd like that. I want to be sure I'm doing the right thing even though my husband says it will be all right.

They leave the office and the counselor escorts Mrs. Jackson to Dr. De May's office. On the way down the hall the counselor sets the next appointment. Following a brief break, the counselor sees her next client.

Case Commentary

A comparison of Mrs. Jackson's presentation at the beginning of the interview with the way she was able to summarize at the end illustrates how effective the counselor was in this session. She had good rapport or positive transference. She appeared to be very empathic to the client's

feelings at just the right times. She helped the client in telling the story
as the client experienced it. With one minor exception she was nonjudgmental and quite neutral. She did not intrude with too many informational
questions and was in many ways very much in tune with the client.
Because of this as well as all the other variables that contribute to a
successful first session, Mrs. Jackson was much clearer and better organized by the end of the interview. The counselor had helped her clarify
some of her feelings and eventually focus on the most important problem
in this crisis, her mother.

As we pointed out throughout the interview, the counselor's interviewing technique was excellent. She encouraged Mrs. Jackson to express
herself fully, accepted these feelings, and showed a great deal of compassion.

There were several areas that the counselor appeared to avoid, however. First, she did not pick up on Mrs. Jackson's fear that she might
harm the baby. Second, she tended to focus on the client's guilt over
leaving her mother at the end, but neglected Mrs. Jackson's anger at her
mother for "running out" on her. We feel that the counselor was uncomfortable with both areas, in which anger was the central issue. All
of us have such blind spots. Supervision is the only way to learn about
such countertransference problems.

The third issue the counselor avoided was the impulsive side of Mrs.
Jackson's personality. This could have been fatal, and with other such
persons, it has been. You cannot let a client leave the office without
giving him some support in case he finds himself in such a suicidal
situation. There are some very good techniques for dealing with a situation
such as this. The behaviorists have developed a concept they call *thought-
stopping*. In Mrs. Jackson's case, you would have her vividly imagine
her baby whenever she found herself in a severely suicidal state. This is
what stopped her before, and there is every reason to believe that it would
work again. This can be the extra insurance the counselor needs in order
to go beyond the positive feelings she had about the case. As it turned
out, the counselor was right and the client did not commit suicide between
appointments. But in our view it is unnecessarily risky and not clinically
sound to leave a client without coping mechanisms.

One important fact that was overlooked by both counselor and supervisor had to do with Mrs. Jackson's (and Mr. Jackson's) previous
mental-health treatment. When, where, with whom, why, and the outcome were questions that should have been addressed. This should be
pursued in future sessions.

The counselor did not cover other issues the supervisor suggested
either. This was due primarily because the psychiatrist had to squeeze
Mrs. Jackson in between her other appointments that day. Therefore the

counselor had to make some clinical decisions about balancing the remaining time with the key issues of the case. Hindsight would dictate that she handle it a bit differently the next time, but all in all she did not do too badly.

Second Session

Mrs. Jackson arrived for her appointment on time. She looked very much the same as she had the previous week. As Kay escorted her into the office, Mrs. Jackson began talking even before she sat down.

Client: I just found out from my family that Dad has a 20 percent chance of living four or five days, though Yvonne says he's getting better, but I don't know what to do.

Counselor: This is your family? Where?

Client: In Wisconsin. I talked to my brother east of the mountains and he said Dad's getting better. They called me and said that he's getting better, and I talked to my sister-in-law who is right there in Wisconsin and she says the doctor says there is 20 percent chance of his living, and only four or five days, so I don't know.

[Whoa! Wait a minute. I wasn't prepared for this. I've been primed to help her with grieving, the crying and all that. What's going on here? I'm prepared to do grief work with Mother. Now here's Father. Is this a smoke screen? Or is this real? Stay flexible until you know for sure. What a switch.]

Counselor: What's happened to your dad?

Client: He's had a heart attack, a bad one, then they put him in the hospital, and he had another bad one.

Counselor: In the hospital?

Client: Yeah, they had him all well, last I talked to her Saturday. They had him on IVs, oxygen, and all the rigamarole, and then my husband called yesterday for me, and they just had him on oxygen, they took everything else off. Now whether he's getting better and they took it off or he's getting worse and they just gave up, I don't know.

Counselor: Did your husband talk to the doctor when he called?

Client: No, he talked to my sister-in-law, and she's the one that's been talking to the doctor. I guess they are going through her. I don't know.

Counselor: Is your father conscious?

Client: Yes, they said he was talking yesterday, they talked to him for a while. They said he was getting ornery, so I guess maybe he's getting better, I hope. But I don't know whether I should go or not. You know, in a way I want him to die. It's awful sad, but he's so lonely. He will be seventy-nine. He's lived a long full life and he's been so

lonely since Momma has been gone, but yet you don't
want to see him die, and I don't know whether I should
go back or not. Whether I can take it or not. Daddy and
I were always close. I mean we didn't have the friction
that my mother and I did, so I feel I've done a lot more
for him when he's alive, and it wouldn't hurt if I didn't
go back for the funeral, but then I talked to my sister-in-
law this morning and I couldn't afford the plane fare anyway. It's such a mess, but they have now got, my brother's
got, a big Greyhound bus he bought. He used to shuttle
airmen back and forth between the bases. When he bought
it he rebuilt it into a camper, and they've got it set up now
that they take the bus and load up everybody on the bus
and make it back and they can make it in forty hours, so
they could go back to the funeral. I don't know if I'm
strong enough to go back there or not—if I could take it
again. That's what worries me. I don't know, I'm just
sitting on a fence. I didn't want to go, I flatly refused to
go, and now I'm debating. I think now I'd rather go, so
I can't seem to be able to make up my mind one way or
the other what to do. If he gets better, well then there is
no problem. But if he dies I'm really faced with one,
whether I go or not. I have such short time to make up
my mind, because I'll have to leave here immediately and
go to my brother's. It takes me about four hours to get
there, because they will want to leave right away. And I'll
have to make a decision in a matter of minutes, whether
it's a right one or a wrong one, and that's what bothers
me, if it's going to be the wrong decision.

[It's exhausting to have to listen to her ambivalence. Back and forth.
She's so torn about what to do. Sometimes I really want to step in and
just tell her "GO!" But I simply can't do that. I've got to let her work
this out by herself. I've got to stay neutral. What I can do is help her
look at both sides, the pros and the cons.]

Counselor: So today you would like to talk about both sides of it and
             maybe think . . .
Client: Whether it's going to hurt to go back and watch Daddy
             die, you know the funeral. I won't be watching him die
             because he will be gone.
Counselor: You wouldn't go except if he died?
Client: Except if he died, and that's why I'm debating whether
             I should go even then. 'Cause I have lots of stuff here,
             a lot of responsibilities. Well of course, I'd be taking the
             baby with me, but then I'd be shoving the woman I take
             care of on to my husband, because he wouldn't go, he
             would stay here with her. We'd be gone about a week
             because it would take two days to get there and then the
             funeral . . . oh thank you. (Reference to counselor giving

client a Kleenex) I ran out of the house just flying. My husband is still sitting up . . . he had to take the car in to get it aligned. I called him at 10:30 and he was still sitting there. I had to find a babysitter and run. But . . . I don't know . . . my husband doesn't think I should go.

Counselor: Why does he say that?

Client: Because he doesn't think I can take it mentally.

Counselor: What do you think?

Client: I don't know whether I could or not. I really don't know. I think I've handled it fairly well, but what if I actually get back there and saw him, I don't know what I would do. And going back, that's like the last straw. As long as he was alive, I mean, I had a tie with home, and if he goes there's no ties left, that's breaking it completely. It's kind of scary, since I'm kind of shaky anyway.

Counselor: Mmm . . . I think you're far more capable than you feel you are to handle things at this point.

Client: When I talked to my sister, what they said about the bus, I felt much more at ease and I felt more like going then. Otherwise I'd have to fly on an airplane and then a six-hour bus ride and that's a lot of money. If we all went in the bus it would be just the gas and oil and the food. They figure they'd have to feed the family at home anyway. So there would be no cost for food and there's beds in it so it's just like a home on wheels.

[She's getting bogged down in details: money, food, and so on. I'd better bring her back to her feelings.]

Counselor: What good would happen by going?

Client: Well, I'd know I'd seen Daddy for the last time. I haven't seen him for two years. I only wish I could go now when he is alive so that he could see the baby. That's one thing I regret. He didn't get to see the baby, so far. Maybe he will, maybe he will pull out of it, but I don't know, I have a negative attitude toward it. I feel he's going to go, because I don't think he's going to fight hard enough. He's really lonesome. He keeps saying he wishes he was with Mom, so I don't feel he's going to fight very hard, but maybe he's getting better. They say that the fourth day afterward is the worst day. Tomorrow would be the day whether they know or not because he had one on Tuesday, then he had one on Friday, and another one on Friday; so if he has another one, he just won't be here, so I don't know. One way or the other. He's been around a long time. I hate to see the loneliness in him. At least he was so lonely, that's all I ever heard about, that's all he ever talked about, how lonely he was. How he wished it was all over with and was with Momma. There's a lot of family

Counselor: there now. I don't think I should see him now because it
would remind me too much of Momma and Lloyd, and
I'd be through that again. I think it would be much better
after he's gone if I go to the funeral, because the family
is very strong on going to the funeral. They would look
on it as something bad if I didn't go. My sister has a two-
week-old baby. I know that she isn't physically well, she's
a very sick girl, but she's going, and I think if she's going
I can go too. If I could stand having the baby with me and
being with the family, I think I could take it, but to go
alone, I couldn't. I think it would be all right for me to
go with the family. I think I could take that. I think I could
stand it because I could have someone to lean on.

Counselor: It sounds as if you're saying that it's a necessary thing for
you to do.

Here is an example of the use of clarification and summary put to very
effective use. By waiting until she had plenty of information, the counselor thus is in a strong position to focus on the essence of what Mrs.
Jackson is wrestling with. She picks up on the heart of the matter. The
one time the client talks about herself stands out and the counselor remembers and picks up on it, and she hits the nail squarely on the head.

Client: I feel it is.
Counselor: Something that you have to do!
Client: Uh huh, whether I want to or not, it's something that I
feel I have to do.

[Now that we have that pinned down, I'm going to ask her specifically
how she's going to manage herself. There are likely to be some old
ghosts stirred up and that could cause real problems.]

Counselor: OK, maybe we could talk about some things that might
occur and how you would cope with them.
Client: Well, I know one thing's going to happen. There is going
to be a family fight, over who is going to get what and
what is going to go where. I know that's going to happen.
But mostly the family is pretty well knit together, like we
did with Mother. I mean we're all knit together and those
grudges against the others were put aside and they all
bunched together, all comforting each other. But as far as
the rest goes, let them fight, I don't care.
Counselor: What are you going to do when this goes on?
Client: The fighting? Just stand back and let them fight. I don't
want any part of it. I've got all I want from the place.
Counselor: How do you really feel about it though?
Client: Well, there's not that much there, and if they want to fight
about it, let them fight about it. I don't . . . let them
divide it up any way that they want to. I don't care about
it. I have no use for the place. If there is anything left
over, fine. If there isn't, that's fine with me. That was

Counselor:

Mom and Dad's, I mean, sure us kids gave them a lot of stuff, a lot of us went in on gifts and things, but I don't care who gets them. I've gotten what I want.

Counselor: What might be bad for you?

This question completes her neutral stance position. Earlier she asked what good going would do. Now she asks what might be bad if the client went. Once you decide to take the neutral position make sure that your interviewing style and technique are faithful to this stance. Rogers (1961) calls it *congruence* and it plays an important though very subtle part in whether clients find you believable or not.

Client: Seeing caskets again, seeing that, seeing Daddy laying there and then putting him in the ground. That's the thing that might bother me the most. Because I'll be right back where Mother was and I'm afraid walking into that house I might go back into it with Mother again.

Counselor: You very likely might.

Client: But I think I've handled her now to where if I went back to face them it might help me even more.

[What's this? What did she say? Is she beginning to understand what it means to grieve? Did she remember what we focused on in the last session? There's been so much else to concentrate on with her father and all, it's slipped my mind a bit to go back and check on whether or not she's worked on the stuff about her mother. And then there's all the suicide stuff. What's happened to that? How am I going to get that into this session? It's not right to just bring it up now. But when? But I am impressed about what she says about the grieving.]

Counselor: You would go back with the idea that you intend to grieve.

Client: Oh yeah! Oh sure, yeah, I was close to Daddy. I like Daddy very much. I was closer to him than I was with my mother, because I had hostilities for my mother, but I seem to be able to handle Daddy's death a little bit better. I don't want to talk about him like this. I've got him dead already, and he's not. That's the bad thing, right there, but I'm handling the situation with Daddy a lot better than with Mother. I mean it's like I found out. I called Saturday to find out how he was, got the worst prognosis, went out over Saturday night to his sister's and I didn't think about him, I mean I didn't worry too much about him. I thought about him once in a while, but I wasn't worried about him constantly, and I don't worry constantly about Daddy. If it's going to be, it's going to be, and I feel it is. For some reason I just feel like he's gone, and I don't know if that's right or not.

Counselor: With the information you've got you might feel that way.

Client: My sister seems and my brother seems to think that he's going to make it, but they are ready to go at a moment's notice.

Counselor: So they're not quite as convinced as they are saying?
Client: No! They're not quite as convinced as I think they think
              they are. I think they're talking themselves into the fact
              they're convinced he's going to get well, yet they are
              preparing for the worst. I'm prepared for the worst.
Counselor: Are you prepared?
Client: Yes, I'm prepared for the worst already, and if he doesn't
              die then it's just that much more happiness and joy. If he
              lives, my brother is going to get him out of there and bring
              him out here, or down by my sister's, one or the other.
              He can't be alone anymore, so, one way or the other he
              will be taken care of. I feel better already. I can talk with
              my husband, yet he sees the financial side of it, and the,
              well, how it's going to affect him if I take off. He's going
              to have the responsibility of her and the finances and
              things, and he sees more of that side. He's more partial
              to me not going and I see both sides of it, that I feel I'm
              duty-bound and it's a necessity for me to go because,
              another thing, I feel that's the only way I can cope with
              everything, if I go right back to where it all started, and
              go through it.

[This is extraordinary. She's absolutely correct. It's like out of a textbook. She's saying all the things I was told I'd never see in a client.
But there it is. Just the way it was diagrammed on the board. And she
says it with such affect. I'm sure it is more than just positive transference. She's not saying all these neat things just to please me. I think
it's more than that.]

Counselor: To go through the whole thing?
Client: Uh huh. I have to go through it because then I'll go back
              and realize Mother is gone and she's dead and there is
              nothing there anymore. Because as long as I'm away, I
              still have a feeling maybe, just maybe, you know there
              is a hold for me and this way it will be a clean break and
              maybe I can lean more on my husband, I want to lean
              more on him. But as long as there is a little bit of a hold
              of a home for me, there's a chance I can get mad and
              leave my husband. This way it's going to stand me on my
              two feet now and I'm going to live with my husband and
              take him for what he is because I've got no place else to
              go.
Counselor: Have you had a chance yet to explain to your husband
              how you feel?
Client: No, I haven't because I just started talking to you. It's
              coming out that I feel that I should go, and I won't go
              now, just to the funeral. I'll go if he dies. I may not have
              to go if he gets better. My husband's just afraid it would
              be too much for me mentally. He doesn't think I'm strong
              enough mentally to cope, but in fact I think I am because

I have been so good, I've been up ever since I talked to you.

Counselor: What would your feelings be if you didn't go? What would go on with your husband?

[Oops! That's two questions. Well, too late now.]

Client: I would probably feel very guilty. He explained to them back there that I'd had a minor breakdown and not to expect me because he didn't think it was right. Well, that's what I told him to tell them. Now I'm seeing more and more if I don't go, I'm going to feel so guilty and it's going to be worse if I don't go than if I did go, because I think if I go, I can handle it. If I stay home I'm going to feel so guilty for not going to Daddy's funeral. Everybody else could go and I couldn't. I'm just going to have to do it, and I think I can. Under the circumstances, the way things are set up, if it wasn't for the bus I wouldn't go. This way there is a chance for me to go that isn't going to cost that much money. I think I should go.

Counselor: You would have the baby with you too?

Client: The baby would be with me. And I would be taking care of the baby so my husband wouldn't have that.

Counselor: And you would have someone with you?

Client: Yes, there will be my brother and his wife and their family and her sister and her husband and their kids. There's seven kids besides mine, so all the kids will be together, well they've got quite a big bus. Once we get back there, we can live in it so we wouldn't be putting anybody out. We can cook our meals and everything right in the bus and sleep there in the bus. The last time at my mother's it was so . . . oh that was a mess. There was ninety-two people.

Counselor: It does sound like your family believes in gathering for a funeral.

Client: They do. Everyone was there, and it's almost a necessity to go. I think, not because it's a necessity, but it would do me good to go back to where Mother was and to see all that again, and realize this time that she is dead. You know, it's done, it's finished.

Counselor: It sounds like you still might be running a bit from that.

This may have sounded a bit too direct for some counselors, but that's a matter of style and tone. It works in this instance and we cannot argue with success.

Client: I am, just a bit, and I think this would be the best thing in the world to put an end to it.

Counselor: Grief, you know, reawakens previous griefs, so grieving

about your father will bring back feelings about your
mother and other people you have cared about.

With this educational comment the counselor clarifies the key point necessary to the resolution of the crisis. She focuses not only on the central
issue of the first session, but does the same for this one as well. Indeed
she is completely accurate when she says that grief reawakens old grief.
Now she has given her client something to hang on to, some explanation
that would allow her to understand how her past ties in with her present.
A very touching, holding and containing statement by the counselor.

Client: Yeah, so it's bringing it back and I think if I go back and
               face it once and for all and really have it over with, I think
               that would be the best thing in the world for me. Because
               it's so easy for me to come away from there and come
               back here and not worry about it, just push it out of my
               mind and forget it.
Counselor: It doesn't stay out of your mind though does it?
Client: No, and I feel if I go back it will settle a lot of things for
               me and I won't run anymore. I may grieve and think about
               her, but I won't run anymore because it's done.
Counselor: Well, it sounds like you've made a decision then of what
               you want to do.
Client: I think so. I think I will go back when he dies. I will go
               back there and I think it will be for the best all the way
               around, because the woman I take care of is well now and
               I'm going to have to have her at the doctor's this afternoon.
               But she's doing fine, and my husband is a good enough
               cook now, he can make meals for her now. He was making
               spaghetti the other night. He made supper all by himself.
               It was really good, I was surprised. He's been watching
               me so he can cook for her. No problem there. And he had
               to do it when I was in the hospital having the baby. And
               if I'm gone over a little more then a week, he can handle
               it. And so my biggest problem will be to get ready to go
               over there. He has to drive me four hours over and then
               four hours back. That's one thing that's going to put pres-
               sure on him.

[Now wait a minute. He's not that fragile, schizophrenic or not. He
can take care of himself much better than she things. But then she sees
everyone as helpless. That's three years of therapy right there. But
that's not for me to deal with. Not here and not now.]

Counselor: Are there any short-term arrangements that you can make
               for the woman so that he can drive back the next morning?
Client: That's what I was thinking of, and, well I sort of . . . it
               all depends on what time they call, if they call. I could
               have someone stay with her, but I think she could stay
               alone by herself for that length of time. I've got TV dinners

in the freezer, so she can just pop one of those in the oven when he is gone, and if it happened right after lunch, he could go and come back late at night. She gets her own breakfast anyway, so that's no problem. It would be just lunch and supper, and for lunch I got a tamale in the refrigerator. She can heat that up herself. If it happened at lunch time, there's a TV dinner. That would take care of her, she could handle herself for that period of time, so I wouldn't worry about that. (Pause) It would be hard on him to drive me all the way over and then come back. Then he would have to come pick me up, or I could catch a bus back from Moses Lake. It isn't that far, about a three- or four-hour drive by bus, and I could handle the baby that long I think. I was going to bring you pictures of him but I forgot. He had a birthday, his first birthday Friday.

Counselor: I remember in our last session you said he was almost ready to be a year old.

Client: Yeah, so we took pictures of him and I was going to bring them over, but I forgot. I forget things so easily. I think I will go back. I think that's the best decision all the way around. My husband may not like it, but for my satisfaction, for my own, I'm the one that I have to think about right now. As far as this goes.

Counselor: Perhaps just explaining to him the reasons why you arrived at that decision will be helpful.

Client: Yeah. Well I think he would understand and as long as we're going in the bus and it wouldn't be so much . . . he said if I could go by train or bus he would let me go. Because it would be cheaper. If I had seen Daddy within the last six months, I wouldn't go at all, because I have seen him when he's alive. There's no sense in my going to the funeral. But since I haven't seen him in two years, and they feel it's a duty to go to the funeral, I mean it's just something you don't do. You just don't do that. You go. The family is kind of funny in their morals, their duties and their obligations. Everybody felt it was my duty and my obligation to stay with my mother and dad, and take care of them because I was the only one that didn't have my own children; the rest of them had children. Well I came up with a child of my own and came up with this job so someone else had to take care of them and they've been a little bit snooty about that. They feel I'm shirking my duty as far as the folks went. But that's the way my mother wanted it.

Counselor: She wanted you to have your own life?

Client: She wanted me to have a good life because I had a chance of having a good life. I'm getting something in the end that the rest of the girls didn't have, a good start in life, and that's what she wanted.

Counselor: It sounds like you've done what she wanted you to do.

Client: I have, I've done what she wanted. She wanted me to stay,
             so I stayed. You see that's where the duty comes in. You're
             bound by what the whole family—they're all that way—
             if it's our obligation, we'll do it, I mean we don't shirk
             it. We stand up to our obligations and duties.
Counselor: It sounds like you pay a pretty high price if you don't do
             it.
Client: Yeah, you get thirteen, you get twelve other members of
             the family on you, you just don't think about not doing
             it. I try to do what I think is right, what I should do, and
             of course when you get critical of yourself, then you pull
             out all sorts of answers. You see all different sides of it.
             But under the circumstances, the way it's set up, with
             going back to them, I can't afford not to go to the funeral.
             Mentally I'm pretty sure I can take it.
Counselor: The question you have to answer for yourself is, "Is it
             easier for me to grieve if I don't go or is it easier for me
             if I do go?"

This is called "leading the client." But in the context of the resolution
work and the crisis model it is proper. It may sound repetitive to have
the counselor keep hammering on one theme over and over again, but
it is part of the process of what psychotherapists call "working through"
the conflict. It is the digestion of information, the bringing together of
what has been fantasy with what is now reality. It is the gradual process
of letting go of childhood dreams and experiencing the frustrations that
are necessary in order to enter into adulthood. It is the pulling together
of fragmented parts, and moving in the direction of the whole person we
all strive to find. This is the healing process of successful crisis intervention.

Client: It would be easier mentally for me to cope if I do go.
Counselor: Well then, that's probably your answer, though it's prob-
             ably not going to be easy.
Client: No it's not. It's going to be difficult.
Counselor: But you feel it will be easier than coping with the other
             way.
Client: I think it would be, yeah. It would be a lot easier for me
             to cope with it mentally by going and going through all
             this with the family.
Counselor: It's a necessary part, really, of dealing with the grief.
Client: Yeah, I've got to go back and work with the family, as
             well as with myself. Mother's death was a little harder
             because she was the mainstay of the family. More than
             Dad was. But I think Dad's . . . the day Dad passes away,
             it will affect them a lot differently. I love my dad very
             much. Sure he made a mistake, but everybody makes
             mistakes. I understand that. I see that he's only human,
             but my sister can't see that. She can't see that he's a human

being and can make a mistake. All she can see is that when
she wanted him, he wasn't there, so she hates him for it.
Sure, I needed him when he wasn't there, but he came
back and made up for it, as far as I'm concerned, so Dad
and I got along fine. In fact I was Dad's baby, I was Dad's
pet. We used to have fights, my younger sister and I used
to have fights. Dad would take my side and Mom would
take her side. (Pause) I think I've made my decision now.

Counselor: It sounds like you have.

Client: I think it's about the best of anything. It's the best under
the circumstances. (Long pause)

Counselor: How do you feel about your medication?

Client: OK. I continue to take it, one a day, and it's worked fine,
I mean even now it's still working.

Counselor: Before we stop let me tie a few loose ends together.

Client: Uh huh.

Counselor: In our first session you mentioned that you had suicidal
thoughts. How are things going in that area now?

Client: I haven't got upset or shaky or anything. Right now I feel
like I have so many other things on my mind that I don't
have time for those kind of thoughts.

Client: OK.

[From the tone of the interview she's probably right. I'm a little nervous
though because I still don't know what might set her off.]

Counselor: Then we'll continue the medication as Dr. De May recommended and we have another appointment next week.

Client: Yeah, next week.

Counselor: If anything happens and you're leaving town, give me a
call so we can talk before you leave.

Client: I'll do that. I'll call and let you know. It depends on what
happens. I'll probably come in anyway. If I'm here I'd
like to keep my regular appointment.

Counselor: OK, so we'll leave it with the one in the book for next
week and then you call in the interim and give us a hol-
ler. . . .

Client: I got it pretty well settled now as to what I want to do.
I feel better.

Counselor: I'm glad you do. (Counselor says good-bye to the client)

Case Commentary

Because of the way this interview went, we felt it unnecessary to repeat
the content of the consultation meeting. The counselor reported to us
pretty much what actually happened in her office. However, there are
several issues we would like to comment on in retrospect.

As with the first session, the counselor maintained her clinical grasp
of the case even though she was caught somewhat offguard by Mrs.

Jackson's opening. Although this could have thrown her completely, she nevertheless managed to maintain her composure and shift her attention to the client's immediate concerns. The interviewing techniques were excellent as were her timely interpretations, reflection of feeling, summary statements, educational explanations, and focused comments. To our way of thinking it was no accident that Mrs. Jackson made some of the psychological connections she did. This was in part because of the counselor's skill, sensitivity of comment, and exquisite timing.

From the first session the counselor had a conceptual grasp that, while complicated, this case was one of grief work. Through both sessions she has retained this understanding. Without superimposing this idea too soon in the second interview, she allowed Mrs. Jackson to tell her story fully. By waiting until everything had been expressed, the counselor inserted the original treatment plan so that it fit with what her client was dealing with and when she was most receptive to it. Kay picked up very early in this session that Mrs. Jackson was quite ambivalent about what to do, and Kay declared her neutral stance and stuck with it. By staying with this position she was able to focus on one of the core issues without getting swept up by all the others.

This allowed Kay to help Mrs. Jackson explore both sides of her conscious feelings without making any decisions for her. While we do not know for sure how Mrs. Jackson interpreted this, a case could be made that the counselor in this situation strengthened her client's ability to feel some mastery over her life. To some this may not appear to be a significant gain, but in this case, with this client's history and chronic problems, it could have been felt as a sizable gain.

Reviewing this case critically, we can see that the client's opening statement proved to be the key statement. (this was when she said, "But I don't know what to do."). By remembering this remark the counselor was also able to avoid two potential clinical dead-ends by 1) not focusing on her helplessness too soon in the interview and 2) changing the client's wish to decide what is right and what is wrong to "let's talk about both sides of the decision you'll have to make." This last point helped Mrs. Jackson shift from a strict interpretation to one that was more balanced and less black-and-white.

It is very difficult to enter a crisis interview expecting one thing only to find something different. Yet Kay managed to shift her preparation almost without batting an eye. She was surprised, but once she caught her breath she was able to follow her client's lead through the rest of the session. This is clearly one of the more demanding elements of crisis work.

By now you have been sufficiently schooled in the realities of how much you are expected to accomplish in an interview. Given this expectation Kay could have abandoned the process of the session for the technical elements and forced Mrs. Jackson to tell her about the grief work. But she did not. This required considerable skill and sensitivity, knowing that the process was more important than the content, and following the client's lead rather than adhering strictly to the agreed-upon treatment plan of the previous session. The counselor had to use her judgment that the client was not simply avoiding the grief work, but was actually dealing with a more immediate situation. Any clinician faced with this decision must do some second-guessing.

Kay confided that she was not particularly satisfied with the way she eventually got back to the state of Mrs. Jackson's suicidal potential, nor did she like the rather superficial way the client answered her. But at the time it did not feel appropriate to do things differently. This variation from the established treatment plan, however, left several loose ends. Therefore, it was important to consult with her supervisors to help her work through this session, so she could give her full attention to the next client.

Mrs. Jackson called during the week to say that she would have to cancel the next appointment. The lady she was caring for had taken a turn for the worse and she had to take her in for a doctor's appointment. Her father was recovering, so it appeared that she would not have to go back. Mrs. Jackson rescheduled her appointment for one week later at the same time.

Third and Final Session

It has been two weeks since Kay last saw Mrs. Jackson. Mrs. Jackson arrived promptly for her appointment and looked cheerful, quite unlike the first session when she was so depressed and anxious. Kay had the immediate reaction that this would probably be the last session.

Client: I feel pretty good, except the other day when I had to cancel. I got a little upset. She got real sick Saturday. I had to take her to the doctor and they had to give her three shots of adrenalin. I got real scared for a few minutes. They sent her home with a whole mess of prescriptions. I think she should have gone to the hospital. That's what bugged me. I knew she was going to come home with all this medication and I thought I was going to have to play nurse again. I got through it all right though. Yesterday morning there was nine different pills she had to take at 7:00 a.m. I don't like to see her sick. I like to see her well. She'll fend for herself when she feels better. Taking care of herself and a certain routine of doing things keeps her

mind going. Other than that everything's been fine. In fact
I bowled the best I have in weeks! I had a 412 series, so
I feel pretty good and I got everything straightened out
with my husband too, so that's settled.

[There were so many problems going on with him. Which ones could
she be talking about?]

Counselor: What was that?
Client: Oh, I told him how I felt about him, about things, and we
             got it all out in the open and we got it over with. We were
             starting in on a debate when I was putting the baby to bed,
             and I said, "Wait till I get him down, then we'll talk about
             it." He went out in the kitchen and sat until I got the baby
             asleep and then we talked it over and we settled it all and
             everything is fine now. So I haven't got much to talk
             about. I'm doing good, I think I'm doing better than I
             have in a long time. I'm back to where I was before it all
             started.

[Wait a minute. All of this sounds too pat, too complete. This is flight
into health if I've ever heard it. But her voice is so firm and definite,
I'm afraid she means what she says. She probably won't let me talk
about anything else. But I'll give it a try anyway.]

Counselor: How far back is that?
Client: Oh about six months. I'm back to where I was six months
             ago. I haven't even taken my Stelazine this morning. I
             forgot it. I feel fine. Oh, that's what I was going to ask
             you, if I'm going to keep on it much longer. I'm going
             to need a prescription because my husband gets short on
             his and refilling it at the drugstore, well then they start
             hollering if you get it too often. That's about all I can
             think of. I'm fine.

[Well, I tried but I can't push her too much.]

Counselor: Do you feel you want to stay on it for awhile yet?
Client: Well, I'd like to start tapering off. I'm not nervous or
             tense or sweaty like I usually am, which is good. The baby
             isn't bothering me as much as he was. Of course the baby
             now is starting to talk. He's picking up new words all the
             time. And then there's the lady I take care of. I have to
             take her to the doctor this afternoon so they can make sure
             she's all right. They want to see her again. She was really
             in trouble. I felt really bad because she couldn't rest. She
             had emphysema and congestive heart failure and she had
             trouble breathing from about 7:00 in the morning until we
             got hold of the doctor. She saw the doctor at 2:30. Boy,
             they had to give her adrenalin. That scared me when they
             started shooting adrenalin into her. I thought, oh boy,
             what's coming off now. But right away it started improving

her breathing. That's so weird, she wasn't getting any rest. She lost weight. She was in Thursday to see the doctor and she weighed 84½ pounds and I weighed her Saturday and she was down to 82. So that's why I watch her so that she doesn't slip down. Otherwise she's fighting a losing battle. She'll be eighty-three in August and I've kept her this long. I'm going to keep her another two years or longer. Hang on tight you know! I wish my dad could see the baby, but oh well, a lot of those things can't be helped.

Counselor: About the problems that you had when you came, do you remember some of them?

Client: Yeah, I remember some of them. Mostly my mother bugging me and talking with her and the fantasies about my husband. That's one thing I have cleared up. A dream used to set me off. Now I can dream and it doesn't bother me and I don't even think about the dream once it's over and done with. I don't build on it anymore or anything. I say "Oh, it's just a dream." Before I would build on it and go from there and now I don't. I know it's just a dream, so there's nothing to build on, so I don't build. I feel much more comfortable about it.

Counselor: How about your dad?

Client: Well, I'm pretty over that now. He's doing just fine and Yvonne says none of us ought to worry (with a laugh). He'll live to be one hundred, so that's fine with me.

Counselor: When you first came in you had thoughts of suicide. How's all that now?

Client: I'm capable enough now to control it. I know what I can do and what I can't do and I'm capable in what I can think and what I can't think. I'm about as normal as anyone I can think of. Oh, I get upset and get worried, but I can control my thinking much better now. You really have helped me.

[That's a flight into health if I've ever heard one. She's been saying that a lot. But she's ending the interview so I'd better go along with it. I'll get her plugged into follow-up with me and Dr. De May just in case. But one more try.]

Counselor: Your husband's still not working?

Client: No, he's still not working. He wants to work on the Eastside. Well, it wouldn't pay for him to go into Seattle on short hours, because of parking and the expenses are too great for what he gets, and there's just nothing nowhere. So he just has no prospects. The only way we can get work is to buy into a job, go into a business, and we can't do that anywhere around the town for another three years. So I can't see any way out except us relocating if he wants to go into pharmacy, and we can't do that until she's gone

> so we're just sitting there and he's collecting unemploy-
> ment so that's all there is to it. That's the way it's going
> to have to be until we can get a job break somewhere along
> the line.

This can be one of the more difficult times for any counselor. The client
has moved into the termination phase, even though it is obvious everything
has not been addressed. But as we have advised you, those loose ends
must be left alone. Regardless of what questions you ask, the client will
answer in such a way that he will not allow you to conclude anything
else, unless you are prepared to argue with him. To interpret or to confront
is a waste of time as well as being unprofessional. You will simply make
the client more defensive and then termination becomes an abrasive rather
than a positive experience.

[I can hardly stand to let all this chronic stuff go by. Does this lady
have any idea of the kinds of problems she's got in the future? The old
lady can die any time and who knows what that will do to her. Then
there are her father's health problems and all that mess, and on top of
this her husband's so-called schizophrenia. Oops! I just remembered
I haven't asked anything about his mental-health history. But wait a
minute. In one of the other sessions I did try but she didn't really want
to go into it. So what do I do? Do I bring it up now? At this late hour?
What will it accomplish? But it's important so I better ask at least a
few questions.]

Counselor: Before we stop I did want to ask a few questions about
             your husband's counseling. When was it?
Client: Oh he's had mental problems on and off for years—ever
             since I've known him. He's the nervous type you know.
             The last time he talked with a counselor was let me see,
             about the time the baby was born. His counselor gave him
             the Stelazine to take to calm his nerves. And then he didn't
             go back no more. He's been fine ever since. Now it's me.
             (Laughs)
Counselor: For future visits do you think he would come with you?
Client: I don't know. I think so. Ya, I think he would for one or
             two visits. Do you think it would help?
Counselor: Yes. From what you've told me today. Getting things off
             your chest has already helped and talking with him here
             might help even more.
Client: I sure hope so. I'll ask him when we get home.

[Well, let's keep our fingers crossed.]

Counselor: I'm looking at the time, and I want to check with Dr. De
             May before you go, so maybe we ought to talk about when
             you would like to be seen again.
Client: I think I'm fine enough now. Before I didn't know what
             it was. I just had the shakes. Now I can realize what's

giving it to me and I can take it and look at it and know what it is and put it back where it belongs.

Counselor: That's quite a skill. Well, I think that If Dr. De May is going to continue medication, he will request that you come in and let him monitor you. We would do something like have you come in every other week for a half-hour appointment. Dr. De May and I could check out where you are and then you could be on your way. In fact today we could make this one a half-hour.

Client: That's just fine.

Counselor: Unless you feel there's something else you want to work on.

Client: No, there's nothing I want to work on. I've got it pretty well organized. That's what surprises me.

Counselor: Why are you surprised?

Client: That it would work out so quickly and so easily. That surprised me because once I got everything off my chest about my husband and our marriage and Mom and Dad, everything just seemed to fit right in, to fall right into place. I was right back to where I started, which was fine.

Counselor: You have had a lot of things to deal with.

[First there was grieving for Mom. Then you faced Dad's possible death. Then there was the impulse to kill yourself. And now you have talked about working on a better marriage. If you mean this last point, it's frosting on the cake. But I doubt you have the resources to pull it off.]

Client: Yes, things had built up and I think Mom's death caused everything to come to the surface, and now I got it all out and all put back and I can see everything the way it should be, so I think a half-hour session every other week would be fine.

Counselor: OK. Well, let me go check right now with Dr. De May.

The counselor excuses herself and consults with her supervisor and Dr. De May. Both agree with her treatment plan and Dr. De May will see her for a brief medication check. The counselor escorts Mrs. Jackson to Dr. De May's office and a half-hour session is planned for two weeks hence.

Case Commentary

Several days prior to the follow-up appointment Mrs. Jackson called to cancel. She told Kay that everything was going so smoothly she didn't want to waste the counselor's time. Besides that her husband and she had been doing a lot of talking and they were really helping themselves a lot. After a few brief attempts to get Mrs. Jackson to change her mind, Kay relented and asked that she keep in touch. By chance, several years later Kay ran into her in a store. Mrs. Jackson reported that she had had her ups and downs but generally everything was going OK. She thanked Kay for helping her and said that if anything came up again she would call.

In a follow-up call to Mrs. Jackson's physician, Dr. Tuelly, it was confirmed that she was indeed managing all right. He saw her occasionally and she voiced how helpful the counselor had been and promised to return if things ever got so bad again. She took herself off the Stelazine but agreed to go back on it if Dr. Tuelly felt she should.

In this specific interview, Kay did the best she could given the client's mental set. It could be argued that Kay should have dealt with the incongruency of the client's claim to feeling better and her unresolved conflicts. But that would not have been appropriate in the crisis model, which focuses on the acute situation(s). Unless the nature of the denial is designed to screen a suicidal plan, you must allow your client to terminate when he says he wants to. In those instances in which you suspect the client might commit suicide, use confrontation and if need be the threat of involuntary hospitalization, fully planning to follow through if your client thinks you're bluffing. Use whatever ethical counseling strategy you have at your disposal to protect and preserve his life. Do not let him terminate counseling with you until the danger has passed. But this was not the case with Mrs. Jackson, therefore Kay gave way to the client's wish to terminate counseling, knowing many of the central and chronic issues were never dealt with.

Overall, this case was managed about as well as it could have been given the client's problems and resources. The husband was clearly the target of her anger, in the suicide impulse in the car as well as in the bathroom. But this was not readily accessible to Mrs. Jackson's consciousness. In the context of her marital balance, it would have served little purpose to point out her anger, though it was one of the core issues. In the brief counseling model there would have been little time to do anything with it. The client would have been unable to deal with it in a healthy and integrative fashion and would have probably terminated counseling. If she had not, and instead returned with all the subsequent material about her father, Kay would have inadvertently added to rather than decreased her state of crisis. Instead of shoring up Mrs. Jackson's defenses, she would have weakened them. The crisis model has its limitations and cannot be expected to accommodate every problem in the client's life. Kay tried to save the chronic problems—the marital problems and Mrs. Jackson's misplaced anger—for longer-term counseling. This was not suggested in a direct and confrontive manner but, responding to the client's ambivalence and reluctance, by offering a half-hour session with the husband. With skill she and Dr. De May would have been able to coax them into ongoing counseling, and then the long-standing conflicts could have been dealt with in a therapeutic way.

It seems to us that there were four things that positively contributed to this case's successful outcome: the medication; the ventilation of feelings with someone who would empathically listen; the normalization of Mrs. Jackson's perceptions about death and her mother's lingering memory; and education about the grief process. In addition, Kay possessed the nonspecific personal qualities we deemed essential to be an effective crisis counselor (Getz 1974): emotional maturity; communication skills; self-awareness; empathy; warmth; and genuineness.

References

Physicians' Desk Reference. Oradell, New Jersey: Medical Economics, Inc., 1982.

Rogers, C. *On Becoming a Person*. Boston: Houghton Mifflin, 1961.

16 "I Haven't Been Feeling Very Well"

Linda is a seventeen-year-old high-school student who is an only child and lives with her parents. She is an attractive, slightly overweight young lady who comes to the north side Teen Drop-in Center casually and neatly dressed and well groomed. She moves and speaks slowly and looks very sad. She speaks in a soft, nearly inaudible voice and avoids the counselor's gaze. She sits slumped in her chair, wringing her hands, and fidgeting.

Counselor: To start off with I don't really know a whole lot about why you are here. Maybe we could start with you just telling me what brings you in today.

What seems like a fairly simple statement by the counselor actually contains many good elements of an open-ended invitation to talk. In the first sentence the counselor establishes generally how much she already knows. The second sentence, also a statement rather than a question, sets a nonthreatening tone and lets the client know that the counselor is willing to join with her in a counseling alliance. Finally, the opening suggests to the client where and how she might begin.

Client: Well, I uh, I just haven't been feeling very well lately, so I told my mom that I thought I should talk with somebody.

Counselor: "Not feeling very well"; can you describe that a little bit more for me?

This is a good bridging statement that uses the client's own words and focuses on the feeling aspects of the statement.

Client: I'm feeling really sad. Nothing seems to be going right for me.

[It's always hard for adolescents to talk, but there seems to be more to it than that. She seems real depressed and it looks like I'm going to have to be more active and structure my questions a bit more.]

Counselor: Can I ask you to be a little more specific? Can you tell me an example of some things that are making you sad?

Client: I don't have any friends at school. Lately I can't sleep at all. I have been reading a lot at night. My mom and dad aren't letting me do anything.

237

Counselor: You're living at home with your mom and dad. Do you
             have any brothers or sisters?
Client: Just me.
Counselor: How old are you Linda?
Client: Seventeen.

[Oops, I've gotten too specific. I'd better get back to open-ended questions about her feelings.]

Counselor: You're seventeen, and some things aren't feeling very
             comfortable at home right now. Can you tell me how long
             you've been feeling especially sad like this?
Client: Well for a long time I felt really lonely, but . . . I don't
             know, the last year.
Counselor: About a year.
Client: It's hard for me at school this year because there is so
             much going on and I see everybody doing things and
             having lots of fun. Somehow I just, I don't fit in, I don't
             feel like studying or doing my homework. I used to get
             pretty good grades.

[So this has been going on for a long time. Why did she finally decide
to come in today?]

Counselor: And you say this has been going on about a year. Has
             something happened real recently that kind of made things
             worse, that made you feel sadder?
Client: Well, about five or six months ago, I guess it was right
             after Thanksgiving, I, uh, tried to slit my wrists.
Counselor: You felt really desperate at that point.
Client: But, I'm just feeling low. Since then my mom and dad
             won't let me go anywhere or do anything. I have to come
             home right away from school, my mom comes and picks
             me up and I can't . . .
Counselor: Do you see that as related, Linda, to the wrist slashing?
             Since that time, your mom and dad are being more re-
             strictive with you? Does that feel like a punishment to
             you?

It is much too early to begin to make these kinds of connections. The
counselor does not have enough information and besides at this point in
the interview the emphasis should be on further exploration of feelings.
This is confirmed in the client's next statement. She is unable to use the
counselor's interpretation on a cognitive level and she directs the counselor back to feelings.

Client: I just feel like I've been put in a room and there is nobody
             in there with me. Now I just, I want to stay in corners or
             something, I don't know, I just feel really empty. I don't
             have any feelings about anything or anybody.
Counselor: Are you spending a lot of time by yourself? How about

at school? You say you're not doing very well at school. Are you having some trouble concentrating on your school work?

The counselor has asked more than one question at a time. The first question stayed closer to the client's feelings. The question about school focuses away from feelings and back on facts. A statement such as, ''Tell me more about that feeling,'' would be more open-ended and would have encouraged her to talk about feelings.

Client: I don't seem to care anymore. Nothing seems interesting.
Counselor: And is this different from before? At one time you liked school and did OK in school, and now you don't?
Client: I'm doing OK. I mean I've never been very popular, I never had any boyfriends or anything. I had a couple of people that I did stuff with, one girl I like a lot, she's my best friend. We go to the same church together, but now I only see her on Sundays. I don't go to the youth group stuff anymore. I don't know, I just, I just feel really empty and . . . I don't know.
Counselor: Well, it sounds as if you're not getting much pleasure from anything in your life right now. Yes, I really hear that kind of emptiness that you're talking about.
Client: My mom and dad are real quiet too, and they just read, you know. They're not the kind that go anywhere, go away or do anything. They go to church and . . .
Counselor: Do you talk with them about your feelings at all?
Client: They don't understand, you know, I mean they're not the type of people who show their feelings. If they are mad, they won't say anything. Dad just shuts up and my mom, I don't think I've ever seen her cry or anything. And so I look like a goon you know. They expect me always to be happy.

[She feels like nobody understands her. She probably feels like that about me too. I seem to be having a hard time really understanding her feelings. I may have tried to get too many facts too quickly. I'd better slow down and go back to feelings.]

Counselor: It's hard for you then to express feelings when you see they don't really deal on that kind of level very well. (Pause) Do you have anyone that you talk to?
Client: Well I try to, but as soon as church is over, we have to go home. We don't even stay for the coffee hour anymore. I don't know what they think. I think they are afraid of leaving me alone.
Counselor: It sounds like they are real concerned about you. If I can, Linda, I'd like to go back to the time that you slashed your wrists back in November. Can you tell me a little bit more about that?
Client: It was last Thanksgiving weekend and everybody that I

knew was going off and doing something and by Sunday afternoon I just . . . I couldn't stand it anymore. I just, I didn't want to be around, there was nothing else to do, so I just got the idea and thought I would try it. I don't know if I really wanted to die or not.

Counselor: Was anyone home when you did it?

Client: Both my mom and dad.

Counselor: And what happened after you made that decision?

Client: I just went into the bathroom and got one of my dad's razors. My mom came in.

Counselor: How did your mom know to come in?

Client: I don't know. I was in there for a while I guess, and she must have looked for me, just walked in and didn't say anything. She just took it out of my hand.

Counselor: Had you actually cut yourself, or were you just thinking about it?

Client: I did.

Counselor: Did you have to go and have some stitches?

Client: Taped. Then we just came home again.

[It doesn't sound like a real serious suicide attempt. There's lots of ambivalence, but the passage of time may have allowed her to deny what may have been more a serious intent at the time. I wonder if those feelings aren't returning now, causing her to panic a bit.]

Counselor: So at that time, it sounds like the holiday season was really getting to you. What I'm concerned a little bit about now is whether you've been thinking any more about doing something to yourself, maybe slashing your wrists again, or something else to take your life.

Client: I think about it sometimes. Sometimes I don't really want to hurt myself, I just wanna cut myself open to see if there is anything inside. I don't think there is anything.

[What a fascinating statement, but it also makes me wonder if there's some psychotic process going on here.

A good intervention here would be to try to answer the counselor's question about psychosis. A question like, "Do you really believe there is nothing inside, or is that just a way of describing your feelings?" may help clarify the issue. It may also be helpful to the client as an interpretative attempt to help her with reality testing.

Counselor: Have you thought about how you would do it?

Client: I don't think . . . I just would wait until maybe they weren't home and maybe . . . I don't know . . . try cutting myself again, because it didn't hurt and then I would see something, maybe try to take some pills and I would just go to sleep, and then . . . I've just thought about it. I haven't decided whether I would do one or the other. It just scares me, that's all, that I'd even think about it.

Counselor: That scares me too. Are you feeling that way right now?

Client: I feel, I'm afraid now . . . but it's nice to talk to somebody.

[That's good to hear. I feel pretty good about our relationship, so it might be a good time to break and consult with my supervisor. I'd better get some more information about depression first, though.]

Counselor: I'm glad that you came in today, too. We're going to need to break here pretty soon, but first there are a couple of things that I'd like to ask you about. Are you able to eat at all, are you eating something every single day?

Client: I'm eating too much, but I can't sleep.

Counselor: Have you been gaining some weight?

Client: Yes, I really look ugly, nobody will ever like me now.

Counselor: How much weight have you put on in the last month?

Client: Oh, I don't know, fifteen pounds, but there is nothing else to do. I eat and then I really don't feel good afterwards, I feel sick, then I feel good because I feel sick.

Counselor: And you mentioned also that you hadn't slept much. How much sleep did you get last night?

Client: I don't know, a couple of hours.

Counselor: A couple of hours. Is that something that is happening quite regularly now?

Client: There is nothing to be tired from.

Counselor: I would like to talk with my supervisor for a few minutes. Would that be OK with you?

Client: Yeah, you just want me to wait here?

Counselor: Yes, you can wait right here, and I'll be back in just a few minutes.

Client: OK. (The counselor steps out of the office for consultation)

What would you say to your supervisor about this case? Before you read what took place, fill out the consultation model (figure 16–1), then compare your model with the counselor's presentation of the case.

Consultation Discussion

Counselor: This is a seventeen-year-old female high-school student who is an only child and lives at home with her parents. She is self-referred and presents depression of at least one year's duration, and suicidal ideation. She reports that she made a suicide attempt about six months ago. She inflicted superficial cuts on her wrists in the bathroom while her parents were at home and was discovered immediately. She denies any other attempts but continues to think about cutting herself. There is no clear precipitant for her decision to come for help at this time but it sounds like she is beginning to feel the same way she did six months ago when she slit her wrists. She comes to the office casually

Name   Age   Marital Status
If Significant: Nationality, Race, Religion
Living Where
With Whom
Came to Agency for What Reason
Brought by
Referred by   Family Dr.

Counselor's statement of the problem(s) and the dynamics involved including a
mental status and suicidal status plus a proposed treatment plan.

Figure 16–1. Consultation Model

but appropriately dressed. She is an attractive, slightly
overweight young woman who appears to be tired. She
speaks slowly with depressed affect, she is vague, and
seems to be having some trouble organizing her thoughts
and expressing herself. She is oriented to person, place,
and time. She made the unusual comment that she feels
like there is nothing inside of her and said that she thinks
about cutting herself open to see if there's anything inside.
I'm not sure if this is a hallucination or delusion or what.
There is no other evidence of thought disorder. She appears to be moderately depressed, with sleep disturbance
and recent weight gain of fifteen pounds. I am still a little
unclear about her suicidal ideation and I am worried about
her suicidal potential.

Supervisor: That's a pretty complete assessment. You need to go back
and check out the precipitating events and circumstances
of the first suicide attempt and get a lot more detail about
her current suicidal thoughts and plans.

Counselor: OK, I realize now how tough it is to get specific information from her. I'm going to have to pin her down more
when I go back in. She has a tendency to talk in fragments
and stop in the middle of a thought. Other times she
doesn't really answer my questions.

Supervisor: How about her psychiatric history? Any other counseling?
I'm especially interested what was done following the
previous suicide attempt. What do you know about the
family dynamics?

Counselor: Not a whole lot. She describes her parents as cold and
distant and has a lot of complaints about rules and reg-
ulations at home.

Supervisor: Since she is seventeen years old and a high-school senior,
separation is probably a big issue here. Why don't you
check into some of the typical issues like curfew, dating,
friends, and plans after graduation?

Counselor:	I think there are a lot of problems at home.
Supervisor:	What do you want to do with her?
Counselor:	I'd feel better if she were in the hospital.
Supervisor:	She doesn't sound like an appropriate candidate for hospitalization, but if you're still worried by the end of the interview you might mention the idea to see how she would feel, in case we decide to hospitalize her later. What do you think about that?
Counselor:	If I decide to work with her as an outpatient I want to have a good suicide contract. I should probably contact her parents to get them to cooperate and support Linda's counseling.
Supervisor:	That's a touchy issue. Be careful not to come on too strong with them. Some parents are threatened and can be defensive about their children's problems. I think part of the treatment plan has to deal with her depression. Find out about her social support system. We need to get her moving, doing things that she finds pleasurable again. See if she can plan some activities. Physical exercise might help her sleep better.
Counselor:	I think she does need some help structuring her days. I think I'll be pretty specific.
Supervisor:	I agree and I think you should see her again before the weekend.
Counselor:	OK, thanks, I'd better get back to the office. (The counselor returns to the office)
Counselor:	Hi, Linda, thanks for waiting for me. How are you doing?
Client:	Fine.
Counselor:	I feel like there are a few things that I really need to talk to you more specifically about. You mentioned to me earlier, that you've been having these kinds of feelings for at least a year now. Did anything happen about a year ago that you can think of, say a death of someone close to you, or a major change in your life of any kind?
Client:	It's just that . . . I just think I suddenly, you know . . . you get old enough and you look at your mom and dad, you don't see them just as mom and dad anymore, you see them as other people. I mean I love them, but I don't like them very much.

This is an excellent example of the individuation crisis issue we discussed in chapter 13 on adolescents. We can hear her ambivalent feelings about her parents, and would speculate that she is feeling a sense of loss that would contribute to her depression.

Client:	I mean they are so cold and so I just decided that, I thought that I didn't have to be more like them because I'm not happy and I wanted to be different, I wanted to get out and do things, and have fun . . . I like drama at school.

> My dad doesn't think that's a good thing to be in. He
> doesn't want me to go to dances. He says that the kids
> just do things that are bad, and when I finally felt good
> about this year at school, I got into some things and was
> going to help with the Tolo and they just don't think that
> I should do anything like that. And all of a sudden they
> came down really hard on me.

Here we see another aspect of this developmental crisis, the parental
difficulty in allowing Linda to separate and grow up. Systems theory
holds that Linda's problem can only be understood in the context of the
family dynamics. One possibility is that there are marital problems and
that Linda and her difficulties are useful in helping all to avoid some
serious marital issues.

Counselor: I'm still a little bit unclear. You started saying that there
              wasn't anything specific that you can remember that made
              you feel especially bad.
Client: I got a job, I think that was, I got a job that I like, and
              started going out after work. This was the summertime
              and I was doing stuff and all of a sudden they just got
              really mean. They started telling me, you know, that I
              couldn't, well I guess, I've always asked, I've always
              been afraid to do anything wrong . . . can I do this
              . . . can I do that, and I guess I never asked that many
              things, and then I just started not coming home right after
              work. We weren't doing anything wrong, just a couple of
              girls and I would go downtown and go shopping a little
              bit or maybe stay at work. I mean it seemed like for the
              first time that somebody liked me and then just right away
              they say, my dad said, that I had to come right home.
Counselor: So about the same time that you were going out, and
              getting a job and starting to do some things on your own,
              you felt your parents pulling you in a little bit tighter.
Client: I guess; nothing else is different.
Counselor: OK. Are you a senior in high school now? (Client nods)
              Are you thinking at all about what you will be doing once
              school is finished in June? (Shakes head) You haven't
              started thinking much about that?
Client: I wanted to go away to school, but they don't want me
              to go away. I've applied to a couple of places, but my
              grades aren't very good this year. They just want me to
              go to a junior college, live at home, and I don't want to
              do that, but I don't know if I have the money.
Counselor: Well, one thing you mentioned a little earlier, your parents
              don't talk very much about feelings. I'm wondering if
              you're even able to talk to them about your likes and
              dislikes and what you want to do with your future.

Client: Just everything is done for me. They don't . . . I don't
               think they want me to think for myself, I don't know.
               They love me though. I know they love me, I guess.
Counselor: Linda, whose idea was it for you to come in for some
               counseling?
Client: They didn't want me to do it, but I did it anyway.
Counselor: The first thing is, I'm glad that you came in today, even
               in spite of the fact that your mom and dad weren't real
               supportive of that. I'm glad that you came in because it
               sounds like you've got a lot of feelings going on inside
               of you that you need to talk about. Would you be willing
               to come back for some counseling maybe once a week or
               even twice a week while you're feeling this way?

The counselor does a nice job introducing the treatment plan. She ac-
knowledges that it was difficult for Linda to come in for help despite
parental reluctance. She also lets Linda know that her feelings were
important enough for the counselor to take her seriously. This supports
her decision to seek help and is the basis for offering additional sessions.
However, the counselor might have been more specific about Linda's
feelings and her understanding of the reasons for them, to say, for example, "I think you and your parents are having some trouble dealing
with the fact that you're growing up. You've talked about some big
changes that go along with growing up like getting a job, spending more
time with friends, graduating and then going to college, and whether or
not to live at home. I'm sure your folks are feeling like they're losing
their little girl. I think it's hard on you too. You're beginning to see them
differently and you've been feeling like they're cold and distant. I think
that is real sad for you and kind of scary too." This statement summarizes
feelings and interprets some of those feelings as well.

Client: If you think that's all right.
Counselor: What do you think?
Client: Yeah. I don't know what they will do, but . . .
Counselor: Would it be helpful for you at all if I talked with them?
Client: What if they get mad?
Counselor: What if they get mad?
Client: Oh, they won't act, you know, they won't yell at you.
               They will be just really cold.
Counselor: I think that I can handle that, but if you would prefer that
               I not talk with them right now, then I won't.
Client: No! That's OK.

[Things feel pretty good, but I still don't have a good enough handle
on her suicidal potential because she's been so vague. Just to be on the
safe side, I better make a verbal suicide contract with her.]

Counselor: OK, but before you go, would you be willing to make an agreement with me that you won't do anything to hurt yourself between now and the next time I see you? And if you felt strongly that you wanted to do something that you call me on the phone instead?

Client: Yes.

Counselor: I want to make something clear, that any contact that I would have with your parents would not be to tell them what you and I have been talking about, but just to help get you some support for coming to counseling. I want you to know that.

Client: OK. I think it will be all right. I think they will let me do stuff; I mean, they want to help, I think.

Counselor: At some time down the road it may be helpful to have them come in so that we can talk about what's going on. OK, one last thing since we are out of time. Today is Wednesday, maybe we could make an appointment to see each other on Friday, since that would be before the weekend. Can you think of something that would be a lot of fun that you would like to do, that you could come back and tell me about?

Client: OK.

Counselor: What can you think of?

Client: I don't know, I would just like to see Carolyn for a day and go downtown and have lunch and just get out and walk around.

Counselor: Is Carolyn a friend from church?

Client: Yes.

Counselor: Would that be possible for you to give her a call?

Client: Well, if they would let me go. She would want to go if they let me do that. Otherwise on Saturday I'd have to sit home all day and work out in the yard and stuff.

Counselor: So that might be something that you would do on Saturday. How about between now and Friday? How about talking to your parents about it and that way when you come in we'll know whether or not you will have some plans on Saturday.

Client: OK.

Counselor: Does that sound good?

Client: OK, I like that.

Counselor: Why don't we go out and look at the book and see when we can set up an appointment for Friday then. And also, I'll really hold you to that contract that you're not going to do anything to hurt yourself between now and then and that you will call me instead. That's just two days away.

Client: All right.

The client leaves the office and heads toward the appointment desk. After the date and time is set the counselor joins Linda to say good-bye. She does not appear quite as sad as when she came in and gives the counselor a firm handshake. She signs the release-of-information forms so that her parents could be contacted and says she will see her counselor on Friday.

Case Commentary

Overall, the counselor did an excellent job with a fairly difficult client. She was able to gather the information necessary for her evaluation and use interviewing techniques in a way that fostered excellent rapport with Linda. She developed and implemented a thorough treatment plan. The strength of the counseling alliance contributed significantly to a successful counseling outcome. The counselor worked with Linda for five sessions on depression management and the separation issues involved in growing up. They had one family conference in which Linda was able to verbalize some thoughts and feelings to her parents for the first time. The counselor was able to work with the parents' feelings about further help for their daughter. The termination process provided Linda and the counselor an opportunity to explore her feelings about separation and loss in the counseling relationship as an example of the kinds of issues she was dealing with in her relationship with her parents. The counselor and supervisor decided to refer them to a therapist who could work individually with Linda and later with the three of them in family therapy.

Appendix A:
Mental Status Exam
Record (MSER)

Form M59 (9/70)

MENTAL STATUS EXAMINATION RECORD (MSER)*

Read instructions on reverse side.

Page 1 of 4

Patient's last name	First name	M.I.	Facility	Ward

IDENTIFICATION

:0:: ::1:: :2:: :3:: :4::   :5:: :6:: :7:: :8:: :9::
Case or consecutive number

:0:: ::1:: :2:: :3:: :4::   :5:: :6:: :7:: :8:: :9::

:0:: ::1:: :2:: :3:: :4::   :5:: :6:: :7:: :8:: :9::

:0:: ::1:: :2:: :3:: :4::   :5:: :6:: :7:: :8:: :9::

:0:: ::1:: :2:: :3:: :4::   :5:: :6:: :7:: :8:: :9::

:0:: ::1:: :2:: :3:: :4::   :5:: :6:: :7:: :8:: :9::

Facility code

:0:: ::1:: :2:: :3:: :4::   :5:: :6:: :7:: :8:: :9::

:0:: ::1:: :2:: :3:: :4::   :5:: :6:: :7:: :8:: :9::

:0:: ::1:: :2:: :3:: :4::   :5:: :6:: :7:: :8:: :9::

Rater code

:0:: ::1:: :2:: :3:: :4::   :5:: :6:: :7:: :8:: :9::

:0:: ::1:: :2:: :3:: :4::   :5:: :6:: :7:: :8:: :9::

:0:: ::1:: :2:: :3:: :4::   :5:: :6:: :7:: :8:: :9::

Last day of week being evaluated

Jan	Feb	Mar	Apr	May	Month	Jun	Jul	Aug	Sep	Oct
1	69	70	71	72	Year	73	74	75	Nov	Dec
2	3	4	5	6		7	8	9	10	11
12	13	14	15	16	Day	17	18	19	20	21
22	23	24	25	26		27	28	29	30	31

Sex of the patient

male   female

Patient's age

:0:: ::1:: :2:: :3:: :4::   :5:: :6:: :7:: :8:: :9::

:0:: ::1:: :2:: :3:: :4::   :5:: :6:: :7:: :8:: :9::

TRANSACTION

initial evaluation	reeval-uation	partial reeval	correc-tion	dele-tion

ATTITUDE TOWARD RATER

unknown

very positive	positive	neutral	ambivalent	negative	very negative

RELIABILITY AND COMPLETENESS OF INFORMATION

very good	good	only fair	poor	very poor

Barriers to communication or reliability were due to   quality of speech

refuses information	massive denial	dialect or foreign language
physical illness	preoccupation	lack of response
sensorial or cognitive disorder	conscious falsification	deafness

IBM M62.389

APPEARANCE

Patient looks	his age	older		younger	good looking

Apparent physical health   very good   good   only fair   poor   very poor

		slight	mild	mod	mark
Physical deformity					

Weight   underweight   average   overweight | gaining   losing

Height   very short   short   average   tall   very tall

Ambulation disturbance   walks with assistance   must use wheel chair   bed-ridden

Dress and grooming

	slight	mild	mod	mark
Unkempt				
Inappropriate				
Seductive				
Neat and appropriate for occasion				

Posture

	slight	mild	mod	mark
Stooped				
Stiff				
Bizarre				

Face

	slight	mild	mod	mark
Impassive				
Tense				
Perplexed				
Suspicious				
Angry				
Sullen				
Bored				
Worried				
Sad				
Tearful				
Elated				
Silly				
Grimacing				
Hypervigilant				
Facial expression unremarkable				

Eyes

	occa-sional	often	very often	most of time
Avoids direct gaze				
Stares into space				
Glances furtively				

Set no. 0052107   Mark last 3 digits of Set number in area below.

:0:: ::1:: :2:: :3:: :4::   :5:: :6:: :7:: :8:: :9::

:0:: ::1:: :2:: :3:: :4::   :5:: :6:: :7:: :8:: :9::

:0:: ::1:: :2:: :3:: :4::   :5:: :6:: :7:: :8:: :9::

Developed by Robert L. Spitzer, M.D., and Jean Endicott, Ph.D., Biometrics Research, New York State, Department of Mental Hygiene. Reprinted with permission.

MSER 1b

PURPOSE

The purpose of the Mental Status Examination Record (MSER) is to enable a rater to record the results of a mental status examination. Proper use of this form encourages the rater to consider all of the items on the MSER when conducting his examination. The recorded information can be used by a computer to produce a narrative description of the results of the examination. In addition, it will also be possible to use the information for the systematic evaluation of individual patients and for studies of groups of patients.

The rater may add narrative comments to the clinical record for any information for which there are no items on the form.

DATA SOURCE

The data upon which the judgments are based should be mainly from direct contact with the patient; however, other information available to the rater, such as nurses' reports or personal observation of the patient on the ward, should be used.

TIME PERIOD

The evaluation covers behavior and symptoms which occurred during the week prior to and including the day of evaluation whether the evaluation is done on admission or at a later time.

ITEMS OF INFORMATION

Some items must be marked for all patients. These items are printed in **bold type** and contain a category indicating no pathology. For example:

Psychomotor none slight mild mod mark
retardation

All of the remaining items are marked only when applicable for the patient being evaluated. These items should be left blank if there is no information or if there is no psychopathology. Examples are:

sus-
pected slight mild mod mark
Drug abuse

hallucinogen barbiturate

Note that a shaded line, linking a series of terms in an item requiring a scaled judgment, indicates that the rater should select no more than one term from the list.

All scaled judgments of severity should take into account how intense the behavior was as well as how much of the time it was present during the week. Thus, the ratings are a weighted average for the entire week and not necessarily the highest intensity exhibited at any one time. When making these judgments, the rater should think of the full range of the behavior that people sometimes exhibit.

NOTING JUDGMENTS

Note all judgments with a No. 2 pencil. Make a heavy dark mark between the lines of the grids. Example: ▬ To change a judgment, completely erase the incorrect mark. In filling out **IDENTIFICATION** section and **Set number,** numbers should be written in the boxes as well as noted in the grids. The numbers read from top to bottom so that the last digit is in the bottom row. If the number has fewer digits than the number of rows alloted, one or more of the top rows are left blank.

SET NUMBER

Each page of the MSER is preprinted with a seven digit Set number. The last three digits of this number are used to link the four pages together for data processing. Be sure to mark the last three digits from the Set number on all four pages.

PRINTOUT

The computer printout will contain in a narrative all of the information that the rater has noted. This will include information based on ratings of "none" as well as positive indications of psychopathology.

If a rater fails to mark an item that is supposed to be completed for all patients, the printout will note that information for this item is missing. Inconsistencies between ratings will also be indicated.

DEFINITIONS AND INSTRUCTIONS for sections and items which may be unclear.

IDENTIFICATION

Rater code Code number for person completing this form.

Last day of week being evaluated The last day of the one week being evaluated. Not necessarily the same as date the form is completed.

TRANSACTION

Initial evaluation for first time entire form used for this admission.
Reevaluation for subsequent use of entire form.
Partial reevaluation Entry of IDENTIFICATION and one or more sections of the form to indicate a change in patient's condition since the last entry. The printout will be limited to those sections.
Correction To make a correction in a previously submitted form, because of clerical or judgmental error, or new information, correct old form or completely fill out a new form. The case or consecutive number and date in the IDENTIFICATION section must be identical to the previously submitted form. The previously submitted form will be completely replaced in the file by the new form.
Deletion To delete from the file a previously submitted form, e.g. wrong case or consecutive number, wrong date, or duplicate record. Form requesting deletion must have identical case or consecutive number and date in IDENTIFICATION section as record to be deleted.

ATTITUDE TOWARD RATER

Unknown as might be the case with a mute patient.
Ambivalent At times positive, at other times, negative.
Neutral No particular emotional reaction.

RELIABILITY AND COMPLETENESS OF INFORMATION

Rater's overall judgment of accuracy and completeness of information. Example: a mute catatonic would not give information about the content of his thoughts, thereby lowering the completeness of the overall information.
Barriers to communication or reliability were due to the specific reason(s) listed.

   Quality of speech Any disturbance of speech listed later under "Quality of speech and thought" which is a barrier to communication.
   Preoccupation Exclusive focus on a topic or thought so that inadequate information is given on other topics.
   Massive denial Extensive use of the defense mechanism of denial where aspects of external reality are not acknowledged so as to avoid anxiety, as distinguished from lying which is conscious.
   Lack of response Failure to reply to questions.
   Sensorial or cognitive disorder Any disturbance listed under "Sensorium" or "Cognitive functions" which is a barrier to communication.

APPEARANCE

Apparent physical health Outward appearance of health.
Physical deformity Visibility of physical deformity causing disfigurement.
Dress and grooming Clothing, hair, makeup, jewelry, accessories.
   Unkempt Untidy or dirty.
   Inappropriate Odd or eccentric or unsuitable for the occasion.
Posture
   Stiff Holding body rigidly.
   Bizarre Odd or eccentric.
Face Facial expression. It need not be consistent with "General attitude and behavior," as with a patient who looks angry but does not act angry.
   Impassive Expressionless. When marked may be like a "zombie."
   Grimacing Distorted facial expression.
   Hypervigilant Excessive watchfulness and attentiveness, as staring closely at interviewer.
Eyes
   Glances furtively Looks about quickly and surreptitiously.

Form M59 (9/70)
MSER   Page 2 of 4

MOTOR BEHAVIOR

	none	slight	mild	mod	marked
Psychomotor retardation					
catatonic stupor	catatonic rigidity				waxy flexibility

	none	slight	mild	mod	marked
Psychomotor excitement					
	catatonic excitement				

	slight	mild	mod	marked
Tremor				
Tics				
Posturing				
Pacing				
Fidgeting				
Gait Unsteadiness				
Rigidity				
Slowness				

Motor abnormality possibly because of

medication	orthopedic problem	neurological disorder

GENERAL ATTITUDE AND BEHAVIOR

Positive characteristics

helpful	responsible	good sense of humor
cheerful	pleasant	likeable

	none	slight	mild	mod	marked
Uncooperative					
Withdrawn					
Inappropriate					
Impaired functioning in goal directed activities					
Suspicious					
Anger (overt)					

sarcastic	critical	argumentative
sullen	assaultive	physically destructive
irritable	threatens violence	

	slight	mild	mod	marked
Provokes anger				

	none	at least threats	at least gesture(s)	attempt(s)
Suicidal behavior				

Self mutilation (degree of disfiguring)	slight	mild	mod	marked

	2	3	4	5
Antisocial				
Impulsive				
Passive				
Dependent				
Domineering				
Guarded				
Complaining				
Ritualistic				

GENERAL ATTITUDE AND BEHAVIOR (continued)

	slight	mild	mod	mark
Obsequious				
Despondent				
Apathetic				
Fearful				
Dramatic				
Sexually seductive				
Homosexual behavior				
Alcohol abuse	suspected			
Drug abuse	suspected			

hallucinogen	barbiturate	stimulant
narcotic	other	

MOOD AND AFFECT

	none	slight	mild	mod	mark
Depression					
Anxiety					

with episodes of panic

	slight	mild	mod	mark
Anger				
Euphoria				
Anhedonia				
Loneliness				

Quality of mood and affect

	none	slight	mild	mod	mark
Flatness					
Inappropriate					
Lability					

Diurnal mood variation				
	worse in morning			worse in evening

QUALITY OF SPEECH AND THOUGHT

Voice	shouts	screams
very loud	monotonous	overly dramatic
whining	very soft	

	very slow	slow	average	fast	very fast
Rate					
Productivity	markedly reduced	reduced	average	increased	markedly increased

	none	slight	mild	mod	mark
Incoherence					
Irrelevance					
Evasiveness					
Blocking					

Set no. 0052107   Mark last 3 digits of Set number in area below.

0	1	2	3	4		5	6	7	8	9
0	1	2	3	4		5	6	7	8	9
0	1	2	3	4		5	6	7	8	9

IBM M62391

MSER 2b

MOTOR BEHAVIOR

Characteristics of bodily movements that are observable.

Psychomotor retardation Generalized slowing down of physical reactions and movements.

    Catatonic stupor Marked decrease in reactivity to environment and reduction of spontaneous movements and activity. May appear to be unaware of nature of surroundings.

    Catatonic rigidity Maintaining a rigid posture against efforts to move him.

    Waxy flexibility Maintaining postures into which he is placed.

Psychomotor excitement Generalized overactivity.

    Catatonic excitement Apparently purposeless and stereotyped, excited motor activity not influenced by external stimuli.

Tics Involuntary, brief, recurrent, movements involving a relatively small segment of the body.

Posturing Voluntary assumption of an inappropriate or bizarre posture.

GENERAL ATTITUDE AND BEHAVIOR

The attitude and behavior that the patient displays in his interaction with others. This may or may not be consistent with "Content of speech and thought." For example: he may be physically assaultive but not indicate or acknowledge thoughts of doing violence to others.

Withdrawn Avoidance of contact or involvement with people.

Inappropriate Behavior that is odd, eccentric or not in keeping with the situation. Examples: exposing self, talking to self, frequent giggling.

Impaired functioning in goal directed activities Impairment in work (if work was expected) or in other goal directed activities, e.g. chores, leisure time activities, or getting dressed.

Suspicious From mild distrust to feelings of persecution. May be markedly suspicious and yet not delusional.

Anger (overt) Overall rating of overt expression of anger. Inferences of unconscious anger should not be used in making this rating.

    Assaultive Physical violence against a person.

    Physically destructive Destroys or breaks things.

Provokes anger Attitude or behavior that provokes anger in others, e.g. teases, touches others, argumentative.

Suicidal behavior As distinguished from suicidal thoughts. Include evaluation of threat to life and seriousness of intent.

Self mutilation Disfigurement resulting from deliberate damage to the body (not associated with a suicide attempt).

Antisocial Antisocial attitude or behavior, e.g. lying, encouraging breaking of rules, stealing, complacent attitude towards his own or others' antisocial behavior.

Impulsive Acts immediately without reflection.

Passive Permits himself to be acted upon without his making efforts to control the course of events.

Dependent Seeks undue assistance, praise or reassurance from others.

Domineering Examples: tries to control interview, orders others around.

Guarded Acts in a defensive or protective manner, e.g. reluctant to give information.

Ritualistic Displays compulsions or other repetitive stereotyped behavior that is not directly adaptive, e.g. hand washing rituals, endless recheckings, formalized procedures for eating or dressing.

Obsequious Servile attentiveness or marked inclination to please.

Despondent Acts discouraged, dejected, or depressed.

Apathetic Lack of feeling, interest, concern or emotion.

Dramatic Artificiality of action with exaggerated emotionalism.

Homosexual behavior Overt homosexual approaches or acts as distinguished from homosexual thoughts.

Alcohol abuse Use of alcohol during the past week which is excessive, causes physical symptoms, causes alteration in mood or behavior, or interferes with performance of expected daily routine or duties.

Drug abuse Excessive self medication; unprescribed use of drugs with effects as described above for alcohol abuse.

MOOD AND AFFECT

Emotion or feeling tone that is either observable or reported by the patient. This may or may not be consistent with the content of speech, e.g. looks sad and tearful but says he is not depressed. Inferences based on psychodynamic formulations should not be used in making these ratings, e.g. unconscious anger because the patient is overly polite.

Depression Sadness, worthlessness, failure, hopelessness, remorse, or loss.

Anxiety Apprehension, worry, nervousness, tension, fearfulness, or panic.

    With episodes of panic Circumscribed periods of intense anxiety.

Euphoria Exaggerated feeling of well being, not consonant with circumstances.

Anhedonia Absence of pleasure in activities that ordinarily would be pleasurable.

Flatness Generalized impoverishment of emotional reactivity, often described as "emotionally dull," or "unresponsive."

Inappropriate Affect is not appropriate for situation or is incongruous with content of speech, e.g. giggles during interview, cheerful while discussing threats to his life.

Lability Unstable emotions that shift rapidly without adequate control, e.g. sudden bursts of anger or crying.

Diurnal mood variation Consistent change in mood from morning to evening.

QUALITY OF SPEECH AND THOUGHT

Voice monotonous Lack of normal variation in pitch.

Rate Rapidity of speech and thought.

Productivity The amount of speech.

Incoherence Impairment in the form of speech which makes it difficult to understand or follow. (A bizarre delusional belief may be explained in a coherent manner.)

Irrelevance Content of remarks is not related to questions being asked or topic under discussion.

Evasiveness Deliberately avoids answering questions directly.

Blocking Sudden cessation in the train of thought or in the middle of a sentence. The patient is unable to explain the reason for the sudden stoppage.

Form MS 9 (9/70)

MSER

QUALITY OF SPEECH AND THOUGHT (continued)

	slight	mild	mod	marked
Circumstantiality	2	3	4	5
Loosening of associations	2	3	4	5
Obscurity	2	3	4	5
Concreteness	2	3	4	5

Other

echolalia	clang associations	neologisms
flight of ideas	excessive profanity	plays on words
persever-ation	unintelligible muttering	suggestive of neurological disorder

CONTENT OF SPEECH AND THOUGHT

	unknown	none	slight	mild	mod	marked
Grandiosity	7	1	2	3	4	5
Suicidal ideation	7	1	2	3	4	5
Ideas of reference	7	1	2	3	4	5
Bizarre thoughts	7	1	2	3	4	5
Phobia(s)	7	1	2	3	4	5
Compulsion(s)	7	1	2	3	4	5
Obsession(s)	7	1	2	3	4	5

		slight	mild	mod	marked
Guilt		2	3	4	5
Alienation		2	3	4	5
Pessimism		2	3	4	5
Distrustfulness		2	3	4	5
Self pity		2	3	4	5
Inadequacy		2	3	4	5
Diminished interest		2	3	4	5
Indecisiveness		2	3	4	5
Isolation		2	3	4	5
Helplessness		2	3	4	5
Failure		2	3	4	5
Loss		2	3	4	5
Self derogatory		2	3	4	5
Resentful of others		2	3	4	5
Death		2	3	4	5
Loss of control		2	3	4	5

Harm	being harmed by others	doing harm to others
Sexual symptoms	frigidity	homosexual impulses
	potency disturbance	fears of homosexuality

Delusions	absent	unknown	suspected	likely	definite

	slight	mild	mod	marked
Persecutory delusions	2	3	4	5
Somatic delusions	2	3	4	5
Delusions of grandeur	2	3	4	5

CONTENT OF SPEECH AND THOUGHT (continued)

	slight	mild	mod	mark
Religious delusions	2	3	4	5
Delusions of guilt	2	3	4	5
Delusions of influence	2	3	4	5
Nihilistic delusions	2	3	4	5

Influence of delusion on behavior	very little	considerable	marked

SOMATIC FUNCTIONING AND CONCERN

Appetite	very poor	poor	normal	excessive	very excessive
		requires urging to eat		requires help to eat	

Energy level	very easily fatigued	easily fatigued	normal	very energetic	extremely energetic
	sleeps excessively			feels little need for sleep	

Change in sexual interest or activity	marked decrease	slight decrease	slight increase	marked increase

Insomnia (overall severity any type)	none	slight	mild	mod	mark
	1	2	3	4	5
	difficulty falling asleep	early morning awakening		awakening during night	

Incontinence	occa-sionally	often	very often	most of time

Seizures (this week)	one	several	daily	several per day
		likely hysterical		likely organic	

Severe sensory impairment (organic)		visual		hearing

Conversion reaction	suspected	likely	definite
Type	hearing loss		visual defect
paralysis	anesthesia		paresthesia
abnormal movements	pain		

Psychophysiologic reactions	none	slight	mild	mod	mark
	1	2	3	4	5
Type	upset stomach			diarrhea	
consti-pation		palpitations		hyperventilation syndrome	
headache		back-ache		urinary frequency	
sweating		itching			

Unwarranted concern with physical health	none	slight	mild	mod	mark
	1	2	3	4	5

PERCEPTION

Hallucinations	absent	unknown	suspected	likely	definite

	slight	mild	mod	marked	un-formed / formed
Visual	2	3	4	5	
Auditory	2	3	4	5	voices noises
Olfactory	2	3	4	5	
Gustatory	2	3	4	5	
Tactile	2	3	4	5	
Visceral	2	3	4	5	

Set no. 0052107

Mark last 3 digits of Set number in area below.

0	1	2	3	4		5	6	7	8	9
0	1	2	3	4		5	6	7	8	9
0	1	2	3	4		5	6	7	8	9

IBM M6239J

MSER 3b

Circumstantiality Proceeding indirectly to goal idea with many tedious details and parenthetical and irrelevant additions.
Loosening of associations Saying things in juxtaposition which lack a logical or inherent relationship, e.g. "I'm tired. All people have eyes."
Obscurity Lack of precision and clarity.
Concreteness A tendency to deal with concepts at a sensory or partial level at the expense of considering general relationships or abstractions, e.g. literal interpretation of proverbs.
Echolalia Repetition by imitation of phrases or words said in their presence.
Clang associations Combining unrelated words or phrases because they share similar sounds, e.g. "I'm sad, mad, bad."
Neologisms Invention of new words.
Flight of ideas Abrupt and rapid changes of topic of conversation so that ideas are not completed.
Plays on words Inappropriate rhyming or punning.
Perseveration Repetition of a single response or idea in reply to various questions or repetition of words or phrases over and over in a mechanical manner.
Suggestive of neurological disorder Impairment in articulation such as those seen in various neurological disorders or expressive aphasia.

CONTENT OF SPEECH AND THOUGHT

The items in this section are descriptive of what the patient says or is thinking about. It may not be in keeping with his attitude and general behavior. For example, he may not act "dependent" yet reports feelings of "helplessness." The information may be offered spontaneously or only after questioning.
Grandiosity Inflated appraisal of his worth, contact, power or knowledge. (A patient may be markedly grandiose and yet not have delusions of grandeur.)
Suicidal ideation From occasional thoughts of killing himself, to preoccupation with method of killing himself.
Ideas of reference Detection of personal reference in seemingly insignificant remarks, objects, or events, e.g. interprets a person's sneeze as a message. (Patient may recognize absurdity of thought.)
Bizarre thoughts Content of thinking is odd, eccentric or unusual (but not necessarily delusional), e.g. preoccupation with flying saucers.
Phobia Irrational fear of a specific object or situation, e.g. fear of crowds, heights, animals; to be distinguished from free floating anxiety or fears of general conditions (getting sick, business failure).
Compulsion An insistent, repetitive, unwanted urge to perform an act which is contrary to his ordinary conscious wishes or standards, e.g. hand washing compulsion.
Obsession Persistent, unwanted thoughts which occur against his resistance, the content of which he regards as senseless, e.g. thoughts of killing child.
Alienation Feelings of estrangement, e.g. wonders who he really is, feels he is different from everybody.
Isolation Feelings of social isolation, rejection, or discomfort with people; preference for being alone.
Loss Feelings or theme of no longer having some person or object of great importance.
Self derogatory Reproaches self for things he has done or not done.
Being harmed by others Thinks of people as mistreating him, as taking advantage of him or as harming him in some way.
Frigidity Impaired pleasure from sexual intercourse.
Fears of homosexuality Fears of homosexual seduction or fears that he is a homosexual.
Potency disturbance Difficulty maintaining an erection during intercourse.
Homosexual impulses Speaks of his homosexual impulses.
Delusions Conviction in some important personal belief which is almost certainly not true.
   Persecutory delusions Examples: believes an organized conspiracy exists against him, or that he has been attacked, harassed, cheated or persecuted or that people talk about him or stare at him, when the circumstances make it almost certainly not true.
   Somatic delusions Conviction about his body that is almost certainly not true, e.g. body is rotting, someone is in his brain.

Delusions of grandeur Claims power or knowledge beyond the bounds of credibility, e.g. has special relation to God; can read people's minds.
Religious delusions A delusion involving a religious theme.
Delusions of guilt Belief that he has done something terrible or is responsible for some event or condition which is almost certainly not true, e.g. has ruined family by his bad thoughts.
Delusions of influence Claims his thoughts, mood, or actions are controlled or mysteriously influenced by other people or by strange forces.
Nihilistic delusions Believes the world is destroyed or that he or everyone is dead.
Influence of delusion on behavior The extent to which the delusional belief influences his behavior. To be left blank if patient is not delusional or if his delusion has virtually no effect on how he interacts with others or how he organizes his life.

SOMATIC FUNCTIONING AND CONCERN

Energy Level Capacity to sustain effort without fatigue. The effort may not be goal directed as with the extremely energetic manic.
Change in sexual interest or activity To be left blank if there is no change from the usual level.
Insomnia Overall rating of difficulty sleeping.
Incontinence Inability to restrain, within normal limits, the natural evacuation of the bladder or bowels.
Seizures A sudden attack of motor or sensory disturbance often involving a disturbance of consciousness.
   Likely hysterical Judged to be on a psychological basis.
   Likely organic Judged to be due to some structural or biochemical abnormality of the brain.
Severe sensory impairment (organic) Examples: blindness, deafness on a physical basis.
Conversion reaction A disturbance of the special senses or of the voluntary nervous system, often expressing emotional conflict in a symbolic manner; to be distinguished from psychophysiologic disorders which are mediated by the autonomic nervous system, from malingering which is done consciously, and from neurological lesions which cause anatomically circumscribed symptoms. Symptoms should not be listed unless they are considered conversion reactions. ("Hysterical hallucinations" should not be noted here but rather under "Perception.")
   Anesthesia Absence of sensation, generally of the skin.
   Paresthesia Perverted sense of touch, e.g. tingling, burning, tickling caused by tactile stimulus.
   Abnormal movements Examples: tremors, tics, seizures, ataxic gait.
Psychophysiologic reactions Physical symptoms usually mediated by the autonomic nervous system, and clearly caused by emotional factors. The physiological changes are those that normally accompany certain emotional states, are generally reversible and therefore do not involve permanent tissue alteration.
   Upset stomach Do not include diarrhea or constipation even if the subject refers to these symptoms as "upset stomach."
   Hyperventilation syndrome Overbreathing which may cause such symptoms as breathlessness, dizziness, paresthesias and feelings of pressure in the chest.
Unwarranted concern with physical health Concern with physical health that is apparently not warranted by actual physical condition. Include concern with one organ (e.g. cardiac neurosis) as well as with multiple organs (hypochondriasis).

PERCEPTION

Hallucinations Sensory perceptions in the absence of identifiable stimulation occurring during the waking state whether judged to be on an organic, functional, psychotic, or hysterical basis.
   Visual hallucinations
   Unformed Visual hallucinations of unformed lights, flashes, or patterns.
   Formed Visual hallucinations of people, animals, or other recognizable things.
   Auditory hallucinations Hallucinations of sounds.
   Olfactory hallucinations Hallucinations of smell.
   Gustatory hallucinations Hallucinations of taste.
   Tactile hallucinations Hallucinations of touch.
   Visceral hallucinations Hallucinations of sensations arising within the body.

Form MS 9 (9/70)
MSER

| PERCEPTION (continued) | INSIGHT AND ATTITUDE TOWARD ILLNESS (continued) |

PERCEPTION (continued)

Content of hallucinations

threatening	accusatory	flattering
benign	religious	self derogatory
grandiose	reassuring	sexual

Conviction hallucinations real — knows unreal / unsure / convinced

Illusions — slight / mild / mod / marked

Depersonalization

Derealization

Deja vu

SENSORIUM

Orientation disturbance — too disturbed to test

	unknown	none	slight	mild	mod	marked
Time						
Place						
Person (self and others)						

Memory disturbance — too disturbed to test / confabulation

	unknown	none	slight	mild	mod	marked
Recent						
Remote						

Clouding of consciousness — slight / mild / mod / marked

fluctuating / continuous

Dissociation

| trance | amnesia | fugue |
| hysterical attack | other | |

COGNITIVE FUNCTIONS

Attention disturbance — slight / mild / mod / marked

Distractability

Intelligence (estimate)

unknown / superior / bright / average / borderline / retarded

JUDGMENT

	very good	good	only fair	poor	very poor
Family relations					
Other social relations					
Employment					
Future plans	no plans (or)				

POTENTIAL FOR SUICIDE OR VIOLENCE

	unsure	not significant	low	mod	high	very high
Suicide						
Physical violence						

INSIGHT AND ATTITUDE TOWARD ILLNESS

Recognition that he is ill — not applicable / unknown

| very good | good | only fair | little | none | says physically ill only |

INSIGHT AND ATTITUDE TOWARD ILLNESS (continued)

Motivation for working on problem — not applicable / unknown

| very good | good | only fair | little | none | | desires refuses treatment offered |

Awareness of his contribution to difficulties — not applicable / unknown

| very good | good | only fair | little | none | | blames circumstances others |

OVERALL SEVERITY OF ILLNESS

not ill / slight / mild / mod / marked / severe / among most extreme

CHANGE IN CONDITION DURING PAST WEEK

marked improv / impr / stable / variable / worse

RATER HAS WRITTEN COMMENTS ELSEWHERE

Signature _____ Date _____

Set no. 0052107

Mark last 3 digits of Set number in area below.

0 1 2 3 4   5 6 7 8 9
0 1 2 3 4   5 6 7 8 9
0 1 2 3 4   5 6 7 8 9

IBM M62394

MSER 4b

Content Theme of hallucinations, including interpretation patient gives to hallucinations.
Conviction that hallucinations are real The extent to which patient is convinced that hallucinations are perceptions of real external events.
Illusions The misinterpretation or alteration of a real external sensory experience to be distinguished from hallucinations, e.g. chime of clock is heard as an insulting remark; wind is heard as someone calling name.
Depersonalization Feelings of strangeness or unreality about one's own body, e.g. feels outside of body or as if part of body does not belong to him.
Derealization Feelings of strangeness or unreality about one's surroundings, e.g. everything is dreamlike.
Deja vu A subjective feeling that an experience which is occurring for the first time has been experienced before.

SENSORIUM
Orientation disturbance
Time Does not know the year, season, month, day, or time of day.
Place Does not know where he is or in what kind of place he is.
Person (self and others) Does not know who he is or misidentifies others.
Memory disturbance General disturbance in memory not limited to a discrete time period (as with hysterical amnesia).
Recent Events of the last few hours or days.
Remote Events of several years ago.
Clouding of consciousness Disturbance in perception, attention and thought with a subsequent amnesia.
Fluctuating Intermittent returning to normal consciousness.
Continuous No return to normal consciousness.
Dissociation A psychological separation or splitting off of behavior or events from consciousness.
Trance Marked unresponsiveness to the environment, usually of sudden onset, with a degree of immobility and a dazed appearance.
Amnesia A loss of memory for a circumscribed period of time on a psychological basis; to be distinguished from a generalized memory disturbance as above.
Fugue A period of amnesia with physical flight from a stressful situation with retention of habits and skills.
Hysterical attack Marked emotional display with a strong histrionic flavor and apparent loss of contact with the environment.
Other Examples: somnambulism, automatic writing, Ganser syndrome.

COGNITIVE FUNCTIONS
Attention disturbance Inability to focus on one component of a situation. Impairment may be observed by the rater or be a subjective complaint of the patient.
Distractability Attention is too easily drawn to unimportant or irrelevant stimuli.

Intelligence (estimate) Takes into account native ingenuity as well as vocabulary, academic achievements and available IQ scores. **Superior:** IQ 120+, **Bright:** 110-119, **Average:** 90-109, **Borderline:** 70-89, **Retarded:** below 70.

JUDGMENT
Ability to evaluate alternative courses of action or to draw proper conclusions from experience.
Family relations Immediate or extended family, e.g. doesn't appreciate how his behavior upsets family.
Other social relations Example: Continually feels mistreated by strangers.
Employment Example: Unrealistic job expectations.
Future plans Note either that the patient has no plans, or note the level of judgment for plans that he does have.

POTENTIAL FOR SUICIDE OR VIOLENCE
Estimate of potential for behavior in the next few days, weeks, or month.

INSIGHT — ATTITUDE TOWARD ILLNESS
Use the **not applicable** category for each item if the patient is not ill now. Use the **unknown** category if patient is ill but his insight or attitude cannot be ascertained, e.g. patient is mute.
Recognition that he is ill Realization that he has emotional, mental, or psychiatric problems or symptoms.
Motivation for working on problem in some realistic manner. May involve changing his life circumstances, attitudes, or behavior. Note whether the patient desires or refuses the treatment that is being offered.
Awareness of his contribution to difficulties Use **not applicable** if the nature of the difficulty appears to be due entirely to external influences, e.g. toxic psychosis because of febrile illness. Note if patient blames circumstances and/or other people for . his difficulties.

OVERALL SEVERITY OF ILLNESS during this one week study period. Consider all of the previous items and any other evidence of psychopathology. Do not include prognosis.

CHANGE IN CONDITION
Note the most appropriate descriptive term (e.g. marked improvement) for the past week.

RATER HAS WRITTEN COMMENTS ELSEWHERE Note if additional comments about the patient's current condition have been recorded elsewhere in the clinical record.

IBM M62395

Appendix B:
The Beck Depression
Inventory

The Beck Depression Inventory   Cut-Off Scores

The Beck Depression Inventory can aid in the recognition and management of the depressed patient who may be seen in medical practice. It is a self-rating questionnaire that can be completed in five minutes. The four alternative statements in each of the 21 groups rate the extent of depression on a four-point scale ranging from not present to present to a mild, moderate, or severe degree.

The patient is asked to describe the way he has felt in the past week. If he is uncertain as to which assessment best characterizes his feelings, he should circle the next higher score.

The Beck Depression Inventory detects the presence of depression and indicates its severity. In addition, if given during the therapeutic process, it can reflect changes that may occur.

There is no arbitrary score that can be used for all purposes as a cut-off point. However, the following ranges may be used as guidelines. When using the inventory as a screening device to detect depression among psychiatric patients, Dr. Beck found a cut-off point of 13 to be appropriate.

None or minimal	0-9
Borderline	10-14
Mild to moderate	15-20
Moderate	21-30
Severe	31-40
Very severe	41-63

BECK INVENTORY

Name_____ Date_____

On this questionnaire are groups of statements. Please read each group of statements carefully. Then pick out the one statement in each group which best describes the way you have been feeling the PAST WEEK, INCLUDING TODAY! Circle the number beside the statement you picked. If several statements in the group seem to apply equally well, circle each one. **Be sure to read all the statements in each group before making your choice.**

1   0 I do not feel sad
    1 I feel sad.
    2 I am sad all the time and I can't snap out of it.
    3 I am so sad or unhappy that I can't stand it.

2   0 I am not particularly discouraged about the future.
    1 I feel discouraged about the future.
    2 I feel I have nothing to look forward to.
    3 I feel that the future is hopeless and that things cannot improve.

3   0 I do not feel like a failure.
    1 I feel I have failed more than the average person.
    2 As I look back on my life, all I can see is a lot of failures.
    3 I feel I am a complete failure as a person.

4   0 I get as much satisfaction out of things as I used to
    1 I don't enjoy things the way I used to.
    2 I don't get real satisfaction out of anything anymore.
    3 I am dissatisfied or bored with everything.

5   0 I don't feel particularly guilty.
    1 I feel guilty a good part of the time
    2 I feel quite guilty most of the time.
    3 I feel guilty all of the time.

6   0 I don't feel I am being punished.
    1 I feel I may be punished.
    2 I expect to be punished.
    3 I feel I am being punished.

7   0 I don't feel disappointed in myself.
    1 I am disappointed in myself.
    2 I am disgusted with myself.
    3 I hate myself.

8   0 I don't feel I am any worse than anybody else.
    1 I am critical of myself for my weaknesses or mistakes.
    2 I blame myself all the time for my faults.
    3 I blame myself for everything bad that happens.

9   0 I don't have any thoughts of killing myself.
    1 I have thoughts of killing myself, but I would not carry them out.
    2 I would like to kill myself.
    3 I would kill myself if I had the chance.

10 0 I don't cry any more than usual.
    1 I cry more now than I used to.
    2 I cry all the time now.
    3 I used to be able to cry, but now I can't cry even though I want to.

11 0 I am no more irritated now than I ever am.
    1 I get annoyed or irritated more easily than I used to.
    2 I feel irritated all the time now.
    3 I don't get irritated at all by the things that used to irritate me.

12 0 I have not lost interest in other people
    1 I am less interested in other people than I used to be.
    2 I have lost most of my interest in other people.
    3 I have lost all of my interest in other people.

13 0 I make decisions about as well as I ever could.
    1 I put off making decisions more than I used to.
    2 I have greater difficulty in making decisions than before.
    3 I can't make decisions at all anymore.

14 0 I don't feel I look any worse than I used to.
    1 I am worried that I am looking old or unattractive.
    2 I feel that there are permanent changes in my appearance that make me look unattractive.
    3 I believe that I look ugly.

15 0 I can work about as well as before.
    1 It takes an extra effort to get started at doing something.
    2 I have to push myself very hard to do anything.
    3 I can't do any work at all.

16 0 I can sleep as well as usual.
    1 I don't sleep as well as I used to.
    2 I wake up 1-2 hours earlier than usual and find it hard to get back to sleep.
    3 I wake up several hours earlier than I used to and cannot get back to sleep.

17 0 I don't get more tired than usual.
    1 I get tired more easily than I used to.
    2 I get tired from doing almost anything.
    3 I am too tired to do anything.

18 0 My appetite is no worse than usual.
    1 My appetite is not as good as it used to be.
    2 My appetite is much worse now.
    3 I have no appetite at all anymore.

19 0 I haven't lost much weight, if any, lately.
    1 I have lost more than 5 pounds.   I am purposely trying to lose weight
    2 I have lost more than 10 pounds.   by eating less. Yes_____ No_____
    3 I have lost more than 15 pounds.

20 0 I am no more worried about my health than usual.
    1 I am worried about physical problems such as aches and pains; or upset stomach; or constipation.
    2 I am very worried about physical problems and it's hard to think of much else.
    3 I am so worried about my physical problems that I cannot think about anything else.

21 0 I have not noticed any recent change in my interest in sex.
    1 I am less interested in sex than I used to be.
    2 I am much less interested in sex now.
    3 I have lost interest in sex completely.

Appendix C:
The Assessment of
Suicidal Potential

This instrument may be useful to you in the evaluation of suicidal risk, but it is only meant to be suggestive and not conclusive. The numbers in parentheses provide a range of numerical values based on a scale of one through nine—nine indicates the greatest suicidal risk. Within each category rate every item that applies to the person you are evaluating and place a numerical value on the line to the left of each applicable item. If any item is not relevant, simply disregard it completely. Next, indicate the overall evaluation for that category by averaging the numerical values (using an arithmetic mean) and placing the average at the end of the category. The suicidal potentiality rating is found by averaging all of the averages (the numbers at the end of each category). The average of the averages, rounded to the nearest whole number, will give you an indication of suicidal potential.

Category One: Age and Sex

____ (7–9) male 50 or older   ____ (5–7) female 50 or older
____ (4–6) male 35 to 49   ____ (3–5) female 35 to 49
____ (1–3) male 15 to 34   ____ (1–3) female 15 to 34

place the average rating for this category here ____

Category Two: Symptoms

____ (7–9) severe depression (in the form of sleep disorders, anorexia, weight loss, withdrawal, despondence, loss of zest, apathy)
____ (7–9) feelings of hopelessness, helplessness, or exhaustion
____ (6–8) delusions, hallucinations, loss of contact with reality, disorientation
____ (6–8) compulsive gambler
____ (5–7) disorganization, confusion, chaos
____ (4–7) alcoholism, drug addiction, homosexuality
____ (4–6) agitation, tension, anxiety

Los Angeles Suicide Prevention Center. Reprinted with permission.

____ (4–6) guilt, shame, embarrassment
____ (4–6) feelings of rage, anger, hostility, revenge
____ (4–6) frustrated dependency
____   other (describe) _____

    place the average rating for this category here ____

Category Three: Stress

____ (5–9) loss of loved ones by death, divorce, or separation
____ (4–8) loss of job, money, prestige, status
____ (3–7) sickness, serious illness, surgery, accident, loss of limb
____ (4–6) threat of prosecution, criminal involvement, exposure
____ (4–6) change(s) in life, environment, setting
____ (2–5) success, increased responsibilities
____ (1–3) no significant stress
____   other (describe) _____

    place the average rating for this category here ____

Category Four: Suicidal Plan

____ (1–9) lethality of proposed method (gun, jumping, hanging, drown-
         ing, stabbing, poisoning, ingesting drugs or aspirin)
____ (1–9) availability of the proposed method
____ (1–9) specific details in the "plan of action"
____ (1–9) specific time planned for the suicide
____ (4–6) bizarre plans
____ (1–9) rating of previous suicide attempt(s)
____ (1–3) has no "plan of attack"
____   other (describe) _____

    place the average rating for this category here ____

Category Five: Acute versus Chronic

____ (1–9) sudden onset of specific symptoms
____ (4–9) recurrent outbreak of similar symptoms
____ (4–7) long-standing traits became more pronounced lately
____ (1–4) no specific recent change
____   other (describe) _____

    place the average rating for this category here ____

Category Six: Resources

____ (7–9) no sources of support (employment, family, friends,
              agencies, etc.)
____ (4–7) family and friends are available, but won't help
____ (4–7) financial problems
____ (2–4) available professional help
____ (1–3) family and/or friends are willing to help
____ (1–3) employed
____ (1–3) finances are not a problem
____   other (describe) _____

     place the average rating for this category here ____

Category Seven: Prior Suicidal Behavior

____ (6–7) one or more prior attempts of high lethality
____ (4–6) one or more prior attempts of low lethality
____ (3–5) history of repeated threats and depression
____ (1–3) no prior suicidal or depressed history
____   other (describe) _____

     place the average rating for this category here ____

Category Eight: Health Status

____ (5–7) chronic debilitating illness
____ (4–6) pattern of failure in previous therapy
____ (4–6) unsuccessful experiences with physicians
____ (2–4) psychosomatic illness (asthma, ulcer, etc.)
____ (1–3) chronic complaints of illness or hypochondria
____ (1–2) no medical problems

     place the average rating for this category here ____

Category Nine: Communication Aspects

____ (5–7) communications were broken and efforts to reestablish com-
              munication by patient and others have met with rejection
____ (2–4) communications have an internalized goal (to cause guilt in
              others, to force behavior, etc.)

____ (3–5) communications directed toward the world and people in general

____ (1–3) communications directed toward one or more specific people

____   other (describe) _____

place the average rating for this category here _____

Category Ten: Significant Other(s)

____ (5–7) defensive, paranoid, rejected, or punishing reactions

____ (5–7) denial of own or suicidal person's need for help

____ (4–6) no feelings of concern for the suicidal person; does not understand the suicidal person

____ (3–5) indecisiveness, feelings of helplessness

____ (2–4) alternates between feelings of anger and rejection and feelings of responsibility and a desire to help

____ (1–3) sympathy and concern plus admission of the need for help

____   other (describe) _____

place the average rating for this category here _____

_____

_____ On the line to the left, place the total of all of the average ratings for the ten categories. Now divide that number by ten, round off the result to the nearest whole number, and circle that number on the assessment scale below to indicate your assessment of risk.

1 2 3	4 5 6	7 8 9
low risk	medium risk	high risk

Source: This scale for estimating suicidal potential was developed at the Los Angeles Suicide Prevention Center. It is only one of many such scales and is therefore not meant to be definitive. Appreciation is expressed for its use in this training outline.

Appendix D:
The Social
Readjustment Rating
Scale

The Social Readjustment
Rating Scale

Life Event	Mean Value
1. Death of spouse[a]	100
2. Divorce	73
3. Marital separation	65
4. Jail term	63
5. Death of close family member	63
6. Personal injury or illness	53
7. Marriage	50
8. Fired at work	47
9. Marital reconciliation	45
10. Retirement	45
11. Change in health of family member	44
12. Pregnancy	40
13. Sex difficulties	39
14. Gain of new family member	39
15. Business readjustment	39
16. Change in financial state	38
17. Death of close friend	37
18. Change to different line of work	36
19. Change in number of arguments with spouse	35
20. Mortgage or loan for major purchase (home, etc.)	31
21. Foreclosure of mortgage or loan	30
22. Change in responsibilities at work	29
23. Son or daughter leaving home	29
24. Trouble with in-laws	29
25. Outstanding personal achievement	28
26. Wife begin or stop work	26
27. Begin or end school	26
28. Change in living conditions	25
29. Revision of personal habits	24
30. Trouble with boss	23
31. Change in work hours or conditions	20
32. Change in residence	20
33. Change in schools	20
34. Change in recreation	19
35. Change in church activities	19
36. Change in social activities	18
37. Mortgage or loan for lesser purchase (car, TV, etc.)	17
38. Change in sleeping habits	16
39. Change in number of family get-togethers	15
40. Change in eating habits	15
41. Vacation	13
42. Christmas	12
43. Minor violations of the law	11

[a]Reprinted with permission from Holmes, T.H., and Rahe, R.H., "The Social Readjustment Rating Scale," *Journal of Psychosomatic Research* 11:213–218, Copyright 1967, Pergamon Press, Ltd.

Appendix E:
Sample Suicide
Contracts

Sample Suicide Contract

1. I, _____, agree not to kill myself, attempt to kill myself, or cause any harm to myself during the period from _____ to _____, the time of my next appointment.
2. I agree not to engage in activities that are harmful to me, such as drinking, smoking pot, driving alone, or going over to my ex-wife's house.
3. I agree to get enough sleep and to eat well.
4. I agree to get rid of things I could use to kill myself; my guns and the pills.
5. I agree that if I have a bad time and feel that I might hurt myself, I will call _____, my counselor immediately, at #_____.
6. I agree that these conditions are part of my counseling contract with _____.

Signed _____
Witnessed _____
Date _____

Sample Suicide Contract

I, _____, agree that I will not kill myself or in any other way harm myself, either accidentally or on purpose until I have seen and talked with _____, my counselor, on _____ in his office.

I will not accidentally or on purpose take an overdose of my medication.

I will drive my car safely and pay attention any time I am behind the wheel.

Signed _____
Witnessed _____
Date _____

Index

About the Authors

William L. Getz, a member of the Academy of Certified Social Workers, and a licensed clinical social worker in California, received the M.S.W. from the University of Washington. He is an instructor in the Department of Psychology and formerly a Field Work Instructor at the School of Social Work, both at the University of Washington. He is senior coauthor of *Fundamentals of Crisis Counseling* (Lexington Books, 1974) and has served as a consultant and trainer in crisis intervention. He maintains a full-time private practice in Bellevue, Washington, as a member of the Hillcrest Group for Psychotherapy.

David B. Allen received the Ph.D. from the University of Washington. He is engaged in the private practice of clinical psychology with the Hillcrest Group for Psychotherapy in Bellevue. He is the former director of a hospital emergency-room, crisis-intervention service and has taught seminars and workshops on suicide and crisis intervention. Dr. Allen has also contributed numerous articles to professional psychology and community mental-health journals.

R. Keith Myers, a member of the Academy of Certified Social Workers, received the M.S.W. from the University of Washington. He is currently in private practice with the Hillcrest Group for Psychotherapy in Bellevue, specializing in the treatment of adolescents and their families. He is an instructor for City University and former codirector of a hospital emergency-room, crisis-intervention service. Mr. Myers has conducted numerous workshops throughout the Northwest and Alaska, and is currently consultant to an innovative drug- and alcohol-treatment program for adolescents at Echo Glen Children's Treatment Center in Washington state.

Karen C. Lindner received the Ph.D. in clinical psychology from the University of Washington. She is coordinator of Diagnostic Services for the Correctional Education and Research Program at the University of Washington and is in private practice with the Hillcrest Group for Psychotherapy in Bellevue. She specializes in working with those who are involved in major transitions in their lives and has worked as a crisis counselor and as a supervisor for crisis counselors.

274